AN INTRODUCTION TO PHILOSOPHY

NECESSARY
QUESTIONS

A N T H O N Y   A P P I A H

NECESSARY QUESTIONS

AN INTRODUCTION TO PHILOSOPHY

PRENTICE-HALL
Englewood Cliffs, N.J. 07632

The author, the publishers and John Calmann and King Ltd would like
to thank the following for permission to reproduce copyright
illustrations:

Camera Press: p.111; Inter Nationes, Bonn: p.65; Mansell Collection:
pp.13, 35 and 123.

North and South American Edition first published 1989 by
Prentice-Hall Inc,
Englewood Cliffs,
N.J. 07632

A John Calmann and King book

ISBN 0-13-611328-1

This book was designed and produced by
JOHN CALMANN AND KING LTD, LONDON

Designed by Pauline Baines
Cover design by Roy Trevelion
Typeset by Communitype Ltd, Leicester
Printed in Hong Kong by Mandarin Offset International Ltd.

Contents

Preface

You learn a lot about your subject when you set out to introduce the range of it to people who are approaching it for the first time. That alone would have made writing this book worthwhile for me. After a while, as you do the detailed work of professional research, you risk losing sight of the forest for the trees. Stepping back for a bit, to think again about the shape of the subject and where your own work fits into it, allows you not just to rediscover connections, but to make new ones. That is why undergraduate teaching is so invigorating.

This book was Larry King's idea; and like any good publisher he made me do the work, kept me to deadlines, and supported me with good advice. But the first thing he did was to persuade me that there was a need for it. So far as I have been able to discover, there is no textbook of philosophy in English that sets out to introduce the subject as it is studied now. There are some good surveys of the history of the subject; there are a few good introductions to important areas of it. There are also some pretty bad surveys and introductions! What I have tried to write is a reliable and systematic introduction to the main areas of current philosophical interest in the English-speaking world. I hope I have also conveyed some of the excitement of the subject.

I find I have now taught philosophy on three continents, and it is astonishing how the same questions arise in such culturally disparate circumstances. I am grateful to all of my students, in Ghana, in England, and in the United States: almost every one of them has taught me a new argument or – what is much the same – shown me an old one in a new light. This book is dedicated to them.

Introduction

People come to philosophy by many different routes. The physicist Erwin Schrödinger, who developed some of the key concepts of modern quantum theory, was drawn into philosophy by the profoundly puzzling nature of the world he and others discovered when they started to examine things on the scale of the atom.

One of my friends came to philosophy when, as a teenager, he was first developing adult relationships of friendship and love. He was perplexed about how easy it was to think you understood somebody and then discover that you had not understood them at all. This led him to wonder whether we ever really know what is going on in other people's minds.

And many people come to philosophy when they are trying, as we say, to "find themselves": to make sense of their lives and to decide who they are.

If, for these or any other reasons, you come to have an interest in philosophy, it is natural to turn to the works of great philosophers. But for most people the contents of these works is rather a shock. Instead of offering direct answers to these questions – What is physical reality really like? Can we ever be sure we know what other people are thinking? Who am I? – a philosopher is likely to start with questions which seem to him or her more basic than these – but which may seem to others far less interesting. Instead of beginning by asking what we can know about other people's thoughts, a philosopher is likely to begin by asking what it is to know anything at all: and thus to begin with epistemology, which is the philosophical examination of the nature of knowledge. Despite the natural disappointment it produces, I think that starting with these funda-mental questions makes sense. Let me suggest an image that might help you to see why.

Imagine you are lost in a large old European city. Every way you turn there is interest and excitement. But you'd like to know where you are. The trouble is that just when you think you have found your way out of one maze of alleys, you are plunged into another. If, in your wanderings, you climb to the top of a tall tower, you can look down over the streets you have been lost in; and suddenly everything begins to make sense. You see where you should have turned one way but went another; you realize that the little shop you walked past, with the wine in the window, was only yards away from the garden in the next street, which you found hours later. And when you get back down into the maze you find your way easily. Now you know your way about.

In this book we shall find ourselves discussing the nature of morality, when we set out to decide whether it is always wrong to kill an innocent person; we shall end up talking about what it is for a theory to be scientific, when we started out wondering about the claims of astrologers. And when this happens, I think it will help to bear in mind this image of being lost in an old city. When we move to these abstract questions, apparently remote from the practical concerns we started with, what we are doing is like climbing up that tower. From up there we can see our way around the problems. So that when we get back down into the city, back to the concrete problems that started us out, we should find it easier to get around.

People are normally introduced to philosophy by one of two routes. The first is through the reading of the more accessible of the great historical texts of philosophy – Plato's dialogues, for example, or Descartes' *Meditations.* The second is by examining some central philosophical problem: What is knowledge? Is morality objective? In this book I shall be following this second route, but I shall discuss the views of some of the great philosophers on the central questions on the way. Still, it is important to keep in mind that I will always be trying to move towards a philosophical understanding of the problem I am looking at, rather than trying to give an historically accurate account of a past philosopher.

It is fashionable, at the moment, to stress the way that the central problems of philosophy change over time. People say that no one nowadays can really be concerned with all of the problems that worried Plato. There is some truth in this. There are things in Plato that it is hard to understand or get excited by: much of the theory in the *Symposium* about the nature of love, for example, is likely to seem hopelessly wrong to a modern reader. Fortunately, however, a good deal more in Plato *is* extremely interesting and relevant: his *Theaetetus*, which is a dramatic dialogue about the nature of knowledge, remains one of the great classics of philosophy, and I shall discuss it in Chapter 2.

So the reason we philosophers continue to read Plato and many other philosophers between his time and ours is not simple curiosity about the history of our subject. Rather, we find in the great works of the past clues to a deeper understanding of the philosophical questions which trouble us now. That's why mentioning Plato and Descartes isn't some kind of concession to the proponents of the historical route into philosophy. It isn't even just a concession to old habits in the teaching of philosophy. It is simply a reflection of the facts that make the historical route work.

My aim in this book is twofold, then: first, I would like anyone who reads it carefully to be able to go on to read contemporary philosophical discussions. Second, I would like such a reader to be able, when he or she comes to read Plato, say, or Descartes, to see why their work remains an enduring contribution to our understanding of the central problems of philosophy. I shall always have in mind a beginning philosophy student, who knows none of the technical language of philosophy, but is, nevertheless, willing to think through difficult questions. There are bibliographical notes and some advice on further reading at the end of the book; and there is also a glossary, which allows you to look up the various key terms in the book. These should help you find your way around.

The book is organized around seven central topics: Mind, Knowledge, Language and Logic, Science, Morality, Politics, and Law. I'm going to start straight in with Mind and this may seem surprising. You might have thought a good question to answer at the beginning of an introductory philosophy book is: What is philosophy? But I think that is a mistake; and if we consider the same question about a different subject I think you will see why.

So consider the question: What is physics? If someone asked what physics is, they might well get the answer that it is the study of the physical world. In some ways this isn't a very helpful answer. One trouble is that if you take the answer broadly, then biology is a branch of physics: living organisms are part of the physical world. But this just shows that not every part of the physical world gets studied in physics. Which aspects *are* the physical aspects? Well, if you knew *that*, and were thus able to rule out biological questions, you would already be well on the way to knowing what physics is.

Nevertheless, there is a reason why most of us don't find this answer just unhelpful. We learned some physics in high school and so we already have lots of examples of physical experiments and problems to draw on. These examples allow us to understand what is meant by "the physical world": it consists of those aspects of the world that are like the ones we studied in high school physics. If we tell someone who has never done any physics that physics is the systematic study of the physical world, we should not be surprised if they find our answer rather unhelpful.

There is a lesson here for how we should begin to develop an understanding of what philosophy is. What it suggests is that rather than tackling the question head on, we should look at some examples of philosophical work. With these examples in mind it won't be so unhelpful to be given an answer like the one we got to: What is physics? For if we end up by saying that philosophy is the study of philosophical problems, that won't be uninformative if we have an idea of what some of the major philosophical problems are. So I'm not going to start this book by telling you what I – or anyone else – think philosophy is. I'm going to start by doing some. Just as you are in a better position to understand what physics is when you have done some, so you will be better able to see how philosophy fits into our thought and our culture when you have a "feel" for how philosophers argue and what they argue about.

I began this introduction by mentioning various questions that might lead you to philosophy in the first place; but perhaps you have never been bothered by any such questions. That is no reason to think that philosophy is not for you. Many people do, of course, live their lives without ever thinking systematically about philosophy. But I shall be arguing that many problems that trouble us in ordinary life – down in the city, rather than up in the tower – can only be answered if we first ask the more fundamental questions that are the hallmark of philosophy.

1 Mind

What is a mind?

Could we make a machine with a mind?

What is the relationship between minds and bodies?

1.1 Introduction

In countless movies, computers play a starring role. Some talk in synthesized voices; others write a stream of words on a screen. Some manage space-ships; others, the "brains" of robots, manage their own "bodies." People converse with them, are understood by them, exchange information and greetings with them. Much of this is still science fiction. But real computers advise lawyers on relevant cases, doctors on diagnoses, engineers on the state of atomic reactors. Both the fantasy and the fact would have astonished our grandparents. *Their* grandparents might have thought that this could only be achieved by magic. Yet most of us are getting used to it, taking the silicon age for granted.

Still, a suspicion remains. We human beings have always thought of ourselves as special. We all assume *some* contrast between the world of material things and the world of spiritual things. If the computer really is a "material mind," then not only must we re-think this distinction, but we have broken it with our own creations. We should be careful to avoid such an important conclusion until we have really thought it through. However natural it seems to take it for granted that computers can think and act, then, we *shouldn't* just assume it. In philosophy we often find that what we normally take for granted – the "common sense" point of view – gets in the way of a proper understanding of the issues. So let's see if the way I spoke about computers in the first paragraph is accurate.

I said that they talk. But surely they don't *really* talk in the sense that people do. It isn't enough to say that they produce something that sounds like speech. Tape-recorders do that, but *they* don't talk. When people talk they mean something by what they say. To mean something, they need to be able to understand sentences. Now I also said that computers understand what we say to them. But do they really? The sounds of our speech are turned into electrical impulses. The impulses pass through the circuits of the machine. And that causes the speech synthesizer to produce sounds. It may be very clever to design a machine that does this, but what evidence have we that the machine understands?

Well, could a machine understand? There are two obvious responses to this question. The first response I'll call **mentalist**, for the sake of a label. It's the response you make if you think that understanding what people say involves having a **mind**. The mentalist says:

> Computers can't really understand anything. To understand they would have to have conscious minds. But *we* made them from silicon chips and *we* programmed them. We didn't give them conscious minds. So we know they don't have them.

At the other extreme is the response I'll call **behaviorist**. The behaviorist says:

> Some computers don't understand, of course. But there's no reason why a computer shouldn't be made that *does* understand. If a machine responds in the same ways to speech as a person who understands speech, then we have just as much reason to say that the machine understands as we have to say that the person does. A machine that behaves in every way *as if it understands* is indistinguishable from a machine that understands. If it behaved in the right way that would show that it had a mind.

It is clear why I call this response "behaviorist." For the behaviorist says that to understand is to *behave* as if you understand.

What we have here is a situation that is quite familiar in philosophy. There are two extreme views – the mentalists' and the behaviorists', in this case – both of which seem to have something in their favor, but neither of which looks completely right. Each of these views has a bit of common sense on its side. The mentalist relies on the common sense claim that machines can't think. The behaviorist relies on the common sense claim that all we know about other people's minds we know from what they *do.* It looks as though common sense here isn't going to tell us if the mentalist or the behaviorist is right.

In fact, if you hold *either* of these views you are likely to find yourself in difficulties. Let's start with a problem you get into if you are a mentalist. Suppose the computer in question is in a robot, which, like "androids" in science fiction, looks exactly like a person. It's a very smart computer, so that its "body" responds exactly like a particular person: your mother, for example. For that reason I'll call the robot "M." Wouldn't you have as much reason for thinking that M had a mind as you have for thinking that your mother does? You might say, "Not if I know that it's got silicon chips in its head." But did you ever *check* that your mother has got brain tissue in her head? You didn't, of course, because it wouldn't prove anything if you did. Your belief that your mother has a mind is based on what she says and does. What's in her head may be an interesting question, the behaviorist will say, but it isn't relevant to deciding whether she has thoughts. And if it doesn't matter what is in your mother's head, why should it matter what's in M's?

That's a major problem if you're a mentalist: how to explain why you wouldn't say an android had a mind, even if you had the same evidence that it had a mind as you have that your mother does. Surely, it would be absurd to believe your mother has a mind on the basis of what she does and says, and refuse to believe M has a mind *on the very same evidence?* This is one line of thought that might lead you to behaviorism.

But if you decide to be a behaviorist, you have got problems too. You and I both know, after all, since we both do have minds, what it is like to have a mind. So you and I both know there's a difference between us and a machine that behaves exactly like us, but doesn't have any experiences. Unless M has experiences it hasn't got a mind. The difference between having a mind and "faking" that you've got one seems as clear as the difference between being conscious and being unconscious. (Of course, only something with a mind could really *fake* anything – which is why I put the word in quotes.)

The upshot is this: If you look at the question from the outside, comparing M with other people, behaviorism looks tempting. From the point of view of the evidence *you* have, M and your mother are the same. Looked at from the inside, however, there is all the difference in the world. You know you have a mind because you have conscious experiences, an "inner life." M may have experiences, for all we know. But if it doesn't, no amount of faking is going to make it true that it has a mind.

We started with a familiar fact: computers are everywhere and they're getting smarter. It looks as though there will soon be intelligent machines, which will understand what we say to them. But when we look a little closer things are not as simple as that. On the one hand, there is reason to doubt that behaving like a person with a mind and having a mind are the same thing. On the other, once we start asking what and how we know about the minds of other people, it seems that our conviction that people have minds is no better based than the belief that there could be understanding computers. We call someone who starts with questions about what and how we know an **epistemologist**. And if we ask how we know about the minds of other people it seems plain that it is from what they say and do. We simply have no direct way of knowing what – if anything – is going on in other people's minds. But then, if what people say and do is what shows us they have minds, a machine that says and does the same things shows us that it has a mind also. From the epistemologist's point of view, other people's minds and the "minds" of computers are in the same boat.

When we look at the question from the inside, as we have seen, the picture looks different. Someone who looks from the inside we can call a **phenomenologist**. For "phenomenology" is the philosopher's word for reflecting on the nature of our conscious mental life. From the phenomenologist's point of view, M, and all machines, however good they are at behaving like people, may well turn out not to have minds.

From thinking about computers in science fiction we have found our way to the center of the maze of problems that philosophers call the philosophy of mind or **philosophical psychology**.

As I said in the introduction, philosophical perplexity is a little like being lost in an old city. It is time now to find our way up that tower to have a look around. We have already been forced back to two of the most fundamental philosophical questions, "What is it to have a mind?" and "How do we know that other people have minds?" So let us put aside the concrete question about M, and take up these fundamental questions directly. At the end of the chapter, I'll get back to M, and we'll see then if our trip up the tower has helped us to find our way about.

DESCARTES

René Descartes (1596-1650) was born in the small town of La Haye in France, and educated by the Jesuits at La Flèche, where he learned traditional Catholic theology and, also, science and mathematics. In his early twenties he enlisted in the Dutch army. While he was serving with the army in Germany he had a dream which he took as a sign from God that he should found a new science of nature; and he devoted most of the rest of his life to science and philosophy. Not only was he perhaps the greatest philosopher of his era, he also made important contributions to mathematics and physics: you have probably used his Cartesian coordinates in geometry. Like Galileo, his famous Italian contemporary, Descartes was one of the first people to write serious works not in Latin but in the vernacular. Though his first important work, the *Rules for the direction of the Mind*, was written in Latin and is usually known by the Latin word *Regulae* (which means "rules"), some of his best-known works – in physics, *The World*, and in philosophy, *The Discourse on Method* – are in French and were aimed at the general educated public. But his most famous work was the *Meditations*, written in Latin, which was very widely studied as soon as it appeared in 1641. His last work, *The Passions of the Soul* (also in French), was published in the year before his death. Descartes was very famous in his own day and died in Sweden as the guest of Queen Christina. Despite his philosophical skepticism, Descartes remained a devout Catholic throughout his life.

1.2   Descartes: The beginnings of modern philosophy of mind

The dominant view of the mind for the last three hundred years has been one that derives from the French philosopher René Descartes, one of the most influential philosophers of all time. His method is to start looking at questions by asking how an individual can acquire knowledge. He starts, that is, by asking how *he* knows what he knows; and if you want to see the force of his arguments you will have to start by asking yourself how *you* know what you know. The fact that Descartes starts with how we know things marks him as one of the first modern philosophers. For, since Descartes, much of Western philosophy has been based on epistemological considerations.

Descartes' most famous work, the *Discourse on Method*, is written in a clear, attractive style. This may make what he is saying seem simpler and more obvious than it really is, so we need to consider what he says very carefully. Here is a passage from the fourth part of the *Discourse*, published in 1637, where he sets out very clearly his view of the nature of his own self:

> I thought carefully about what I was, and since I noticed that I could suppose that I didn't have a body, and that there was neither a world nor any other place that I was in; but that I could not therefore suppose that I didn't exist; and that, on the contrary, from the very fact that I doubted the truth of other things, it followed clearly and certainly that I existed; while, on the other hand, if I just stopped thinking, I would have had no reason to believe I existed, even if all the other things which I had ever imagined had really existed; I concluded that I was a substance whose whole . . . nature consists only in thinking, and which needs no place in which to exist and is not dependent on any material thing; so that this "I", . . . the mind which makes me what I am, is totally distinct from my body, is more easily known than my body, and . . . would still continue to be all that it is, even if my body did not exist.

This passage contains practically every central component of Descartes' philosophy of mind.

First, Descartes is a **dualist**. This means he believes that a mind and a body are two quite distinct sorts of thing.

Second, what he thinks you really are, your *self*, is a mind. Since you *are* your mind, and minds are totally independent of bodies, you could still exist, even without a body.

Third, your mind and your thoughts are the things you know best. For Descartes it is possible, at least in principle, for there to be a mind without a body, unable, however hard it tries, to become aware of anything else, including any other minds. Descartes knew, of course, that the way we do in fact come to know what is happening in other minds is by observing the speech and actions of "other bodies." But for him there were two serious possibilities which would mean that our belief in the existence of other minds was mistaken. One is that these other bodies could be mere figments of our imagination. The other is that, even if bodies and other material things do exist, the evidence we normally think justifies our belief that other bodies are inhabited by minds could have been produced by automata, by mindless machines.

Fourth, the essence of a mind, which is the property which every mind *must* have, is to have thoughts; and by "thoughts" Descartes means anything that you are aware of in your mind when you are conscious. In other places Descartes says that the essence of a material thing – the property, in other words, every material thing must have – is that it occupies space. This means that, for Descartes, the essential differences between material things and minds are that minds think, which matter does not, while material things take up space, which minds do not. Descartes' claim, then, is that what distinguishes the mind from the body is the negative fact that the mind is not in space and the positive fact that the mind thinks.

It is not surprising that Descartes believed that matter does not think. Very few people think that stones or tables or atoms have thoughts. But why did he think that minds were not in space? After all, you might think that my mind is where my body is. But if I had no body, as Descartes thought was possible, I would still have a mind. So he couldn't say that a mind *must* be where its body is, simply because it might not have a body at all. Still, if I do have a body, why shouldn't I say that that is where my mind is? If I didn't have a body, that would be the wrong answer: but, as it happens, I do.

I think the main reason for thinking that minds are not in space is that it does really seem strange to ask, "Where are your thoughts?" Even if you answered this question by saying "in my head," it would not be obvious that this was literally true. For if they were in your head, you could find out *where* they were in your head, and how large a volume of space they occupied. But you cannot say how many inches long a thought is, or how many centimeters wide.

There is a fifth and final characteristic of this passage which is typical of Descartes' philosophy of mind: throughout Descartes insists on beginning with what can be known for certain, what cannot be doubted. He insists, that is, on beginning with an epistemological point of view.

These are the major features of Descartes' philosophy of mind, and, as I said, this has been the dominant view since his time. So dominant has it been, in fact, that by the mid-twentieth century the central problems of the philosophy of mind were reduced, in effect, to two. The first was a problem M made us think about, the **problem of other minds**: What justifies our belief that other minds exist at all? And the second is the **mind-body problem**: How are we to explain the relations of a mind and its body? The first of these questions reflects Descartes' epistemological outlook; the second reflects his dualism.

Now it is just this dualism that raises some of the major difficulties of Descartes' position. For anyone who thinks of mind and body as totally distinct needs to offer an answer to two main questions. First, how do mental events cause physical events? How, for example, do our intentions, which are mental, lead to action, which involves physical movements of our bodies. Second, how do physical events cause mental ones? How, for example, is it possible for physical interaction between our eyes and the light to lead to the sensory experiences of vision, which is mental? And, as we shall see, the answer Descartes gives to these questions seems not to be consistent with his explanation of the essential difference between body and mind.

Descartes' answer to these questions *seems* clear and simple enough. The human brain, he thought, was a point of interaction between mind and matter. Indeed, Descartes suggested that the pineal gland, in the center of your head, was the channel between the two distinct realms of mind and matter. That was *his* answer to the mind-body question.

But this theory comes into conflict with Descartes' claim that what distinguishes the mental from the material is that it is not spatial. For if mental happenings cause happenings in the brain, then doesn't that mean that mental events occur in the brain? How can something cause a happening in the brain unless it is another happening in (or near) the brain? Normally, when one event – call it *A* – causes another event – call it *B* – *A* and *B* have to be next to each other, or there has to be a chain of events which *are* next to each other in between them. The drama in the television studio causes the image on my TV screen miles away. But there is an electromagnetic field which carries the image from the studio to me, a field which is in the space between my TV and the studio. Descartes' view has to be that my thoughts cause changes in my brain which lead to my actions. But if the thoughts aren't in or near my brain, and if there's no chain of events between my thoughts and my brain, then this is a very unusual brand of causation.

Descartes wants to say that thoughts aren't anywhere. But, according to him, at least some of the *effects* of my thoughts are in my brain, and none of the direct effects of my thoughts are in anybody else's brain. My thoughts regularly lead to my actions and never lead directly to someone else's. We have now reached one central problem for Descartes' position. For it is normal to think that things are where their *effects* originate. And on this view my thoughts are in my brain, which is the origin of my behavior. But if mental events occur in the brain then, since the brain is in space, at least some mental events are in space also. And then Descartes' way of distinguishing the mental and the material won't work. Let's call this apparent conflict between

(a)   the fact that mind and matter do seem to interact causally, and
(b)   Descartes' claim that the mind is not in space

Descartes' problem. There are four main ways you might try to deal with this problem.

The first would be to deny that causes and their effects have to be in space. Descartes' is only one of the possible dualist solutions to the mind-body question which takes this approach. Because he thinks that mental and material events interact, even if only in the brain, his view is called **interactionism**. But if you want to keep Descartes' view that the mind is not in space, and if you do not think that causes and effects of events in space have themselves to be in space, you might also try one of the other forms of dualism. There are two kinds of dualism you might try in which the causation goes only one way. You could hold either that mental events have bodily causes but not bodily effects, or that mental events have material effects but no material causes. Each of these positions deserves consideration. But each of these two kinds of dualism claims that minds are both causally active in space and yet somehow not in space themselves. As a result, they need to offer some way of thinking about causation which is very unlike the way we normally think about it.

A second way out of Descartes' problem is to deny that there *are* any causal connections between mind and matter at all. On this view there are corresponding material and mental realms, which run in parallel, without any causal interaction. **Psycho-physical parallelism**, as this theory is called, certainly escapes Descartes' problem. But we are left with a mystery: why do the mind and the body work together, if there is no interaction between them? Psycho-physical parallelism says mind and body run in parallel without explaining why. So you might next try a third way out.

This third way out of Descartes' problem would be to try a different way of distinguishing mind and matter. If you think that both causes and their effects have to be in space, and that mental events have material causes or effects, you cannot maintain Descartes' claim that minds are not spatial. Starting with some new way of distinguishing mind and matter, however, you might still be able to keep dualism, while taking into account the fact that causes have to be in space if their effects are.

But however you distinguish the mental and the material, if you believe they are two different kinds of thing you will have to face the "other-minds" problem. If your mind and body are utterly distinct kinds of thing, how can I know anything about your mind, since all I can see (or hear or touch) is your body? You brush off the fly, and I judge that you want to get rid of it. But if there is no necessary connection between what your body does and what is going on in your mind, how is this judgment justified? How can I know your body isn't just an automaton: a machine which reacts mechanically, with no intervening mental processes? If you find this thought compelling, you might want to try a solution to Descartes' problem that is not dualist at all.

So the fourth and last way out of Descartes' problem is just to give up the idea that mind and matter really are distinct kinds of thing, and thus to become what philosophers call a **monist**. Monism is the view that reality consists of only one kind of thing. For monists, beliefs and earthquakes are just things in the world. Things in the world can interact causally with each other, so there's nothing surprising about my belief that there's a table in my way causing me to move the table. The movement of the table is partly caused by the belief. That's no more surprising than a movement of the table caused by an earthquake.

I've suggested that thinking about the other-minds problem might lead you to give up dualism. And if you consider the very evident fact that we *do* know that other people have minds, you may be led, with many philosophers and psychologists of our own century, to the form of monism called "behaviorism." Behaviorism, which we noticed as one possible response to the problem of deciding whether a computer could have a mind, is simply the identification of the mind with certain bodily dispositions. A **behaviorist**, then, is someone who believes that to have a mind is to be disposed to behave in certain ways in response to input. On one behaviorist view, for example, for an English speaker to believe that something is red is for them to be disposed to say "It is red," or to reply with a "Yes" if asked the question "Is it red?" And dispositions like this are a familiar part of the world. Being sharp is (roughly) being disposed to cut, if pressed against a surface; being fragile is (roughly) being disposed to break, if dropped.

There's a strong contrast between behaviorism and Descartes' view. Descartes thought belief was a private matter. That had two consequences. First, that you know for sure what you believe. Second, that *only* you know for sure what you believe. And the trouble with Descartes' view of the mind is that it makes it very hard to see how we can know about other minds at all. For the behaviorist, on the other hand, belief is a disposition to act in response to your environment. If you respond in the way that is appropriate for someone with a certain belief, that's evidence that you have it. Since your response is public – visible and audible – others can find out what you believe. Indeed, as the English philosopher Gilbert Ryle argued in his book *The Concept of Mind*, we sometimes find out what we ourselves believe by watching our own behavior.

It is a big step from saying that *some* of our mental states are things that other people can know about, to saying, with the behaviorists, that *all* of them must be in this way public. Yet one of the most influential philosophical arguments of recent years has just this conclusion. The argument was made by the Austrian philosopher Ludwig Wittgenstein, whose work we will discuss again in the chapter on language.

Wittgenstein began by supposing that anyone who believed in the essentially private thoughts of Descartes' philosophy of mind would find it quite acceptable to suppose that someone could *name* a private experience; one, that is, that nobody else could know about. And indeed, as we shall see in Chapter 3, Thomas Hobbes, who was an English philosopher influenced by Descartes' ideas, thought that we used words as names of our private thoughts, in order that we should be able to remember them. He called them "marks" of our thoughts. To use marks in this way, someone would have to have a rule which said that they should use the name just on the occasions where that private experience occurred. Wittgenstein argued that obeying such a rule not only required that there should be both circumstances when it was and circumstances when it wasn't appropriate to use the name. He thought that it also required that it should be possible to *check* whether you were using the name in accordance with the rule. And he offered a very ingenious argument which was supposed to show that such checking was impossible. If Wittgenstein was right, there could be no such "private languages." And his argument is called, for that reason, the **private language argument**.

1.3   The private language argument

Wittgenstein's objection to a Hobbesian private language depends, as I have said, on a claim about what is involved in following a rule. The *Philosophical Investigations* begins by introducing the idea of a **language-game**, which is any human activity where there is a systematic rule-governed use of words – and this could include, of course, a language like English. One of the conclusions Wittgenstein suggests we should draw from his consideration of language-games is that the notion of following a rule can only apply in cases where it is possible to check whether you are following it correctly. If someone uses a word or a sentence in a rule-governed way, Wittgenstein argues, it must make sense to ask how we know that they are using the rule correctly; or, as he puts it, there must be a "criterion of correctness."

Suppose, for example, Mary claims to be using the word "table" in a language-game. We watch her for a while, and she says the word "table" from time to time but we cannot detect any pattern to the way she uses the word. So we ask her what rule she is following. If Mary claims simply to know when it is appropriate to use the word, but we cannot discover what it is that makes her use of the word appropriate, then we have no reason to think she is following a rule. Unless we can check on whether it is appropriate for Mary to use the word "table," we cannot say that there is a difference between Mary's following a rule, on the one hand, and Mary's simply uttering a word from time to time, on the other.

Let us now see how Wittgenstein can put the claim that rule-following involves a criterion of correctness to use in attacking the Hobbesian private language.

We can start by considering in a little more detail the kind of private use of language that Hobbes thought was possible. Suppose I have an experience that I have never had before. For a "Cartesian" (this is the adjective from "Descartes") there can be no doubt in my mind either that I am having the experience or what the experience is. Still, since it is new, I might want to give it a name, just so that, if it ever comes along again, I can remember that I have had it before. So I call the experience a "twinge." I know exactly what a twinge is like, and I just decide to refer to things like that as "twinges." Of course, I cannot show you a twinge and, since I don't know what caused it in me, I don't know how to produce one in you either. My twinge is essentially private: I know about it and nobody else can.

This story seems to make sense. But Wittgenstein thought that if we analyzed the matter a little further, we could see that it does not. Here is the passage where Wittgenstein makes his objection to the sort of Hobbesian private language that I have described.

> Let us imagine the following case. I want to keep a diary about the recurrence of a certain sensation. To this end I associate it with the sign "S" and write this sign in a calendar for every day on which I have the sensation. – I will remark first of all that a definition of the sign cannot be formulated. – But still I can give myself a kind of ostensive definition. – How? Can I point to the sensation? Not in the ordinary sense. But I speak, or write the sign down, and at the same time I concentrate my attention on the sensation – and so, as it were, point to it inwardly. – But what is this ceremony for? for that is all it seems to be! A definition surely serves to establish the meaning of a sign. – Well, that is done precisely by the concentrating of my attention; for in this way I impress on myself the connection between the sign and the sensation. – But "I impress it on myself" can only mean: this process brings it about that I remember the connection *right* in the future. But in the present case I have no criterion of correctness. One would like to say: whatever is going to seem right to me is right. And that only means that here we can't talk about "right".

Before we try and work out what the argument is that Wittgenstein is making here, we should notice a number of features of the way this passage is written. What Wittgenstein has written is in many ways like dialogue in a play. Some philosophers, like Plato, whom we'll discuss in the next chapter, actually wrote philosophical dialogues in order to make their arguments. Wittgenstein doesn't give different names to the people expressing different points of view. Nevertheless you can see that in this passage there is, in effect, a discussion between someone who believes that Hobbes's story makes sense and someone who does not. This means, of course, that we have to be careful to decide which of the positions is the one that Wittgenstein is actually defending. In fact, he was defending the point of view of the position which has the last word in this passage: the point of view of the person who says that "this means that here we can't talk about 'right'." We must try to see what Wittgenstein means by this claim and how he argues for it.

So, how *does* he get to this conclusion? Let's make explicit the fact that two opposed positions are represented here, by identifying each of them with a character. We might as well call one of these characters "Hobbes" and the other "Wittgenstein." Then we can paraphrase this passage as if it were a philosophical dialogue; and, for the sake of concreteness, let's call the sensation a "twinge," as we did before, rather than using Wittgenstein's rather neutral term "*S.*"

HOBBES: For there to be a private language, all that is required is that I associate some word, "twinge," with a sensation and use that word to record the occasions when the sensation occurs.

WITTGENSTEIN: But how can you define the term "twinge"?

HOBBES: I can give a kind of "ostensive definition." In an **ostensive definition**, we show what a term means by pointing to the thing it refers to. Thus, suppose we were trying to explain to someone, who didn't know English, what "red" meant. We could point to some red things and say "red" as we pointed to them. That would be an ostensive definition of the word "red."

WITTGENSTEIN: But for an ostensive definition to be possible, one must be able to point to something and in this case pointing is not possible. I cannot point to my own sensations.

HOBBES: Of course, you cannot *literally* point to a sensation, but you *can* direct your attention to it; and if, as you concentrate on the sensation, you say or write the name, then you can impress on yourself the connection between the name, "twinge," and the sensation.

WITTGENSTEIN: What do you mean by saying you "impress the connection on yourself"? All you can mean is that you do something which has the consequence that you remember the connection correctly in future. But what does it mean, in this case, to say that you have remembered it correctly? In order to be able to make sense of saying that you have remembered it correctly, you must have a way of telling whether you have remembered it correctly, a criterion of correctness. And how would you check, in this case, that you had remembered it right?

This is the key step in the argument. Wittgenstein asks Hobbes in effect to consider the question: "How do you know, when you say 'Aha, there's another twinge,' that it is the same experience you are having this time?" "Well," Hobbes might answer, "since nothing is more certain than what is going on in your own mind, there can be no doubt that you know."

But if it is possible for you to remember correctly, then it must be possible that you remember incorrectly. After all, according to Hobbes, it is the fact that we may forget an experience that makes names useful as marks. So suppose you *have* misremembered. Suppose that this experience is in fact not the same experience at all. How could you find out that this was so? And, if you can't find out, what use is the word "twinge"? The name gives you no guarantee that you have remembered correctly, if you have no guarantee that you know what the name refers to.

You might put Wittgenstein's objection like this. Hobbes's idea is that the name can help you remember that you have had the experience before. If it is possible that you have forgotten the experience of the *twinge*, however, then it is surely possible that you have forgotten the experience of *naming the twinge*. Do you need another "mark" which names the experience of naming the twinge? If every memory needs a name to help us remember it, then we seem to be caught in what is called an **infinite regress**. Hobbes's use of marks seems to be like the old Indian theory that the world is supported on the back of an elephant. If the world needs supporting, then the elephant needs supporting, too. And if the elephant doesn't need support, then why does the world?

An infinite regress argument like this shows

(a) that a proposed solution to a problem – in this case the problem of how the world stays in place – only creates another one – in this case, the problem of how the elephant stays in place, and
(b) that every time we use the proposed solution to deal with the new problem there will automatically be yet another one to solve.

This shows that the proposed solution leads to the ridiculous position where we accept a strategy for solving a problem that creates a new problem for every problem it solves.

This infinite regress argument is the one that shows that there is no possibility in this case of checking that you are using the term twinge correctly. And, once this point is established, we have reached the center of Wittgenstein's argument. Using the word "twinge" to refer to a private state involves conforming to the rule that you should say to yourself "twinge" only when you experience that private state. But the idea of trying to conform to a rule essentially involves the possibility that you might *fail* to apply it correctly: and in this case there is no such possibility. "Whatever is going to seem right to me is right. And that only means that here we can't talk about 'right'." If we have mental states that are private, the argument shows that we can't talk about them, even to ourselves! Since it doesn't make sense to talk about such private states, Wittgenstein drew the conclusion that there could not be any: after all, if the sentence "There are private states" makes no sense, it certainly can't be true!

There has been a good deal of philosophical argument about whether Wittgenstein was right to make his claim about rule-following. As I have said, much of the first part of his *Philosophical Investigations* is concerned with an attempt to defend this claim. If it is right, this seems to be a very powerful argument against the Hobbesian view that the primary function of language is to help us remember our own experiences. So you might want to think about whether you should accept Wittgenstein's view that following a rule requires a criterion of correctness. If you *do* accept Wittgenstein's claim about rules, you have good reason to prefer behaviorism to Cartesianism.

The behaviorist view of belief solves Descartes' problem: there is no difficulty for the behaviorist about the causal relations of mind and body. So it has an answer to the mind-body question, namely that having-a-mind is having a body with certain dispositions. And behaviorism certainly isn't open to the private language argument. So it solves the other-minds problem because it says that we can know about other people's minds just as easily as we know about any dispositions. We can know about your pain just as easily as we can know that a glass is fragile.

But behaviorism seems to create new problems as it solves these old ones. Here is one of them. The behavior that most obviously displays belief is speech: if you want to know what I believe, the first step is to ask me. So, as I've said, some behaviorists have held that to believe something is to be disposed (in certain specific sorts of circumstances) to say it. The trouble is that this theory makes it impossible, for example, to explain the beliefs of non-speaking creatures (including infants,) and has led some philosophers to deny that such creatures can have beliefs at all. Though there is something rather unsatisfactory about the privacy of the Cartesian mind, there is something simply crazy about the publicity of the behaviorist one. "Hello; you're fine. How am I?" says the behaviorist in a well-known cartoon; and the cartoonist has a point. We *do* know better than others about at least some aspects of our mental life. And the question for behaviorism is: Why? It isn't just that we see more of our actions than others. For in interpreting the minds of others we rely very much on their facial expressions; but we hardly ever see our own facial expressions at all.

Neither behaviorism nor Descartes' theory seems to be quite right.

1.4 Computers as models of the mind

In recent years, a new alternative to behaviorism has been suggested, which treats the mind neither as absurdly public, in the way behaviorism does, nor as completely private, in the way Cartesianism did. It is, in other words, a halfway house between behaviorism and Cartesianism, and it is called **functionalism**. Its recent appeal derives from the development of the very computers with which we began. For one way of expressing what functionalism claims is to say that it is the view that having a mind, for a body, is like having a program, for a machine.

A good way to start thinking about functionalist theories, however, is to look at similar "theories" of a simpler kind. Consider, then, what sort of theory you would need to give if you were trying to explain the workings not of something really complex, like a mind, but of something fairly simple and familiar, like a thermostat designed to keep the temperature above a certain level. What should a theory of such a thermostat say?

It should say, of course, that a thermostat is a device which turns a heater on and off in such a way as to keep the temperature above a certain level. Consider a thermostat which keeps the temperature above 60 degrees. An analysis of what something has to be like to do this job can be stated in a little "theory" of the thermostat.

A thermostat has to have three working parts. The first, which is the *heat-sensor*, has to have two states: in one state, the heat-sensor is ON, in the other it is OFF. It should be ON, when the external temperature is below 60 degrees and OFF when it is above. It doesn't matter how the heat-sensor is made. If it is a bimetallic strip, then maybe whether it is ON or OFF will depend on how bent the strip is; if it is a balloon of gas, which expands and contracts as the temperature changes, then ON will be below a certain volume, OFF will be above. The second part is the *switch*, which needs to have two states also. It should go into the ON state if the heat-sensor goes into its ON state; and into its OFF state if the heat-sensor goes OFF. Finally, we need the *heat-source*, which should produce heat when the switch goes ON and stop producing heat when the switch goes OFF. What I said about the heat-sensor applies to the other parts too: it doesn't matter what they are made of as long as they do the job I have just described.

Now this explanation of what a thermostat is also shows what a functionalist theory is; for this little theory is a functionalist theory. And what makes it functionalist is that it says how a thermostat *functions* by saying:

(a) what external events in the world produce changes inside the system – here, changes in temperature cause the sensor to go ON and OFF;
(b) what internal events produce other internal events – here, changes from ON to OFF in the sensor produce changes from ON to OFF in the switch; and
(c) what internal events lead to changes in the external world – here changes from OFF to ON in the switch lead to increased heat-output; changes from ON to OFF produced reduced heat-output.

Now anything at all which meets these specifications functions as a thermostat, and anything which has parts which play these roles can be said to have a heat-sensor, a switch, and a heat-source of the appropriate kind. In other words, at the most general level, a functionalist theory says what the internal states of a system are by fixing how they interact with input, and with other internal states, to produce output. What I mean by saying that the theory says what states *are* can be explained by way of an example: our thermostat theory says what a heat-sensor is by saying that it

(a) changes from ON to OFF (and back again) as the external temperature falls below (and rises above) 60 degrees, and
(b) causes changes which lead to an increase in heat-output if it is ON, and to a decrease when it is OFF.

A heat-sensor is thus characterized by its **functional role**; which is the way it functions in mediating between input and output in interaction with other internal states. And we can say, in general, that a functionalist theory says what a state *is* by saying how it functions in the internal working of a system.

We can apply this general model to computers. They have large numbers of internal, usually electronic, states. Programming a computer involves linking up these states to each other and to the outside of the machine so that, when you put some input into the machine, the internal states change in certain predictable ways and, sometimes, these changes lead it to produce some output. So, in a simple case, you put in a string of symbols like "2 + 2 =", at a terminal, and the machine's internal states change, in such a way that it outputs "4" at a printer. We can now see why computer programs can be thought of as functionalist theories of the computer. For a computer program is just a way of specifying how the internal states of the computer will be changed by inputting signals from disk or tape or from a keyboard, and how those changes in internal state will lead to output from the computer.

From one point of view – the engineer's – all that is going on in a computer is a series of electronic changes. From another – the programmer's – the machine is adding 2 and 2 to make 4. People who are functionalists about the mind – which is what I shall mean by **functionalists** from now on – believe that there are similarly two ways of looking at the mind-brain. The neurophysiologist's way, which is like the engineer's, sees the brain in terms of electrical currents or biochemical reactions. The psychologist's way, which is like the programmer's, sees the mind in terms of beliefs, thoughts, desires, and other mental states and events. Yet, just as there is only one computer, with two levels of description, so, the functionalist claims, there is only one mind-brain, with its two levels of description. In fact, just as we can say what electrical events in a computer correspond to its adding numbers, a functionalist can claim that we can find out which brain-events correspond to which thoughts. Functionalism thus leads to monism. There is only one kind of thing, even though there are different levels of theory about it.

Functionalism starts with an analogy between computers and minds. It doesn't say that computers have minds. But if we go carefully through the functionalist's arguments, we will see how you might end up holding that they could have minds, even if they don't yet.

1.5   Why should there be a functionalist theory?

But before we look in more detail at some functionalist proposals, it will help if we consider why anyone should think that it ought to be possible to construct a functionalist theory.

In section 1.2 I raised two questions that a theory of the mind ought to answer. "What justifies our belief that other minds exist at all?" and "How are we to explain the relations of a mind and its body?" Functionalism answers the second question quite simply: a person's body is what has the states that function as his or her mind. Just so the physical parts that make up the "body" of the thermostat are what function as heat-sensor, switch, and heater; and the physical "hardware" of a computer is what has the states that function according to the program.

But consider, now, what functionalism implies in answer to the first question. To have a mind, functionalists claim, is to have internal states that function in a certain way, a way that determines how a person will react to input – in the form of sensations and perceptions. The answer to the other-minds problem must, therefore, be that we know about other minds because we have evidence that people have internal states that function in the right way. And, of course, we do have such evidence, as the behaviorists pointed out. People with minds act in ways that are caused by what is going on in their minds; and what is going on in their minds is caused by things that happen around them. One reason for being a functionalist is, thus, that it allows you to deny the Cartesian claim that minds are essentially private; that only you can know what is going on in your mind. Wittgenstein's private language argument gives us a reason for doubting that minds can be essentially private. We shall see in the next chapter why many philosophers have held that nothing that exists can be known about only by one person. For the thesis that there are things that cannot, even in principle, be known by anyone appears inconsistent with some very basic facts about knowledge. To make these arguments now, I would have to step ahead of this chapter's topic. But when you have read what I say in the next chapter (section 2.6) about **verificationism**, you might want to think again about whether functionalists are right in holding that it is an advantage of their theory that it denies that the mind is essentially private.

1.6   Functionalism: A first problem

So far what I have said about functionalism is very abstract. If we are to see why it is plausible we will need a more concrete case to consider. Take beliefs.

Beliefs, for a functionalist, are characterized as states that are caused by sensations and perceptions of the appropriate kind, and that can cause other beliefs, and that interact with desires to produce action. Thus, for example, seeing a gray sky causes me to believe that the sky is gray, which may lead me to believe that it will rain, which may lead me to take my umbrella, because I desire not to get wet. Here, the input is sensation and perception, and the output is action; and the internal states that mediate between the two are beliefs and desires.

There is an immediate and obvious problem for anyone who wants to say what beliefs are in a theory of this kind. Remember that a functionalist says what an internal state of the system is by saying what its functional role is: by saying how it functions in mediating between input and output in interaction with other internal states. Suppose we try to do this for some particular belief – say the belief, once more, that the sky is gray. You might think you can say fairly precisely what would cause this belief. Looking up, eyes open, fully conscious, at a gray sky ought to do it. But the trouble is that this is really neither a necessary nor a sufficient condition for acquiring the belief. It isn't necessary, because you can acquire the belief in lots of other ways: looking at the sky's reflection in a pond, for example, or listening to a weather forecaster. It isn't sufficient, because, in suitably weird circumstances, you might reasonably believe that the sky wasn't gray when it looked gray. Suppose, for example, I told you I had inserted gray contact lenses in your eye while you were asleep; suppose you believed me. Then it would be very strange indeed if you came to believe the sky was gray when it looked gray. The general point, so far as input goes, is that whether the evidence of your senses would lead you to some particular belief – here, that the sky is gray – depends on what else you believe.

A similar problem arises with output, though here the issue is even more complex. For what you do on the basis of the belief that the sky is gray, depends not only on what other beliefs you have – do you believe that gray skies "mean" rain, for example? – but also on what desires you have – do you want to avoid getting wet, for example? So whereas for a heat-sensor in a thermostat the effect of input doesn't depend on a complex array of other internal states, in the case of belief in a mind it does.

In finding a way to handle this increased complexity, the analogy with the computer is helpful. For, in this respect, computers are more like minds than like thermostats. The results of inputting a number to a computer depend also on a complex array of internal states. If I put in a "=" to an adding program after putting in "2", followed by "+", followed by "2", then the output will be "4"; but if I put in the same sign, "=", after putting in "4", followed by "+", followed by "2", then the output will be "6". Yet we can still give a functional role to each internal state of the system: we can do it by saying, for example, that when the adding program is in the functional state of *having a "2" stored*, entering "+" followed by any numeral, "*n*," followed by "=" will result in outputting the numeral "*n*+2." The general strategy is this: we must specify the functional role of a state, *A*, by saying what will happen, for any input, if the computer is in state *A*, *but in a way that depends on what the other internal states are.*

So, for a functionalist account of the belief that the sky is gray, we can say, at the level of input, that it will be caused by looking at gray skies, *provided you don't believe that there's some reason why the sky should look gray when it isn't*; and that it will also be caused by acquiring any other belief that you think is evidence that the sky is gray. And we can say, at the level of output, that having the belief will lead you to try to perform those actions that would best satisfy your desires – whatever they are – if the sky was in fact gray. Which actions you think those are will itself depend on your other beliefs.

It may look as though we have still not solved the problem we started out with. For this definition of the belief that the sky is gray still seems to define it in terms of other states of belief and desire, and these other states are ones we want to give functionalist definitions also. So, you might ask, isn't this sort of definition going to be circular? We are going to define the belief that the sky is gray partly in terms of what it will lead you to do if you believe that gray skies mean rain; but aren't we going to have to define the belief that gray skies mean rain partly in terms of what it will lead you to do when you believe the skies are gray?

This is a genuine problem if you want to use functionalist definitions; but there is a procedure that allows us to solve it in a way that avoids this circularity. Applying it in the case of beliefs is extremely complex, so it will help, once more, to start with a simpler case.

1.7 A simple-minded functionalist theory of pain

Pain is a mental state. Let's suppose we are trying to produce a functionalist theory of it. We begin by gathering together all the truths we normally suppose a mental state must satisfy if it is to be a pain. The philosopher Ned Block has suggested how we might do it, for what he calls the "ridiculously simple theory," which we'll call *T*, that

> *T*: Pain is caused by pin pricks and causes worry and the emission of loud noises, and worry, in turn, causes brow-wrinkling.

T is ridiculously simple. But we can still use it to elucidate some general points about functionalist theories of the mind. For with this simple theory we can see how the charge of circularity might be avoided.

So, begin with *T.* We write it as one sentence. Then, we replace every reference to pain in the sentence by a letter, and each other mental term by a different letter, to get

> *T: X* is caused by pin pricks and causes *Y* and the emission of loud noises, and *Y*, in turn, causes brow-wrinkling.

(In this case, since there is only one other mental term, "worry," we only need the one extra letter, *Y*; but in other cases, as we'll see, we would need more.) The next step is to write in front of this the words "There exists an *X*, and there exists a *Y*, and there exists a . . . which are such that" for as many letters as we introduced when we removed the mental terms. So, in this simple case, we get

> *R*: There exists an *X*, and there exists a *Y*, which are such that *X* is caused by pin pricks and causes *Y* and the emission of loud noises, and *Y*, in turn, causes brow-wrinkling.

Notice that we now have a sentence, *R*, which has no mental terms in it. It allows us to say how pain works without relying circularly on knowing what "worry" is. It would be circular to rely on our understanding of what "worry" is, because, in a full functionalist theory, we would be going on to define worry later. Now, finally, we can define what it is for someone to be in pain. For we can say

> Someone – say Mary – is in pain if there exist states of Mary's, *X*, and *Y*, which are such that *X* is caused by pin pricks and causes *Y* and the emission of loud noises, and *Y*, in turn, causes brow-wrinkling *and* Mary has *X*.

If Mary has such a state, a state that functions in this way, she is in pain.

Now *T* is, as I said, ridiculously simple. But it has allowed us to see how to define one mental state – pain – that can only be explained in terms of its interactions with another mental state – worry – without assuming that we can define the other mental state first.

1.8 Ramsey's solution to the first problem

Now that we have seen how to solve the problem of defining one mental state without circularly assuming that we have already defined some others, let's see if we can see how to do this for belief. If we were to try to do this for belief, we should need many more letters than *X* and *Y*. We call these letters "variables," and they function in a way I shall explain in the chapter on language. But the procedure would be exactly the same. We would first write down all the claims about beliefs and desires and evidence and action that we think have to be satisfied by a creature that has a mind. We would join them all together with "and"s to make one very long sentence of our functionalist theory of the mind. Call that sentence *MT* (for "mental theory"). From *MT*, we would then take out all the mental terms referring to beliefs and desires and replace them with "variables." The result of this we can call *MT"*. Finally, for each variable we should write "There exists a . . ." in front of *MT"*, and we would have a new sentence, which didn't have any mental terms in it. That sentence is called the **Ramsey-sentence** of the theory *MT*, because this procedure was invented by the British philosopher Frank Ramsey. The Ramsey-sentence of *MT* says, in effect, that something that has a mind has a large number of internal states – one for each variable – which interact with input and with each other in certain specific ways, to produce behavior.

Now in 1.4, I said that many philosophers who have thought about the "other-minds" question have wanted to be able to define mental states in such a way that it was always possible, at least in principle, that somebody else should know what is going on in your mind. Notice that this functionalist theory, set up in the way Ramsey suggested, seems to make this possible. For Ramsey's method allowed us to define pain in terms of its causes and effects, its functional role, in such a way that if we have evidence that someone's internal states would make them react in certain public ways – brow-wrinkling and the emission of loud noises – in response to certain public events – pin pricks – we have evidence that they are in pain. It allowed us to do this without requiring that we know anything about the other internal states – in this case, worry – except that they too would have certain causes and effects, which could, in the end, be seen to show up in what people do. For the Ramsey-sentence of *MT* is true of someone if and only if they have a system of internal states that produces the right pattern of responses in output – in this case, brow-wrinkling and loud noises – to input – in this case, pin-pricks.

In the more complex case of beliefs, as we saw, we can proceed in a similar way. But here, just because the case is more complex and there are so many more internal states, it may be very hard, in practice, to discover that the right complex pattern of dispositions to respond to input exists. So, while allowing us to take mental states seriously, functionalism also allows us to believe that they might be very difficult, or, indeed, practically impossible for anyone but the person who has them, to find out about. And it is in this sense that functionalism is a halfway house between Descartes and behaviorism. For Descartes, as we saw, left open the possibility that someone could have mental states that no one else could know existed even in principle. Functionalism denies this. Any evidence of the existence of the right (extremely complex) pattern of dispositions will be evidence of your mental states. For behaviorism, every mental state is nothing more than a disposition to respond to input. Functionalism denies this also. What someone with a certain belief will do when stimulated depends, the functionalist claims, on other internal states as well.

1.9 Functionalism: A second problem

I said, in 1.1, that from an epistemological point of view, it seemed plausible to say that M had a mind. We have been looking, in the last three sections, at functionalism about minds from an essentially epistemological point of view. We have seen that functionalism offers a plausible answer to the "other-minds" question: we *can* know, at least in principle, what is going on in other peoples' minds. But from the phenomenological point of view, which denied that machines could have minds, functionalism doesn't look so attractive. For if functionalism is right and to have a mind is to have certain internal states that function in a certain way, then anything that has states that *function* in the right way has a mind. That seems to have the consequence that if a computer had internal states that functioned in the right way, it would have a mind. And, phenomenologists say, that is quite wrong. It isn't enough to have internal states that lead you to respond in the right way, you must also have an inner life. That inner life has to have the sort of character that Descartes thought it had. It has to be *conscious mental life.* And a machine could quite well behave in the right way without having any mental life at all.

If the phenomenologists are right, it follows that functionalism has failed to capture the essence of what it is to have a mind. For *if* they are right, a functionalist might say that a creature (or a machine) had a mind, because it had internal states with the right functions, even though it did not, in fact, have a mind, because it had no inner life. To understand this objection to functionalism, we must first try to make more precise what is meant by "having an inner life." The phenomenologist will usually explain this by saying that the difference between a creature with an inner life and one without an inner life is that there is *something that it feels like* to be a creature with an inner life, but nothing that it feels like to be a creature without one. If a person has an experience – say, seeing something red – we can ask what it feels like to have that experience. So, for example, if you, like me, are neither blind nor color-blind, then you know what it feels like to see red.

Suppose there was a machine that was sensitive to red things, and had internal states that led it to say "That's red" and, generally, to do all the things that people do with visual information. The phenomenologist believes we could still not be sure that the machine knew what it felt like to see red. That is why the phenomenologist thinks that a functionalist might mistakenly think that a machine had a mind.

How are we to settle this dispute between the phenomenologist and the functionalist? It will help, I think, to consider it in the light of specific examples again; and, as we shall see, M and your mother provide just the right kinds of examples.

1.10 M again

M was a machine that would behave in every situation exactly like your mother. A machine that is made to have internal states that function like a human mind we can call **functionally equivalent** to a person. M and your mother are functionally equivalent. But phenomenologists might have different attitudes to them. The phenomenologist might say

> How do I know whether M knows, as your mother does, what it feels like to see red? Your mother, I believe, does know, because she, like me, is a human being. I have reason to think that human beings with normal vision know what seeing red feels like. For I know what it is like, and I believe that other human beings are like me.

The functionalist replies:

> All the evidence you have that your mother knows what it is like to see red is from what she says and does. Since M does the same, it is unreasonable to believe that your mother has a mind and M does not.

Notice, first, that we cannot appeal to any *evidence* to settle the dispute. Even if we were discussing an actual machine, instead of a hypothetical one, it wouldn't help, for example, to ask it if it knew what it felt like to see red. For any machine functionally equivalent to your mother would say "Yes" if you asked it if it knew what it felt like to see red, because that is what your mother would say. Of course, if you didn't believe that what the machine said was true, you might try and test it, just as you might try and test your mother, if you suspected that she was color blind. But whatever she would do in the test the machine would do also. So no amount of such testing is going to give you a reason to say something about the machine that you wouldn't say about your mother. The phenomenologist's worry that M may lack mental states will never be settled by the kind of evidence that normally persuades us that people have them.

Now this is already a rather strange situation, since we normally think we can tell whether people know what it feels like, for example, to see red, by testing their responses to red things. Nevertheless, despite the fact that no amount of evidence could settle the issue, the conviction that there *is* a real doubt about whether such a machine would have a mind is very widespread, including among philosophers. In the next chapter I shall be looking at arguments for the view that if no amount of evidence could decide an issue, there is no real issue. Someone who believes this is called a **verificationist**. And, if the verificationist is correct, then the phenomenologist must be wrong.

But even if the phenomenologist is right in thinking that some states, such as seeing that something is red, can only be had by someone with an "inner life," there are other mental states for which this does not seem to be true.

Take beliefs once more. We do not normally talk of "knowing what it feels like to have a belief." Indeed, we can have beliefs – unconscious ones – that we are unaware of altogether, and even our conscious beliefs do not have a special "feel" to them. What does it feel like to believe consciously that the President is in Washington, or that the rain in Spain falls mainly on the plain?

If this is so, then, even if the phenomenologist was right to be suspicious about the claim that M knows what it feels like to see red, that would not give you a reason to doubt that it had beliefs. And, as the functionalist will insist, you would have all the same reasons for thinking that M did have beliefs as you have for thinking that your mother has them. But beliefs are a pretty important feature of people's minds; and if having beliefs is enough to have a mind, then, as I said, we might end up holding that machines could have minds, even if they don't yet.

1.11   Conclusion

In this chapter we have discussed some of the central questions of the philosophy of mind. We started by asking "Can machines have minds?" But that led us to ask how we know that *people* have minds, and what minds are like. Because we asked this epistemological question, I came, at the end, to a point where we could go no further until we had thought more about knowledge. We were also led to consider what the relationship is between a mind and its body. And because causation seems very important to this relationship – because thoughts seem to cause actions, and events in the world seem to cause sensations – we found at another point that we could go no further until we had thought some more about causation. That is one reason why I haven't been able to settle the central dispute of this chapter – between the functionalist and the phenomenologist – decisively in favor of one or the other. But even if I *had* given an explanation of the nature of causation and of knowledge, I should not have been able to settle that question decisively. For it is a question that divides philosophers now, and there is something to be said in favor of both sides. If, when we have gone further with knowledge, you decide to join the phenomenologist, on the one hand, or the functionalist, on the other, I hope you will keep in mind that there are good arguments in support of each of them.

Questions about the relation between our knowledge of minds and minds themselves have been central to our discussion in this chapter. It is time now to approach the nature of knowledge head on.

2 Knowledge

What is knowledge?

How can we justify our claims to knowledge?

What can we know?

2.1 Introduction

Brain surgery is getting better all the time. We can't do them yet, but one day we may well be able to do brain transplants. Let's suppose that we are living in a time when they are possible. Unlike other transplants, of course, the person who survives the operation is the owner of the organ not the owner of the body. But like all organ transplants, brain transplants involve an intermediate stage. For a while, a brain has to be stored outside its old body before it is connected into a new one. Now suppose that someone – call him Harry – is very badly injured in an accident. His body is hopelessly damaged. Fortunately his brain was protected by a helmet, and, as a result, it is unhurt. So a neuro-surgeon sets about removing Harry's brain from his body in order to transplant it to a new one. Let's call this surgeon "Ruth." Ruth carefully removes, along with the brain, both the *sensory* nerves that used to carry information from Harry's eyes, ears, nose, mouth and so on, about the looks, sounds, smells and tastes and the feel of the world around him; and the *motor* nerves that used to carry messages from the brain to the muscles, "telling them" what to do.

Unfortunately, there isn't a spare body available just yet. So Ruth puts Harry's brain into a vat of fluid and connects up the main blood vessels to a supply of blood. This is science fiction, so let's add interest by supposing that Ruth is an unscrupulous scientist. Here's a spare brain, and she just can't resist investigating it while she waits for a body. So she connects up the sensory nerve-endings to an elaborate computer. The computer is designed to feed those nerve-endings with electrical stimuli that are just like the stimuli that Harry got when his brain was properly connected to his body. Thus, when Harry's brain recovers consciousness, the computer feeds it electrical stimuli, which produce in the nerves of his eyes the very same electrical signals that used to make him think he was looking around a room. If Ruth connected the motor nerve-endings to the computer too, she could tell what the brain was trying to do, and the computer could fake the experiences that the brain would have had in a body if it had succeeded in what it was trying to do.

Now here's a question. Is there any way Harry could tell that he was being fooled? Most people would say that the answer is no. But if Harry couldn't tell in that situation, then, if you were in a similar situation, you couldn't tell either. So what makes you so sure you aren't being fooled right now? Maybe you're part of the first experimental program that will eventually lead to regular brain transplants. The researchers know that you would be very distressed to discover that you had lost your body, so they've deliberately wiped out all memories of the accident. They've faked your experience of reading this chapter in order to start you thinking about the idea of a new body! Later on, maybe, they'll tell you the truth; but, for now, you are living like Harry. Of course, if you *are* being fooled now, then all the things you think are going on around you are not happening at all. This book you think you are reading, for example, is just an illusion produced by a device like Ruth's computer.

Philosophers are often caricatured as being worried about things that it is absurd to worry about. They are supposed to ask questions like "How do I know that the book in front of me is really there?"; and, without a context, that really can seem a pointless question. But once we place the question in the context of this science fiction possibility, it does not seem so obviously pointless. Maybe, one day not too far from now, somebody might find themselves asking this question in all seriousness. Once again a piece of science fiction has lead us straight to the heart of a philosophical problem. How *do* we know about the existence of physical objects? Our robot, M, raised the question of how we know that other people have minds. Now we have to ask an even more disturbing question: How do we know that other people have bodies? Indeed, how do we know that anything exists at all?

Questions like these, about the nature of knowledge, belong to **epistemology** – the philosophical examination of the nature of knowledge. And one way to set about answering the sorts of questions raised by this story is to start by asking what we mean by "knowledge." If we can answer that question, we'll be in a better position to discover if – and if so, how – we know that we aren't just brains in fluid, the playthings of an unscrupulous scientist.

2.2 Plato: Knowledge as justified true belief

Plato is the first Western philosopher who left us a substantial body of writing. Yet he never wrote any philosophical treatises like Descartes' *Discourse on Method*. Instead he wrote dialogues: dramatic works in which different characters represent and argue for different philosophical positions. In these dialogues the central character is usually Plato's teacher, Socrates, whose philosophical technique was to proceed not by stating a position but by asking questions and leading those with whom he talked to their own answers. In the dialogue called the *Theaetetus*, Socrates discusses the question "What is knowledge?" with a young man called Theaetetus. Because Plato's discussion of knowledge has been as central to the Western tradition as Descartes' view of mind has been to modern philosophical psychology, I want to begin considering what knowledge is by examining some of the ideas discussed by Socrates and Theaetetus in this famous dialogue.

Theaetetus begins answering Socrates's question "What is knowledge?" by giving examples of knowledge: geometry, for example, and the technical know-how of a shoemaker. But Socrates objects that what he wants is not a set of examples of knowledge, but rather an explanation of the nature of knowledge. In answer to the philosophical question "What is knowledge?" what is wanted is a definition that we can use to decide whether any particular case really is a case of somebody's knowing something.

Theaetetus then makes other attempts at answering the question, which *do* give definitions of this sort. But Socrates argues against all of them. Finally, Theaetetus suggests that to know something is just to believe something that is true. If you know that you are reading this book, for example, then, on Theaetetus's theory,

(a) you must believe you are reading this book, and
(b) you must, in fact, be reading this book.

Socrates points out that it follows from this theory of Theaetetus's that when a skilled lawyer persuades a jury that someone is innocent, then, if the person is in fact innocent, the jury knows he or she is innocent, *even if the lawyer has persuaded the jury by dishonest means.* This consequence, Socrates argues, shows that Theaetetus's theory must be wrong, because in such circumstances we would not allow that the jurors *knew* that the accused person was innocent, even if they *correctly believed* it.

Socrates has a point. Suppose, for example, my lawyers believe that I am innocent and that I am being framed. They might decide that it was more important to protect someone from being framed than to respect the law, which the prosecutors are, after all, abusing. So they might fake evidence that undermines the fake evidence of the prosecutors. Suppose they persuaded the jury: the members of the jury would *correctly believe* I am innocent, but they certainly wouldn't *know* that I am innocent.

Here is the passage where Socrates summarizes his objection and Theaetetus responds:

> SOCRATES: But if true belief and knowledge were the same thing, then the jury would never make correct judgments without knowledge; and, as things are, it seems that the two [i.e. knowledge and true belief] are different.
> THEAETETUS: Yes, Socrates, there's something I once heard someone saying, which I'd forgotten, but it's coming back to me now. He said that true belief with a justification is knowledge, and the kind without a justification falls outside the sphere of knowledge.

Theaetetus realizes that this case shows that we need some third condition for knowledge: knowing does involve believing, and it does involve the truth of what you believe, but it also requires something else. And, since he is nothing if not persistent, Theaetetus suggests that knowledge is true belief along with a justification. The rest of the *Theaetetus* is taken up with discussing what sort of justification is necessary. But the essential idea is that to know something

PLATO

Plato (c.430-347 BC) was born in Athens, Greece, of an aristocratic family. But since Athens was a democracy for most of his life, his family played little part in political affairs. Plato was profoundly influenced by Socrates, who was sentenced to death when Plato was in his early thirties, apparently for undermining the state religion of Athens with his skepticism. In middle age Plato travelled to Egypt and to Syracuse in Sicily (as the guest of the ruler, Dionysus). He then returned home and founded the Academy, a school whose curriculum he describes in Book VII of *The Republic* – perhaps Plato's most famous book, and the first great work of political philosophy. The Academy was originally in Plato's house, and it was the first permanent school for young men in Athens. Unlike earlier Greek schools it had several teachers and a broad curriculum and subjects were not studied as a preparation for a specific vocation. In that sense, the Academy was, in fact, the first Western "academic" institution, pursuing knowledge for its own sake. Plato's writings, with the exception of some letters of disputed authenticity, are dialogues,

usually with Socrates – the central character – and a few others arguing on a question in metaphysics, logic, ethics, epistemology or political philosophy. Aristotle, whose works were the most influential philosophical writings until the Renaissance, was Plato's student at the Academy. Among Plato's best-known works, apart from *The Republic*, are *Theaetetus*, a work of epistemology, *Timaeus*, a work of natural science, and *The Symposium*, which discusses the nature of love.

(a) you must believe it,
(b) it must be true, and
(c) you must be justified in believing it.

It is the recognition that we need this third condition – which I'll call the **justification condition** – that is the *Theaetetus's* major legacy to epistemology. That the justification condition and the first two conditions, taken together, are necessary and sufficient conditions for knowledge is a central philosophical claim of the Western tradition since Plato. This idea is often expressed in the slogan "Knowledge is justified true belief."

Socrates never accepts any of Theaetetus's attempts to define exactly which kind of justification is necessary to turn true belief into knowledge; but the idea provides the starting point for many philosophical attempts to define knowledge since. Typically, philosophers have first argued for the view that knowledge is justified true belief, and then gone on to ask the question: "What *kind* of justification do you need, in order to have knowledge?"

Theaetetus's idea is suggested by a diagnosis of why the jurors don't really know I'm innocent. That diagnosis is, roughly, that though the jurors have a true belief, it isn't one that they are entitled to have, since my lawyers could have used the very same evidence to convince them I was innocent, *even if I had been guilty.* In other words, the evidence my lawyers gave the jury for the claim that I was innocent was consistent with my being guilty, even though it persuaded them that I was not. This diagnosis is at the root of the first of two major ways in which philosophers have tried to say exactly what the justification condition amounts to. The first is found in the epistemology of Descartes.

2.3   Descartes' way: Justification requires certainty

To see how we might get to the first way of interpreting the justification condition – Descartes' way – let's start by examining more precisely what it means to say that the evidence my lawyers present in the hypothetical case we have been considering is *consistent* with my being guilty.

One way of putting more precisely what I mean by saying that the evidence is consistent with my being guilty is that there is a true sentence that reports the evidence and that sentence is consistent with a sentence that says I am guilty. Two sentences are consistent only if it is possible for them to be true at the same time. Throughout this chapter, when I am discussing evidence I shall often talk about sentences that report the evidence. This doesn't mean that I think that having evidence is simply a matter of believing sentences to be true. If I thought that, I'd have difficulty in explaining how a person who didn't know at least one language could know anything. It's just that putting it in terms of sentences makes it easier to express the points I want to make. Suppose, then, that we have a sentence, and we're looking at the evidence for it. Let's call the sentence that reports the evidence the **evidence-sentence**, and the sentence for which it is evidence *S*. What we mean, then, by the evidence being **consistent** with the sentence *S* being false, is that it is possible that the evidence-sentence should be true and *S* should be false at the same time. Thus, for example, the evidence-sentence "John is crying and looking downcast" is quite consistent with the sentence "John is unhappy" being false, since John might be trying to fool us.

Nevertheless, "John is crying and looking downcast" is good evidence that John is unhappy. Evidence like this, which is consistent with the falsity of the sentence it supports, is called **defeasible** evidence. If, on the other hand, you have evidence for the truth of a sentence, *S*, that is so good that it is *not* possible that *S* should be false when the evidence-sentence is true, then you have what we call **indefeasible** evidence for *S*. The evidence-sentence "It looks red to me," for example, is indefeasible evidence for the sentence "I am having a visual experience."

The jury in my story plainly did not have indefeasible evidence that I was innocent: for, as I said, the evidence was consistent with my being guilty. One possible view, then, would be that what the jury in my story lacked was indefeasible evidence, and that if they had had *that*, they would have had knowledge. The justification condition for knowledge, on this view, means that you must have evidence that justifies your belief *indefeasibly*.

This was, as I say, essentially Descartes' view. Descartes didn't know much about how brains work. But he got to this conclusion by considering problems very much like the one raised by Ruth, the unscrupulous neuro-surgeon, with which I began. One problem he raised was how we could know that all our experiences were not just a dream. In many ways this is just like asking how we know that we are not Ruth's victims. But his most convincing way of raising the question of our knowledge of the physical world, in terms that were natural and of immediate concern in his day, was to consider the possibility of an evil demon's fooling us into believing things by careful manipulation of our senses. This demon would be able, like Ruth, to keep us from knowing what it was doing, while essentially fabricating all our experiences for us.

Here are two passages where Descartes first faces the possibility of the evil demon, and then considers how to respond to it.

> I will suppose, then, not that there is a supremely good God, the source of truth; but that there is an evil spirit, who is supremely powerful and intelligent, and does his utmost to deceive me. I will suppose that sky, air, earth, colors, shapes, sounds, and all external objects are mere delusive dreams, by means of which he lays snares for my credulity . . .
>
> But if I did convince myself of anything, I must have existed. "But there is some deceiver, supremely powerful, supremely intelligent, who purposely always deceives me." If he deceives me, then again I undoubtedly exist; let him deceive me as much as he may, he will never bring it about that, at the time of thinking that I am something, I am in fact nothing. Thus I have now weighed all considerations enough and more than enough; and must at length conclude that this proposition "I am", "I exist", whenever I utter or conceive it in my mind, is necessarily true.

This is a very persuasive argument: it is, indeed, one of the most famous arguments in the history of philosophy. What Descartes realized was that, however powerful the demon was, there was one thing the demon couldn't fool him about, namely Descartes' own existence. The evidence each of us has of our own existence is indefeasible: it is obviously impossible both to be aware of yourself and not to exist. Descartes formulated this argument rather pithily in Latin in one of the best known slogans in all philosophy: "*Cogito ergo sum*," which means "I think, therefore I am."

Descartes thought he could escape the demon's tricks if he could find other beliefs that were as certain and indubitable for him as his own existence – the "I am" – and the fact that he had thoughts – the "I think." So long as he had any beliefs at all, he could claim *these* beliefs as knowledge, however hard the demon tried to confuse him.

Descartes, then, suggested that the right way to explain the justification condition was to insist that the evidence you had entitled you to be certain of what you believed. And by "certain" he meant that it had to be impossible to doubt it. This, after all, is a natural extension of the idea that we express by asking people who think they know something, "But are you *sure?*" We want them to consider whether they really have no doubt at all that they are right.

It is only a short step from insisting that a belief that is to count as knowledge must be impossible to doubt, to insisting that you must have indefeasible evidence for the belief. For if it is impossible for you to doubt that S, then you must have evidence that couldn't be true unless S was true. And I defined "indefeasible evidence" as evidence for the truth of a sentence, S, that is so good that it is not possible that S should be false when the evidence-sentence is true. So Descartes is committed to the view that to know something you must have indefeasible evidence for it – or, equivalently, that your evidence must make the belief indubitable. To know something, for Descartes,

(a) you must believe it,
(b) it must be true, and
(c) you must have indefeasible evidence for the belief.

Descartes' view has one surprising immediate consequence. Some sentences – like "Nothing is both in New York and not in New York at the same time" – couldn't be false, and they are called **necessary truths**. It turns out that, given the way *indefeasible evidence* is defined, any sentence at all is indefeasible evidence for a necessary truth. Take a sentence, S, which is a necessary truth. By definition, it can't be false. Indefeasible evidence for S is *defined* as evidence that couldn't be true if S were false. Consider any other sentence at all; say, T. It certainly isn't possible for S to be false, if T is true. For it isn't possible for S to be false under *any* circumstances. So you have indefeasible evidence for any sentence that is a necessary truth, provided you believe anything at all!

It follows, of course, that we *know* any necessary truths we believe. For necessary truths are, by definition, true under *any* circumstances, and, as we have seen, we automatically have indefeasible evidence for them.

As far as necessary truths are concerned, then, Descartes' theory is very permissive. The difficulty with the theory is that it is, by contrast, very demanding, when it comes to beliefs about the physical world. Indeed, it is so demanding that it is hard to think of any beliefs about physical objects that Descartes could claim to know. For, after all, as the story of Ruth and Harry showed – as Descartes' own story of the demon shows – the evidence we actually have is consistent with our being wrong about almost everything we believe, except – as Descartes saw – what we believe about our own existence and our own thoughts. Nothing at all – save the existence of our own minds – is certain. So, on the Cartesian view, nothing at all – save the existence of our own minds – is known. The philosophical position that we can know nothing about some kind of thing is known as **skepticism** about things of that kind. The Cartesian definition of knowledge leads swiftly to skepticism about the physical world.

Descartes thought he could escape the skeptical consequences of his definition of knowledge. His way of avoiding these consequences depends on the belief that there is an omnipotent, benevolent God, who does not want us to be deceived. It is important to state as clearly as possible why this helps, because it allows us to make explicit one of Descartes' assumptions about the way we ought to seek justification for our beliefs. That assumption, as we shall see, is crucial to many philosophical views about justification.

Suppose I have a sensory experience that I can describe by saying:

E: It looks to me as though there is a book in front of me.

I call this sentence E – for "evidence." Since E is about my own mind, Descartes will allow that I can know it to be true: I can have indefeasible evidence of my own state of mind. But how can I come to know, on the basis of this state of mind, that there is, in fact, a book in front of me? Descartes says that if God is both benevolent and all-powerful, then He can make sure that the experiences we have correspond with the way the world really is. But even if my experience in fact corresponds with reality, because God has guaranteed it, I cannot *know* that it does unless I have indefeasible evidence. Suppose, however, that I have indefeasible evidence that God guarantees that sensory experience corresponds to how the world is. Then I know that if it looks, sounds, or, in general, seems to me that something is so, it *is* so. And so I know, in particular, that

R: If it looks to me as though there is a book in front of me, then there *is* a book in front of me.

Now from the two sentences, R and E, it follows logically that there is a book in front of me. (We shall discuss what it means for something to follow logically in the next chapter: see 3.10.) Furthermore, I know, according to Descartes, both R and E. Suppose that if something you believe follows logically from two things you know, then you know *it*, too. If that were true, Descartes could say that I knew that there was a book in front of me.

Descartes' claim that God's guarantee of our senses can form the basis of knowledge, requires, therefore, both

(a) that we know about God's guarantee, and
(b) that the following principle is correct:

Take any two sentences, A and B: if you know that A and know that B, and if from A and B, together, C follows logically, then, if you believe that C, you know that C.

This principle is usually called the **deductive closure principle**. For it says that the class of things you know includes all your beliefs that are logical (or "deductive") consequences of everything you know already.

Notice that the deductive closure principle is really a consequence of Descartes' definition of knowledge. For, on Descartes' theory, if you know both *A* and *B*, then it is true of each sentence that

(a) you believe it,
(b) it is true, and
(c) you have indefeasible evidence for it.

Suppose you believe *C*, which follows logically from *A* and *B*. Since you do know *A* and *B*, it follows that your belief in *C* is true. That gives us conditions (a) and (b). So you know *C*, provided the justification condition (c) is satisfied as well. Does your knowing *A* and *B* mean you have indefeasible evidence for *C*, which follows from them? Obviously. For if *C* follows from *A* and *B*, then the evidence-sentence that makes *A* and *B* true, makes *C* true as well. So the deductive closure principle is correct.

The core of the argument here is expressed in the following principle:

> *PDJ*: If you take any two sentences, *A* and *B*, then, if you are justified in believing both *A* and *B*, and if from *A* and *B* together, *C* follows logically, then, if you believe *C*, you are justified in believing *C*.

The American philosopher, Irving Thalberg, has called this the **principle of deduction for justification** (**PDJ**, for short.) The PDJ is certainly correct if justification means "indefeasible justification." And, given the PDJ and Descartes' definition of knowledge, the deductive closure principle follows.

Descartes requires the deductive closure principle because, without it, even the existence of a benevolent God, attempting to do the opposite of the evil demon, would not allow us knowledge of the world. With both the principle and the knowledge that God guarantees that our senses will not deceive us, however, Descartes is able to allow that we have some knowledge of the physical world.

But there is a serious problem with the Cartesian position. It is that Descartes offers no convincing reason for thinking that we know that God guarantees the evidence of our senses. After all, it seems that our senses can sometimes deceive us: sometimes we seem to have hallucinations. And if we sometimes have hallucinations, then God doesn't always guarantee that the world is as it appears to be. (It won't help here to say that God *sometimes* makes sure our senses don't deceive us, because to know anything, on Descartes' view, we would have to know *when*.)

If God doesn't guarantee our senses, then we don't have indefeasible true beliefs about the physical world. So we know nothing about it. Still, as we saw earlier, we *do* have some knowledge, since we know any necessary truths we believe. The real reason that Descartes thought we knew necessary truths is that we do not need evidence from our senses to justify belief in them at all. His theory leads to skepticism about the physical world because all the evidence of our senses is defeasible. But we can work out necessary truths without relying on our unreliable senses.

Because Cartesianism lays such stress on certainty, it leads to the conclusion that we know only those things that we can work out by reasoning, without appeal to sensory evidence, even though Descartes tried to avoid this consequence. The position that the major or only source of knowledge is reasoning is called **rationalism**. We shall discuss the nature of necessary truths in the next chapter, where we shall see that the rationalist belief that all our knowledge of necessary truths comes solely from reasoning is mistaken.

The main objection to Cartesian rationalism, however, is that it leads to skepticism about the physical world. For it seems absurd to claim that we don't know of the existence of any physical objects at all. The British philosopher G.E. Moore once held up his hands in an expression of exasperation with those who deny the existence of the "external world," the world "outside" our minds, and said that he certainly knew that his hands existed. He was, in effect, assuming that we should reject a theory that had so absurd a consequence as that he didn't know he had two hands. Very often in philosophy, we argue against a position by showing that it has absurd consequences: a procedure called **reductio ad absurdum** (or **reductio**, for short,) which is just the Latin for "reducing to absurdity." Moore's point was that we should reject a philosophical theory of knowledge that leads us to conclude that we do not know that our own hands exist. We should reject such a theory because this consequence reduces it to absurdity.

It is important in a *reductio* proof that the consequence we draw should be not only absurd but false. We shall discuss in the next chapter the fact that if you can draw a false conclusion from a position, the position must be false itself. Because it is the *falsity* of the conclusion that means that the position must be false, we sometimes refer to an argument as a *reductio* simply because it shows that a position leads to a false conclusion.

Now there is no doubt that we have to be very careful with *reductio ad absurdum* as a form of argument. This is because it is not always clear that what we take to be absurd really is false. For a long time, for example, it might have been thought absurd to draw the conclusion that God doesn't exist. Nowadays, even many believers agree that it is not *absurd* to suppose that there is no God, though, of course, they think that it is an error to believe this. So before we reject Descartes' position in Moore's way, we should consider seriously the possibility that it is *not* false that we know nothing of the external world.

But we have at least one strong motive for rejecting Descartes' extremely strict interpretation of the justification condition, if it does have the consequence that we know only of the existence of our own thoughts; namely, that a theory of knowledge that says that we can know nothing about the world in which we live makes the concept of knowledge rather uninteresting. We certainly have beliefs about the world, and some of them seem better justified than others. Even if knowledge is unavailable, we should still need the idea of justified beliefs. And whatever "justified" means, it cannot mean "indefeasibly justified" in this context, because, as we have seen, *no* beliefs about the physical world are indefeasibly justified.

We have, then, good reason for hoping that Descartes is wrong to insist on indefeasible justification, because this theory of knowledge leads to skepticism. But we may be able to develop a theory of knowledge that does not lead to skepticism, if we find another way of interpreting the justification condition. Is there any way of interpreting the condition that is less demanding?

2.4   Locke's way: Justification can be less than certain

The obvious thing to do is to weaken the justification condition, to require not indefeasible evidence, but just *good* evidence. As Moore pointed out, we normally take it that we know that we have hands, even though we do not have indefeasible evidence that we have them. The evidence that we have hands – which is the evidence of our senses – is strong evidence, even if it isn't strong enough to satisfy Descartes.

Let us examine the proposal, then, that to know something

(a)   you must believe it,
(b)   it must be true, and
(c)   you must have good – but not necessarily indefeasible – evidence for the belief.

On this theory, unlike Descartes', I can know, for example, that I have two hands, because I have very good evidence from experience for my true belief that I have two hands. Someone who believes that evidence of this sort is what we require for knowledge of the physical world is called an empiricist. **Empiricism** is the claim that most or all of our beliefs are justified by experience – by empirical evidence, as it is called. Such evidence comes from our senses: our sight, hearing, taste, smell, touch, and so on. Just as rationalists regard necessary truths – sentences that *must* be true – as the model of knowledge, empiricists regard contingent truths – which might not have been true – as the model. (We shall discuss the idea of truths being *necessary* or *contingent* in the next chapter.) For a rationalist, like Descartes, "2 + 2 = 4" would be a very good example of something we know, because reasoning can give us indefeasible evidence that it is true. For an empiricist a sentence like "It is raining here," said by someone standing in the rain, would be a very good example of something someone knows.

Descartes was a leading rationalist. The English philosopher John Locke, who also wrote in the seventeenth century, was one of the founders of modern empiricism. In Book 2, Chapter 1, Section 2, of his *Essay Concerning Human Understanding*, one of the great classics of empiricism, he says:

> *All Ideas come from Sensation or Reflection.* Let us then suppose the mind to be, as we say, white paper, void of all characters, without any ideas: how comes it to be furnished? Whence comes it by that vast store which the busy and boundless fancy of man has painted on it with an almost endless variety? Whence has it all the materials of reason and knowledge? To this I answer, in one word, *experience.* In that all our knowledge is founded; and from that it ultimately derives itself.

Though this is an apparently clear statement of the essentials of empiricism, what Locke is saying is not as simple as it seems. There are two main reasons.

First, Locke held a special view about what our minds contain. Our knowledge, he believed, is stored in our minds in the form of collections of ideas. These ideas are what he calls the "materials" of knowledge: they are, quite literally, what our knowledge is made of. When he says that all our knowledge is *founded* in experience, then, he does not mean that all of our knowledge is *justified* by experience. He means rather that we can have no ideas that are not derived from experience; and that, thereore, every piece of knowledge is made up of materials that come from experience. As we shall see in a moment, it is very important that Locke did not hold that all of our knowledge has to be justified by experience.

A second reason why what Locke says here is not as simple as it seems is that Locke meant by "experience" something rather more than just sensation. In Book 2, Chapter 1, Sections 3 and 4, he argues, there are two sources of ideas in experience:

> *The Objects of Sensation one Source of Ideas.* First, our Senses, conversant about particular sensible objects, do convey into the mind several distinct perceptions of things, according to those various ways wherein those objects which do affect them . . . This great source of most of the ideas we have, depending wholly upon our senses, and derived by them to the understanding, I call SENSATION.

> *The Operations of our Minds, the other Source of them.* Secondly, the other fountain from which experience furnisheth the understanding with ideas is, – the perception of the operations of our own mind, as it is employed about the ideas it has got; . . . I call this REFLECTION, the ideas it affords being such only as the mind gets by reflecting on its own operations within itself . . . These two, I say, viz. external material things, as the objects of SENSATION, and the operations of our own minds within, as the objects of REFLECTION, are to me the only originals from whence all our ideas take their beginnings.

All of our ideas, then, come from experience: either experience, in sensation, of the world outside us, or experience, in reflection, of the workings of our own minds. It is also true that most of our beliefs derive from experience. But, Locke holds, we can also come to know things – mathematical truths, for example, such as "2 + 2 = 4" – by reasoning, which he calls "demonstration." "Mathematical demonstration," he says, "depends not upon sense . . ." (Book 3, Chapter 11, Section 6). Even here, however, our knowledge is *founded* in experience: for our ideas of the numbers 2 and 4, or of addition and the equality of numbers, are just as much derived from experience, according to Locke, as our ideas of tables and chairs. The idea of the number 2, for example, he thought was derived by "abstraction" from our experiences of pairs of things.

It follows, then, that though Locke stresses that our ideas *come from* or are "founded in" experience, he can agree that reason can be as much a source of knowledge as experience. Locke can, therefore, accept all the kinds of knowledge that Descartes' theory allowed: but he is not restricted to truths known indefeasibly. So, he can hold that we sometimes come to know things other than by reasoning.

Empiricism as an approach to epistemology has grown side by side with modern science. Locke was a contemporary of Sir Isaac Newton, the first great modern physicist. This connection between the growth of empiricism and the growth of science is not very surprising. Science depends a great deal on experience in its search for knowledge of the physical world. Even psychology, which sometimes relies on our experiences of our own mental life for its evidence, relies on experience, in Locke's sense. For, remember, Locke regarded "reflection," by which he meant our experience of our own mental lives, as a kind of experience.

The basic idea that much of our knowledge derives from our experiences of the world is, as a result, an attractive one in an age of science. Mathematics is, of course, important to modern science too, and we learn mathematical facts, not from experience, but – as Locke pointed out – by using our powers of reasoning. But even in mathematical physics, which uses more mathematics than most other sciences, the evidence of experience is tremendously important.

Nevertheless, it is one thing to say that we know only those things that we correctly believe and that experience – or demonstration – justifies us in believing; it is another to say precisely *how* our experiences justify our beliefs. Indeed, we have already come across the fact that creates the main problem for empiricism: the evidence of experience is always defeasible. This means that the evidence we have could, in each case, be misleading us. So we have to ask whether there is any way of deciding which evidence we should actually rely on. In answering this question, empiricists have often tried to develop the idea that some of the knowledge we acquire in experience provides the basis for the rest of our knowledge. They have held, in effect, that all of our knowledge is founded on one basic class of things we know. This approach is called **foundationalist epistemology**.

2.5 The foundations of knowledge
According to all foundationalist epistemologies

(a) we need to find some class of beliefs, of which we have secure knowledge; and
(b) once we find this class, we can then honor some of our other beliefs with the special status of knowledge by showing that they are properly supported by the members of this class of **foundational beliefs**.

So every foundationalist epistemology needs to answer two main questions:

(a) *the nature of the foundations*: what are the foundational beliefs? and
(b) *the nature of the justification*: how do the foundational beliefs support the other, derivative, beliefs?

If we could find the right foundational beliefs, and the right explanation of how they support other beliefs, then we might be able to find a way around Ruth, the unscrupulous scientist, and Descartes' demon. With the right answers to these two questions, we might be able to deal with the problems created by the fact that the evidence of experience is always defeasible. The possibility is worth investigating.

I said just now that foundationalism has appealed to many empiricists. But it is a natural view for any rationalist as well. Rationalists believe that reasoning is the best source of knowledge; and, in the most rigorous sort of reasoning – namely, mathematical proof – we start with axioms, as our foundation, and proceed by logical steps to our conclusions. The axioms are certain: they are the foundations. And they support the consequences we draw in the strongest possible way: indefeasibly.

Descartes is typical of rationalists in this respect. For him, the foundational class was just the class of thoughts that could not be doubted, because you had indefeasible evidence for them. His famous slogan – "I think, therefore I am" – was one thing he thought you couldn't doubt. You couldn't doubt it because you couldn't be fooled about it. Even someone as clever as Ruth, our unscrupulous scientist, couldn't be fooling the brain if she got it to think that it was thinking; and if it thought that, it would know it existed, because you can't think without existing.

But, as we have seen, Descartes' foundational class was too small to provide us with a basis for knowledge of the physical world. For there is nothing at all – save our own minds – whose existence is certain. Since Descartes required that all knowledge should be certain, that led to the general attitude of doubt that is the most extreme form of skepticism about the physical world.

For Locke, on the other hand, the foundational class of beliefs, from which we derive our knowledge of the physical world, is the class of perceptual beliefs. Locke was, therefore, an exponent of a form of empiricist, foundationalist epistemology in which our beliefs about the world all have to be supported by sensory experience, just as our beliefs about our minds have to be supported by reflection. That was Locke's view of the nature of the foundations.

Locke was aware of Descartes' arguments, and of the skepticism about the physical world to which they so easily lead. But he had an answer for them, which relies on two main claims:

(a) Our experiences are involuntary. We cannot simply choose what experiences we should have. I can decide whether or not to open my eyes. But I cannot choose whether I will see this book in front of me once I do open my eyes. So something other than my own mind must cause my experiences.
(b) Our experiences are consistent. "Our senses in many cases bear witness to the truth of each other's report . . ." (Book 3, Chapter 11, Section 7). For example, we can check on what our eyes tell us – when we see a fire – by using our hands – to feel its warmth.

These are, indeed, arguments that might satisfy someone who was worried about whether some *particular* experiences were in fact reliable. If I was unsure whether a vision in the desert was a mirage, for example, it would help to check whether my other senses confirmed it. I might run to where the water seemed to be, to find out if I could touch or taste it. Similarly, it seems reasonable to think that if I could make an experience come and go simply by wishing, then that experience could not be evidence for the existence of a physical object. But notice that neither of these points really meets the skeptic's worry. For Harry, the brain in the vat, could think both (a) – that his experiences were involuntary – and (b) – that his experiences were consistent; but he would still be wrong if he believed his senses. And the demon would make Descartes' experiences both consistent and involuntary, too.

The problem is that though the involuntary nature of my experience does show that it must have some cause outside of my conscious mind, the story that I am a brain in a vat seems to account for the involuntary nature of my experience just as well as the story that I am experiencing a real world. And though the consistency of our experience does need explaining, it seems as if the story that I am a brain in a vat just could be the right explanation. It looks as if to say that our experience is only defeasible evidence for the existence of things in the world is just to admit that the suggestion that *all* our experience is faked is a real possibility. If that is right, whatever reason we give for trusting our senses cannot rule out the possibility that they are misleading us. Someone who believes that we have no right to think that any of our beliefs about the world could not be wrong is called a **fallibilist**.

Locke followed this line of argument and so he said that our senses provide us with grounds for *probable* beliefs, not for *certain* ones. But then he claimed that probability is all that we practically require.

> He that in the ordinary affairs of life, would admit of nothing but direct plain demonstration, would be sure of nothing in this world, but of perishing quickly. (Book 3, Chapter 11, Section 10)

Certainty comes only with those truths of reason that we can establish by "direct plain demonstration." If you will accept only these truths and refuse to believe the evidence of your senses, Locke is saying, you will simply end up suffering the consequences. Skepticism may seem a real possibility in the study, but no one could survive as a skeptic in the real world.

Locke's definition of knowledge is closer than Descartes' to the one we normally assume. He allows that we know that we have hands, for example, because we have consistent evidence from our experience that we have hands. We began our search for a definition of knowledge in the hope that we could answer the question whether – and if so, how – we know that we aren't just brains in fluid. Locke's answer has to be that we *do* know this. For, as we saw, the PDJ means that if we believe something, and it is a logical consequence of something we know, then we know it too. And since it is a logical consequence of my belief that I am experiencing my two hands that my experience is *not* being faked by Ruth, I must know that I am not a brain in Ruth's vat.

As for Locke's explanation of why the brain in a vat does not *know* things about the physical world, it must be that the brain's beliefs are *false*, not that they are *unjustified*.

For it is *evidence* that justifies beliefs; and a brain in a vat would have exactly the same evidence that its senses were not deceiving it as I now have that mine are not deceiving me. It follows that the brain is as justified in its beliefs as it would be if they were true.

Here is the problem with this explanation of why Harry's brain does not know things about the world. Suppose Ruth allowed Harry's brain to have some true beliefs. Suppose she made him believe that the sun was shining on a day when it really was shining. Needless to say, Harry wouldn't *know* that the sun was shining. Yet, Locke would have to say that he did know it, since the brain would have a justified true belief. Descartes' view of knowledge – which required indefeasible evidence – led to skepticism. He had to deny that we knew anything about the physical world. So his theory led to the conclusion that we do not know some things that we do know. But if we simply weaken Descartes' justification condition to allow defeasible evidence, we get Locke's theory – which leads to the conclusion that the brain knows things that it doesn't know. If knowledge is justified true belief, skepticism is not so easily evaded.

2.6 Ways around skepticism I: Verificationism

I want to consider, now, a view of knowledge that has been very influential in this century and that seems to offer a way out of the skeptical impasse. It is a view I mentioned in passing in the last chapter, namely, **verificationism**. I described it there as the view that if no amount of evidence could decide an issue, there is no real issue. To decide an issue, in this context, is to decide whether or not a particular state of affairs obtains in the world.

Since we are usually concerned with states of affairs that we can discuss in our language, verificationists usually express their position in terms of the *sentences* that describe states of affairs. Sentences that describe states of affairs, and can therefore be true (if the state of affairs is as they say it is) or false (if it is not) we can call **declarative** sentences. They declare how the person who says them believes the world to be. So we can express verificationism like this:

> For every declarative sentence, there must be some sort of evidence that would provide grounds either for believing or for disbelieving it.

A sentence for which there is the possibility of evidence – either for or against – is called a **verifiable** sentence. Every declarative sentence, the verificationist says, must be verifiable. This thesis, which we call the **verification principle**, is a radical version of empiricism: radical because it says, in effect, that *every* sentence that makes a claim about how the world is has to be subject to the evidence of experience. And, indeed, the Austrian philosopher Moritz Schlick, who was one of the leaders of the school of philosophy called **logical positivism**, which developed verificationism, called his view "consistent empiricism." But on the face of it, the verification principle seems to assume that the universe is arranged for our epistemological convenience. What reasons could there be for believing that this is so?

The best argument for the verification principle depends on some assumptions about language, which we shall be discussing in more detail in the next chapter. But I will outline the basic argument here:

For our sentences to have meanings, there must be rules for how we use them. A sound that you use without following any rule at all cannot be a meaningful sentence. A rule for a sentence will say when you should use it and when you should not. For example, the rule for using the sentence "I am hot" is, roughly, that you should use it when you want to communicate the fact that you are hot, and not otherwise.

One way to defend a position is to show by *reductio* that it is wrong to deny that position. If we can show that denying a claim leads to a conclusion we can recognize as false, then the claim itself must be true. So let's suppose that the verification principle is false, and see if that leads to a false conclusion.

Suppose, then, that there could be a declarative sentence, *S*, which you could not in any circumstances find evidence for or against. So, of course, there would be no circumstances in which you could use it. But then there would be no rule that said under what circumstances you should use it and under what other circumstances you should not. But since, as I said, every sentence that is meaningful must be used in accordance with some rule, it follows that there can be no meaningful sentence like *S*.

This argument led many philosophers to accept verificationism. Verificationism says that the only reality we can meaningfully talk about consists of things that people are capable of detecting. Because they insist on every sentence being one for which we could have evidence, verificationists are particularly likely to adopt the epistemological point of view that led us to functionalism in the last chapter. Indeed, as you will have noticed, the argument for verificationism is very like Wittgenstein's private language argument. That argument said we couldn't refer in a private language to things that people generally can't know about; this one says that we cannot refer to things that people generally can't know about in a public language. This similarity is not so surprising, since Wittgenstein was, like Schlick, a member of the Vienna Circle, the group of philosophers who founded logical positivism.

There are two important things to notice about the argument for verificationism. First, it doesn't show that we must actually be able to *find* evidence for or against every declarative sentence. A rule must establish circumstances in which the sentence would be properly used. But for there to be a rule it does not have to be possible for us actually to get into one of those circumstances. I am not able to get to the nearest star, and I don't know how to measure the temperature of remote objects. But there is a perfectly good rule for when to use the sentence "The nearest star is hot"; namely, use it when you want to communicate the fact that the nearest star is hot. This is a sentence that you could have evidence for, if you went to Alpha Centauri with a thermometer, even if you can't actually get there now. It follows that, if the verification principle is supported by this argument, we must interpret it as requiring that it should be possible for *someone, somewhere, sometime* to have gathered evidence for or against every declarative sentence, not as requiring that it should be possible for you or me to find evidence here and now.

That brings us to the second important thing to notice about the argument, which is that it does *not* assume that the universe is organized for our epistemological convenience. The argument I have given depends on assumptions about what our *language* must be like, *not* on assumptions about what the *universe* must be like. But there is another way of making the argument, which is not based on assumptions about language, but on assumptions about our beliefs.

Consider any property, *P*, about which we have beliefs. For *P* to play any part in our lives we must be able to conceive of circumstances in which we would apply it. Call such circumstances *P*'s **circumstances of ascription**. Under a property's circumstances of ascription, a suitably situated observer may interact with the property in ways that give him or her knowledge that it obtains. Even if we don't actually know whether anything has this property, we can still imagine that if anything does have it, someone *could* have known this if its circumstances of ascription had obtained and they had been in a position to perceive the circumstances of ascription. It follows that we cannot possess the idea of any property that no one could in any circumstances have known to hold.

This argument should be particularly appealing to someone who believes that the kind of functionalism I described in the last chapter is correct. For, if functionalism is correct, then for each belief there should be a way of saying what its functional role is, a way of saying what role it plays in determining what people with that belief will *do* in response to the experiences they have. But if it is impossible for anyone to come to believe that something has the property *P*, then the belief that something is *P* has no functional role: there are no experiences that would cause the person with that belief to do anything.

This line of thought might, if suitably elaborated, lead you to accept a version of verificationism: one that said that every property in a certain class must be one that can be known under some circumstances to obtain. A similar line of thought would lead to the view that every name must have circumstances in which some agent could know that the thing it named had some property.

If this argument is sound, we have reason to believe that the behaviorists and the functionalists were right to deny that there could be essentially private mental states. If there were such a state – call it *S* – someone could have the property of having-*S* even though nobody else could in any circumstances have known that she did.

Verificationism not only provides grounds for rejecting Cartesian philosophical psychology, it also offers an answer to skepticism. The skeptical hypotheses of the evil demon and the brain in the vat are both designed to raise the possibility that there *are* states of affairs that no amount of evidence could detect. But the verification principle says that no sentences that purport to describe undetectable states of affairs can be meaningful; and the argument I have just offered is intended to show that nobody can have beliefs about undetectable states of affairs. So if the verification principle is correct, skepticism will not be a real possibility, because the skeptical stories literally will not make sense.

But because we started with the story of Harry, the brain in the vat, the verification principle is likely to seem implausible. Harry was unable to tell the difference between the following two hypotheses:

(a) that he was moving around in the world having experiences of real things;
(b) that he was a brain in a vat with faked experiences.

And the story seems to make perfect sense. If it *does* make sense, it seems to be a clear case of something that the verificationist says is impossible: an issue that no evidence could decide.

But is it really a case that the verificationist should accept as a counter-example? For example, suppose Ruth found a new body for Harry. Couldn't she then reconnect him to his body and tell him that his experiences since the crash were all faked? And wouldn't he then have evidence that he used to be a brain in a vat? Of course, Harry has no control over whether Ruth *does* provide him with this evidence. But the verificationist didn't say that we had to be able to produce the evidence by our own efforts, only that it had to be logically possible that there should be evidence. And the fact that Ruth could reconnect the brain in the vat with a new body means that Harry could be given evidence that he was once a brain in a vat.

Verificationism doesn't help as a solution to skepticism. The skeptics want a way of checking whether their experience is misleading them, not the reassurance that evidence that they are being misled could eventually show up. And if verificationism is correct it only offers this weaker sort of reassurance.

But there is another way out of skepticism, which has been suggested recently. This new approach was prompted by a class of examples that undermined the long-established principle of deduction for justification.

2.7 Ways around skepticism II: Causal theories of knowledge

We saw that Descartes' definition of knowledge committed him to the deductive closure principle, because he had to accept the principle of deduction for justification. But Locke is committed to the PDJ, too. In fact, everything that we are justified in believing on Descartes' strong interpretation of the justification condition, we are justified in believing on Locke's weaker interpretation. And, indeed, most other epistemologists have assumed until recently that the PDJ is correct. Then, in 1963, in one of the few examples in the history of philosophy where a really new argument changes the course of the subject, the American philosopher Edmund Gettier provided examples that showed the PDJ to be wrong.

Gettier prepared the ground for his examples by making explicit another important assumption that all empiricists had made. It was that one could be justified in believing what was, in fact, false. This is a simple corollary of Locke's empiricist view that your beliefs can be justified by defeasible evidence. For to say that defeasible evidence can justify a belief is to say that a belief can be supported by evidence that is consistent with its being false. If – as Locke supposed – what justifies your belief is the evidence, then you could have the same justification in the cases where the belief was false as you have in the cases where it is true.

Here is one of Gettier's examples: We suppose that two people, Smith and Jones, have applied for a job. Smith has been reliably informed by the president of the company doing the hiring that in the end Jones will be selected. It also happens that a few minutes ago Smith counted the ten coins in Jones's jacket pocket. So Smith has very strong evidence in support of the following sentence:

(d) Jones is the man who will get the job, and Jones has ten coins in his pocket.

From (d) it follows that:

(e) The man who will get the job has ten coins in his pocket.

Now Smith knows perfectly well that (e) follows from (d), and accepts (e) precisely because he believes (d). Because he has strong evidence for (d), Smith is clearly justified by the PDJ in believing that (e) is true.

But now suppose also that, despite what the president said, Smith, not Jones, is going to get the job. Perhaps they decide he is just too impressive to turn down. And suppose, too, that Smith himself has ten coins in his pocket, even though he does not know it. Then (e) is true, though (d), which was his sole reason for believing it, is false.

In Gettier's example, then, all of the following three conditions clearly hold:

(a) (e) is true,
(b) Smith believes that (e) is true, and
(c) Smith is justified in believing that (e) is true.

Gettier concludes:

> But it is equally clear that Smith does not *know* that (e) is true. For (e) is true because of the coins in Smith's pocket, while Smith does not know how many coins are in his own pocket, and bases his belief in (e) on a count of the coins in Jones's pocket, while falsely believing that Jones is the man who will get the job.

Because it requires the assumption that a false belief can be justified, this example only works against a theory that allows that justification is sometimes defeasible. It therefore poses no threat to the rationalist who believes that all evidence must be indefeasible. But it is not too hard to show that the PDJ is inconsistent with rationalist assumptions as well.

Suppose, for example, I believe that some very complicated mathematical theorem is true, just because you told me, and I had mistaken you for a very gifted mathematician. Let's suppose that, in fact, you are a very poor mathematician and just made the theorem up on the spur of the moment, but you happened, by pure chance, to come up with a truth. Suppose, furthermore, I know some mathematical truths from which this theorem follows logically *even though I do not know that it follows from them*. Still Descartes' theory is committed to the principle of deductive closure: anything I believe that follows from things I know, I also know. So on Descartes' account, I know that the theorem is true. But, of course, I know no such thing.

How are we to react to the discovery that the PDJ is not right? We can begin by noticing that, in each of these cases, it is mere chance that the belief that the person has acquired is true. For, though in each case the belief is true and justified, the fact that it is true plays no part in explaining why it is justified. It is the merest chance that Smith is correct in believing (e) or that I am correct in believing the mathematical theorem you told me. Perhaps, then, we should interpret the justification condition as requiring – as the American philosopher Peter Unger has suggested – that the fact that the belief is true should not be a mere accident.

There are some recent theories, prompted in part by Gettier's problems, which try to say what knowledge is in a way that follows up this idea. And, as it happens, they also allow us to find a sort of solution to the skeptical problem with which we began. These theories are known collectively as **causal theories of knowledge**.

The basic idea of causal theories of knowledge is that in order to know that *S*

(a) you must believe that *S*,
(b) it must be true that *S*, and
(c) the fact that you believe that *S* must be caused in an appropriate way.

The causal theories' interpretation of the justification condition amounts to this: your belief is justified if it is caused in the right sort of way.

Originally, it was suggested that your belief must be caused – in an appropriate way – by the fact that *S*. Theories of this sort deal with the example of Gettier's I cited just now. Though Smith correctly believed that the man who would get the job had ten coins in his pocket, he would still have believed it even if the man who had got the job had *not* had ten coins in his pocket. The fact that the man who was going to get the job had ten coins in his pocket was not part of the cause of Smith's believing it. So, on a theory of this sort, we should say that Smith did not know that the man who would get the job had ten coins in his pocket. But we have to give up the idea that the fact that makes the belief true should actually *cause* the belief. For we know many general facts – such as the fact that all men are mortal – and general facts cannot cause things.

Once we give up the idea that the fact that makes the belief true should actually cause the belief, the main problem for causal theories is that talk of a belief's being caused *in an appropriate way* is left rather vague. So we need to answer the question: How exactly do we decide which ways are appropriate?

We can provide an example at once that shows that not just *any* way will do. This example is one from the work of the American philosopher Alvin Goldman, who has played a leading part in developing causal theories. Henry is out driving and he sees a barn. On this basis, he comes to believe correctly that there is a barn. Since there *is* a barn there and his seeing it is part of the explanation for why he truly believes it is there, this might seem to be a clear case of knowledge on the causal theory. Since there is little doubt that in this case, as described, we *would* say that Henry knew that there was a barn there, the theory does all right so far. But now Goldman expands the story with some extra details.

> Suppose we are told that, unknown to Henry, the district he has just entered is full of papier-mâché facsimiles of barns. These facsimiles look just like barns, but are really just facades, without back walls or interiors, quite incapable of being used as barns. They are so cleverly constructed travelers invariably mistake them for barns. Having just entered the district, Henry has not encountered any facsimiles; the object he sees is a genuine barn. But if the object on that site were a facsimile, Henry would mistake it for a barn. Given this new information, we would be strongly inclined to withdraw the claim that Henry *knows* the object is a barn.

Goldman suggests that the reason we shouldn't say that Henry *knows* there is a barn there is that in this district just looking at a barn from a car is not a way of finding out whether there is a barn there. For, in these special circumstances, just looking out of your car window will lead you to believe that there is a barn on many occasions when there isn't one. *Just looking out of your car window* is, in these circumstances, an unreliable way of acquiring the belief that there is a barn.

What this story suggests is that the appropriate way of getting a true belief, if you want to have knowledge, is to get it by a method that is reliable in the circumstances. One form of causal theory, then, says that knowledge is true belief produced by a means that is *reliable in the circumstances.*

Notice that this theory explains why Smith didn't know that the man who would get the job had ten coins in his pocket, and, more generally, why the PDJ is wrong. For Smith came to believe

(e) The man who will get the job has ten coins in his pocket

by deducing it from

(d) Jones is the man who will get the job, and Jones has ten coins in his pocket.

But, in these circumstances, this was not a reliable way of coming to believe that (e). For if Smith himself had not happened, quite by chance, to have ten coins in his pocket, (e) would have been false. We cannot accept the PDJ, because in many circumstances, like this one, deducing a consequence will cause you to have a true belief only by the merest chance. That is possible because you can draw a true consequence from a false assumption, a fact we shall discuss in the next chapter.

There are still many problems to be worked out before a causal theory can be accepted as an answer to our original question: What is knowledge? But causal theories are certainly one important response to Gettier's problems. More than that, however, proposals like Goldman's represent a radical break with the kind of traditional epistemology that Descartes and Locke developed.

There are two major ways in which these theories are unlike the sorts of traditional approaches we have considered. First of all, traditional epistemologies assume that the difference between people who are justified in believing something and people who are not must depend on states of which those people are aware in their own conscious minds. Traditional epistemologies give what we can call **phenomenological** accounts of the justification condition. ("Phenomenological," remember, means having to do with the conscious aspects of our mental life.)

Descartes and Locke, for example, both gave phenomenological theories of justification. Justification, for Descartes, had to be indefeasible: and if you have indefeasible evidence you can tell that you have it, simply by reflection on the contents of your own conscious mind. Locke's justifications came from experience: but experience, too, is something you are aware you have, whenever you have it.

Goldman's causal theory of knowledge, on the other hand, is not phenomenological. It is not phenomenological because the facts that he told us about Henry – the facts that made us change from saying he knew there was a barn there, to saying that he didn't know it – had nothing to do with the nature of his conscious mental life. Rather, they had to do with facts about Henry and his relations with the world around him. If we replaced all the papier-mâché facsimiles of barns around Henry with real barns, then on Goldman's theory, we should say that he *did* know that there was a barn there. And this means that whether or not Henry's true belief is justified can depend on facts of which he is unaware. Because causal theorists explain justification in a way that depends on facts about the world outside the mind of the knower, we can call their theories of justification **objective** theories. The first break with traditional epistemology, then, is that causal theories of justification are objective and not phenomenological.

The second break with tradition is that causal theories are not *foundationalist*. Causal theories do not, of course, deny that one belief can be the basis for reasonably believing another. But they *do* deny that whether a belief is justified depends on whether it is supported by beliefs in some foundational class. Provided the belief is produced by a reliable method, Goldman says, it is suitably justified.

There are many cases where the causal theory works in a non-foundationalist way. If, to use an example of Goldman's, I am able to tell the twins, Trudy and Judy, apart without knowing what it is about them that allows me to do it, then I have a reliable method of forming the belief that this one is Trudy. If I do form that belief correctly, then, the causal theory says – surely correctly – that I know it is Trudy. But, since I am unable to say what it is about Trudy that allows me to tell her apart from Judy, I have no foundational beliefs that justify my claim that it is, in fact, she.

In recent years, many philosophers have become skeptical of foundationalism anyway. For once it is agreed that no beliefs about the world are indefeasible, there seems no point in looking for a secure foundation of beliefs that are certain. And if there is no foundation of certain beliefs,— there is no clear way of distinguishing the foundational class. If both

(a) the foundational class were certain, and
(b) the process of justification could transfer the certainty to the derived beliefs,

foundationalism would be very attractive. But beliefs about the physical world – unlike mathematical beliefs – satisfy neither of these conditions.

Causal theories, then, are both objective and non-foundational. These two features make theories like Goldman's quite different from Locke's and Descartes'. But it is the fact that Goldman's theory is objective that allows it to provide an answer to the double question with which we began: Do you know that you aren't just a brain in a vat – and if so, how do you know it? To see why this is so, we must first provide the causal theory's answer to the question.

That answer, of course, is that you know you aren't a brain in a vat, provided your true belief that you have a body that moves about in the physical world is produced by a process that is reliable in the circumstances. Since, in fact, you are not a brain in a vat, your beliefs about the world are produced by the reliable process of using your eyes, ears, and other senses, and therefore you *do* know that you are not a brain in a vat. Of course, if, like Harry, you *were* a brain in a vat, you would not know that you were. As a matter of fact, you would know nothing about the physical world. All your beliefs about it would be produced by something like Ruth's computer, and that is an extremely unreliable way of forming beliefs, since Ruth, you'll remember, faked all Harry's experiences.

This solution to our original question has something of an air of paradox about it. For we have come to the conclusion that we know we aren't brains in a vat, even though if we *were* we would have had exactly the same experiences. But that, for the causal theory, is precisely the point. To be concerned only with the nature of our experiences – our phenomenology – without looking at whether our ways of getting beliefs are in fact reliable is just to refuse to adopt an objective theory of justification.

If you don't accept an objective theory of justification, then you are bound to allow that the brain in the vat is as justified as we are in believing that it is *not* in a vat, since it has exactly the same sort of experiences as a person who is living a normal human life. I objected to Locke's theory that if Ruth gave Harry the true belief that the sun was shining, that still wouldn't mean that the brain in the vat *knew* the sun was shining. But any phenomenological theory of justification has to say either

(a) that Harry's belief is justified – and thus wrongly conclude that he knows that the sun is shining – or

(b) that Harry's belief is not justified – and thus wrongly draw the skeptical conclusion that my belief that the sun is shining is not justified either.

Causal theorists say that since neither of these conclusions is correct, no phenomenological theory of knowledge can be accepted.

2.8 Conclusion

In this chapter, we have discussed some of the central questions of epistemology. Starting with the question how we know that we aren't just brains in a vat, the playthings of an unscrupulous scientist, we were led to ask what knowledge is. We discussed the very different answers to this question given by Cartesian rationalism and Lockean empiricism. But both of them shared Theaetetus's assumption that knowledge was justified true belief: and both of them, as we have just seen, regarded justification as both phenomenological and foundational. The problem was that Descartes' theory led immediately to the impasse of skepticism, while Locke wrongly allowed knowledge to the brain in the vat.

Finally, we tried a radical way out. We gave up the idea that our theory of justification needed to be phenomenological. The resultant theory is that in order to know that S

(a) you must believe that S,
(b) it must be true that S, and
(c) the fact that you believe that S must be caused in a way that is reliable in the circumstances.

This theory allows us to claim to know that we aren't brains in a vat, even though our experiences could be the very same if we *were* brains in a vat.

The dispute between causal theory and traditional epistemology is a dispute between a theory that looks at minds as causal systems in the world, on the one hand, and a theory that looks at minds from the point of view of the individual "looking out" on the world, on the other. In this respect it is like the dispute between phenomenologist and functionalist that we discussed at the end of the last chapter. Just as Descartes is on the same side – against the "objective" view of mind – in both these disputes, so many philosophers who are functionalists are on the objective side in epistemology. To see mind and knowledge in the way the functionalist and the causal epistemologist do – as a causal system in the world – is to support a form of **naturalism**. It is to see human beings and their philosophical problems as part of the wider world of nature, not as privileged observers of that natural world.

Whether some form of causal theory is right is still a hotly disputed issue – as is the wider issue of whether naturalism is the right position from which to start. As always, I must leave you to make up your own mind.

3 Language and Logic

How do words express thoughts?

What is meaning?

How does language relate to reality?

3.1 Introduction

Ever since Charles Darwin published *The Origin of Species*, biologists have increasingly seen human beings as just one kind of animal. Darwin's theory of evolution claims that we are descended by natural selection from other, earlier, kinds of animals. Biologists are not surprised, therefore, that our respiration, nutrition, and reproduction are typically mammalian; and that our cells look very like the cells of other animals, with their nuclei and cytoplasm and the multiplicity of organelles that we can see under a microscope. But even a biologist would have to agree that we have some important distinctive traits; and one of the most important is that we use language, to speak, to write, and, some would say, to think. So far as we know, we are the only animal, from the amoeba to the elephant, that naturally uses language. Furthermore, many of the other distinguishing features of our species – our social organization, our arts and crafts and sciences – are inconceivable without language. Even if other animals do have languages, what they have done with them seems very limited by comparison. Imagine trying to co-ordinate a bank or an art gallery or an experiment in chemistry without being able to understand, speak, read, or write a word.

Human beings have been using language for hundreds of thousands of years, and most of us learned a language easily and naturally when we were very young. In Chapter 1 I mentioned how easily we have come to take computers, which are relatively new on the human scene, for granted; how much easier it is for us to take language for granted, along with all the distinctively human activities that it makes possible.

We can start to realize just how special language really is by thinking about what it would take to establish that some other creature also had the capacity to use a language. This is not, as it happens, a purely hypothetical problem, because it has been suggested by people who study animal behavior that various other animals do have that capacity. For example, a chimpanzee, Nim Chimpsky (so named because the most important linguist of our time is called Noam Chomsky!), has been taught to use some of the signs of American Sign Language, which was developed for people who are deaf or mute. But the fact that Nim can make movements with his hands that are like the hand-movements of trained users of the sign language, does not, of course, prove that he understands the language. He might be doing what parrots can do with speech: simply copying the sounds without having any idea what they mean. So how would you set about checking whether another creature was using a language?

With the trained chimp, we already have a certain advantage. He was trained to use a language we already know. So let's make the problem even harder by asking how we could discover that an animal was using a language that wasn't invented by human beings. This, too, is not such a hypothetical problem. It is claimed by some people that the sounds dolphins make are actually used by them in communication. If we consider a simple experiment that we might do to test this claim, it will start us thinking about the issues.

One obvious thing we do with language is communicate information. So one obvious way to start checking whether dolphins have a language in something like the way we do is to see if they can communicate. Suppose we put two dolphins in separate tanks where they can't see each other, but connect the tanks by speakers and microphones so that the dolphins can hear each other's vocalizations. Then, we put in each tank a similar switch whose function is to release food for the dolphins to eat and which takes a while to learn to operate. We let the dolphins swim around the switches and we see that neither of them knows how to operate it to release food. In one tank we then place a barrier that keeps the dolphin away from the switch, while we let the dolphin in the other tank figure out how to use the switch. Now we remove the barrier in the other tank. What this dolphin does next may offer us evidence that it has learned from the first dolphin both that the switch releases food and how to operate it. For if the second dolphin swims straight across to the switch and releases the food, we may reasonably infer that the other dolphin made sounds that communicated the necessary information.

If the experiment turned out this way (which, as it happens, it probably wouldn't), that would only be the beginning. Because we should then want to know how to interpret the dolphins' language. And this is a much harder task. For how would we go about telling which of the sounds the dolphins made meant what? Indeed, what, exactly, does it mean to say that a dolphin sound has a certain meaning?

These questions should have a familiar ring for you. Questions like them came up right at the start, when we were considering whether computers can talk. I said there that we shouldn't take it for granted that something is using language properly just because it produces strings of symbols or sequences of sounds that look or sound like sentences of English. I also said that to mean something you have to be able to understand what you're saying. If that is right, then we can only find out whether dolphins have a language if we know what it means to say that a creature understands a sentence; and we need to know what understanding a sentence involves before we set out to translate "dolphinese."

These questions about meaning and understanding are at the heart of the philosophy of language. In this chapter I am going to examine some philosophical attempts at understanding how language works. But I think it will help if I begin by discussing some of the reasons that these questions have come to be so central to philosophical inquiry.

3.2 The linguistic turn

Western philosophy has been concerned from its very beginning with language. There are many reasons for this, and different reasons have been important at different times in the history of the subject. But one perennial source of the appeal that language has for philosophers is the fact that language is the tool with which they do their work. The philosopher's product, in the Western tradition, is a text, a piece of writing. Philosophy is especially concerned with the careful exposition of arguments that illuminate the central concepts with which and through which we understand reality. It is natural, therefore, that philosophers should have attended very closely to how language works, and, more especially, to questions about how to use language in valid arguments.

But everybody has a reason for being concerned to understand language properly. Whoever you are, you will sometimes have to think through difficult questions. And when you do, you will almost certainly have to do it with language. Even if you believe you can do without language for your private thinking, you *will* need to use it if you want to discuss these problems with others, or to look for relevant information or argument in books. So that, though philosophers have to be very careful about language, the fact that language is the tool of their trade does not distinguish philosophy from most other forms of intellectual activity.

Nor does this fact explain the tremendous importance that has been attached to philosophical questions about language in the last hundred or so years of European philosophy. From the work of the German philosopher Gottlob Frege a hundred years ago, to Ludwig Wittgenstein's *Philosophical Investigations* in the middle of this century, some of the most influential philosophical writings have asked questions about how language works. In the philosophy of language, questions about language have been addressed not because care with words allows us to avoid confusion, but because the nature of linguistic meaning, or of what it is for sentences to be true or false, has come to be regarded as intrinsically philosophically important. Philosophy, whose traditional preoccupation is with concepts and ideas, has come, in our own century, to be centrally engaged with questions about words and sentences. As the American philosopher Richard Rorty has put it, philosophy has taken a "linguistic turn."

It will help you to see why language came to be so important to recent philosophy if we begin before the "linguistic turn." So let's begin again with Cartesianism, which (as I have already said) has been the dominant philosophy of mind of the last three centuries. In particular, let's consider the view of language that went with it.

For Descartes, you remember, your mind and the thoughts you have are the things you know best. In this framework – which we find, for example, in Descartes' English contemporary Thomas Hobbes – public language is naturally seen as the expression of these private thoughts. As Hobbes puts it, with his characteristic directness: "Words so connected as that they become signs of our thoughts, are called SPEECH." Whether or not you share Descartes' view of thoughts, this is, surely, a very natural view of one of the major ways that language functions. But, for Hobbes, language had a more important function than its role in communication, one that I mentioned in Chapter 1.

> How unconstant and fading men's thoughts are, and how much the recovery of them depends upon chance, there is none but knows by infallible experience in himself. For no man is able to remember. . . colors without sensible and present patterns, nor number without the names of numbers disposed in order and learned by heart. . . . From which it follows that, for the acquiring of philosophy, some sensible moniments are necessary, by which our past thoughts may not only be reduced, but registered every one in its own order. These moniments I call MARKS.

Hobbes is saying that the major function of language is to help us remember our thoughts, and he says that language is a system of "sensible moniments" – reminders that we can see and hear. Thus, he claims in this passage that no one could remember "number," that is, how many things there are of a certain kind, if they did not have the numerals, the written or spoken signs for numbers; and he implies that no one could count things unless they had learned the numerals in their proper order. He claims, too, that you could not remember what color things were, if you did not have the names of the colors – the words "red" and "yellow" and so on – so that you could store away the memory of a sunset, for example, by storing away the words "The sunset was a spectacular red." In fact, Hobbes believed that almost every word was a *name* of a "thought"; and by a "thought," like Descartes, he meant anything that you are aware of in your mind when you are conscious. The heart of his view of language, then, was that

> the nature of a name consists principally in this, that it is a mark taken for memory's sake; but it serves by accident to signify and make known to others what we remember ourselves.

As I argued in the chapter on mind, Cartesian thoughts are essentially a private matter. For Hobbes, it is just "by accident" that names also have a role in public language. So far as Hobbes was concerned, Robinson Crusoe would have had just as much use for language before Man Friday arrived in his life as afterwards. So far as Hobbes was concerned, then, it was only an accident that human beings do not have private languages, consisting of systems of "marks" that allow each person to remember his or her own ideas and that are not used in communication at all. If Hobbes were right, the fact that chimpanzees in the wild do not appear to use signs to communicate would not show that they didn't use sounds or gestures as marks for their thoughts.

You will remember that I argued in Chapter 1 that the extreme privacy of Cartesian thoughts raised serious problems for Descartes' theory. In particular, his theory raised in an especially acute way the problem of other minds. Wittgenstein's private language argument brought this problem into sharp focus; and this led us to behaviorism and then to functionalism. Now Hobbes's theory is, in essence, that we use languages as private languages. So that behaviorists and functionalists are likely to object to Hobbes's view because they do not believe in the existence of the totally private states – the "thoughts" – that Hobbes, like Descartes, regarded as the one sort of thing that we each know for certain. Blaming the defects of the Cartesian view on its commitment to the existence of *private* mental states, behaviorists placed their confidence in the certain existence of *public* language. A significant part of the appeal that language has had for many recent philosophers as an object of philosophical study is that it is public. Spoken and written languages, unlike the minds of their speakers and writers, are open to the inspection of all.

But there is another, connected, reason why the study of language has come to occupy a central place in recent philosophy: philosophers have come to believe that it is not, as Hobbes thought, an accident that language is a public phenomenon. As we saw in Chapter 1, Wittgenstein's private language argument was supposed to show that Hobbes's notion that we use language as a "sensible moniment" was actually incoherent. But Wittgenstein also offered to show why Hobbes and Descartes might have come to make the mistake of thinking that a private language was possible. His explanation relies, like the verificationist argument of Chapter 2, on an appeal to a fact about public language.

3.3 The beetle in the box

Here is the passage from *Philosophical Investigations*, section 293, where Wittgenstein examines one way in which we might conceive of a private language. He considers why we might think that we use the word "pain" as if it were the name of a private object. He considers, in other words, why we might think that the word "pain" was used like the word "twinge" in my story in Chapter 1.

> Now someone tells me that *he* knows what pain is only from his own case! – Suppose everyone had a box with something in it: we call it a "beetle." No one can look into anyone else's box, and everyone says he knows what a beetle is only by looking at *his* beetle. – Here it would be quite possible for everyone to have something different in his box. One might even imagine such a thing constantly changing. – But suppose the word "beetle" had a use in these people's language? – If so, it would not be used as the name of a thing. The thing in the box has no place in the language-game at all; not even as a *something*: for the box might even be empty. – No, one can "divide through" by the thing in the box; it cancels out, whatever it is.
>
> That is to say: if we construe the grammar of the expression of sensation on the model of "object and designation" the object drops out of consideration as irrelevant.

The analogy between pain, on the one hand, and the beetle in the box, on the other, is meant to reinforce the point of the private language argument. If you really could not, even in principle, get into someone else's box to see if there was a beetle, then whether there was a beetle in the box could not possibly matter to the language-game. Wittgenstein suggests at the end of this passage that we have been misled by the "grammar" of the sentence "I have a pain" into thinking that, when John is in pain, there is a private object that he experiences, just as when Joanna has a beetle in a match box, there is a public object that she possesses. But Wittgenstein thinks that we should regard "I have a pain" as being like "I have a fever." It makes no more sense, he thinks, to say that there is some fever that I have than to say that there is some pain that I have. When I have a fever, there are not two things, me and the fever: there is just one thing, me, in a feverish state. So, too, when I have a pain, there are not two things involved – me and the pain – but only one thing – me – which is in a certain state: the state of *having-a-pain.*

Having-a-pain is certainly not an essentially private state. For if, for example, I stick a pin in you while you are awake and I see you wince, then, in the normal course of things, I know that you are in pain. If Wittgenstein is right, the problems generated by the privacy of pain are all dissolved. Indeed, if we could replace all the Cartesian talk of the allegedly private objects of experience by talk of the public (that is, in principle, detectable) property of having-the-experience, the problem of other minds would disappear. Thus, even though Wittgenstein discusses the issue of privacy in terms of private *language* and not in terms simply of private *objects* of experience, his arguments, if successful, solve a central problem in the philosophy of mind.

Wittgenstein's talk of "grammar" here suggests he thinks that, in this case, clarity about how language works will allow us to avoid the philosophical error of thinking that there can be private states. So you might be led to conclude that Wittgenstein's interest in language was just the sort of interest in language as a tool that I said was *not* the main reason for philosophical concern with language in our own century. The reason why I think you should not draw this conclusion is that I believe that Wittgenstein's concern for issues about grammar is a *consequence* and not a *cause* of his skepticism about the usefulness of trying to explain human action, including human speech, by talking about private mental states. One reason for such skepticism becomes clear if we ask ourselves exactly what Hobbes would say if you asked him what was involved in understanding a sentence.

Hobbes's answer would be that to understand a sentence is to know "what thought the speaker had. . . before his mind." So, according to Hobbes, if I know what Joanna means by the word "table," I know that it "signifies" her idea of a table. There are at least two sorts of objection that one might make to this explanation. The first is that, far from helping us understand what Joanna means, it actually makes understanding Joanna impossible. After all, Hobbes thinks that I cannot know about Joanna's ideas since they are Joanna's private property. Yet, if this explanation of meaning were right, I would *have* to know what Joanna's idea of a table was like in order to know what she meant by her word "table"; which, according to Hobbes, is impossible!

A second objection to Hobbes's theory is that it mistakes a fundamentally subjective question for an objective one. The question of what experiences go with Joanna's use of words is subjective. It depends on Joanna's particular psychology. But the question of what Joanna means is not, in this sense, subjective at all. What Joanna means by the word "table," if she understands English, is the same as what you or I mean by it; it is quite independent of her psychological peculiarities.

This second objection was made by the German philosopher Gottlob Frege in a well-known article called "On Sense and Reference." "Sense" and "reference" are the words that Frege used, as we shall see, to explain what is involved in understanding language. For the moment, let's just take "sense" to mean *meaning*, and "reference" to mean *the thing that a name names.* In this passage, he makes his point by considering what is involved in understanding what someone means when they use the name "Bucephalus," which was the name of Alexander the Great's horse.

> The reference and sense of a sign are to be distinguished from the associated idea. If the reference of a sign is an object perceivable by the senses, my idea of it is an internal image, arising from memories of sense impressions which I have had and acts, both internal and external, which I have performed. Such an idea is often saturated with feeling; the clarity of the various parts varies and oscillates. The same sense is not always connected, even in the same man, with the same idea. The idea is subjective: one man's idea is not that of another. There result, as a matter of course, a variety of differences in the ideas associated with the same sense. A painter, a horseman, and a zoologist will probably connect different ideas with the name "Bucephalus."

One reasonable response to these two objections, both of which are arguments against the *subjective* character of the Hobbesian theory of meaning, is to try and explain what is going on in language not by saying how it relates to our inner subjective experiences, but by saying how it relates to the outer objective world. And Frege was the pioneer of modern thought on this issue.

3.4 Frege's "sense" and "reference"

Frege was a mathematician, and his interest in questions about how language works derived from a concern to give a precise account of how the signs of mathematical languages worked. He thought that if we understood properly how mathematical language functioned, we should be able to avoid certain sorts of mathematical error. But he soon developed an independent interest in how languages function; and, though he did a great deal of work on questions about how mathematical signs like the numerals ("1," "2," "3," and so on) operate, he also worked out a theory that covered proper names, like "Bucephalus," and various forms of words, like "I doubt that —," which are not used in mathematics at all.

Frege's aim was to develop a **theory of meaning**, a philosophical account that would tell us what we had to know about the words and sentences of a language in order to understand the way people use them. His fundamental idea was that the meaning of a word is just what you have to know about it in order to understand how it is used in a language. Since the word *semantic* means "having to do with meaning," what Frege was doing is also called **philosophical semantics**, and his theory is called a **semantic theory**.

One of Frege's most important discoveries was that previous theories of meaning had started in the wrong place. Hobbes, as we saw, started by trying to explain the meaning of individual words, like names. Frege pointed out that, in a sense, words on their own do not mean anything at all. For the meaning of a word is what you have to know in order to understand proper uses of that word in the language; and just saying "dog" is not a proper use of a word in English. Only if I use the word "dog" with other words to form a sentence will I be saying something that you can understand. It is not that the word "dog" doesn't mean anything, it is simply that what it means depends on how it is used in sentences. This discovery of the **primacy of the sentence** is one of the basic insights of Frege's philosophy of language. You might put his discovery like this: to say what a word or phrase means, you have to say how it contributes to the meaning of complete sentences.

With this basic idea established, Frege sets out to discuss how we understand names like "Bucephalus." He says that we must think of them as *referring* to some object. Given the primacy of the sentence, we must now ask what this means in terms of how words contribute to sentence meaning. A simple, preliminary answer is that a word, *W*, refers to an object, *O*, if and only if *W* is used in sentences to determine what those sentences are about. Thus, because the word "Bucephalus" refers to a certain horse, the sentence "Alexander rode Bucephalus" is about that horse. As we shall see, Frege had a better, more precise answer than this preliminary answer; but before I give it, we shall need some more of Frege's terminology.

Once Frege has introduced the idea of reference, he points out immediately that we cannot say that the thing that a name refers to – its **reference** – is all you need to know in order to understand how that name functions in our language. For if it were all that you had to know, then the meaning of two words with the same reference would be identical; and he gives a famous example that shows that this is not so. Here is the example.

The planet Venus is often observable near the horizon both at sunset and at sunrise. In antiquity, people called Venus "the evening star," when they saw it at sunset, and "the morning star," when they saw it at dawn, without realizing that they were talking about the very same heavenly body. (As you can see from the names, they didn't know it was not a star but a planet either.) In the course of the history of astronomy, it was discovered that the heavenly body people saw at sunset and the one they saw at sunrise were the same. This discovery could be reported by saying

F: The morning star is the evening star.

Now suppose we held that the meaning of "the morning star" was just its reference, and likewise for "the evening star." Then it would follow that, since these two names refer to the same thing, they must have the same meaning. If that were true, then the sentence, *F*, could not possibly be informative. For if the two words meant the same, then all you would have to know in order to know that *F* was true was what the two words meant. But the discovery that *F* was true is not something that people knew simply because they knew what the words meant; it was an astronomical discovery.

Frege made the same point in a slightly different way. He offered a *reductio* argument that showed that reference was not the same as meaning. The argument depends on the following assumption:

CT: If two words or phrases have the same meaning, then we should be able to replace one of them with the other in any sentence, *S*, without changing the meaning of *S*.

FREGE

Gottlob Frege (1848-1925) was born in Germany and spent all of his working life as a professor of mathematics in the University of Jena. It was he who invented the idea of using quantifiers and variables to deal with the role of "all" and "some" and, in so doing, founded modern logic. Apart from introducing new standards of mathematical rigor into discussion of the foundations of logic and mathematics, Frege is important for his attack on "psychologism," the idea that mathematics and logic are about things in our minds. His theory of reference tied words directly to the things in the world that they referred to and he was particularly concerned to deny that meaning was subjective. Frege's book on *The Foundations of Mathematics*, published in 1884, demolished all existing theories of the nature of number and set out to define the notions of arithmetic in terms of purely logical ideas. But in the course of this book Frege made many important philosophical discoveries, including the primacy of the sentence.

Unlike many of the other philosophers we have considered, Frege made no contributions to philosophy outside the philosophy of language and mathematics. And the fact that he was a virulent anti-Semite illustrates how someone who is extremely intellectually gifted can nevertheless lack moral insight.

"Bachelor" and "unmarried adult male" mean the same. So "John is a bachelor" and "John is an unmarried adult male" mean the same also. I shall call *CT* the **componentiality thesis** for meanings. The argument for it is quite simple. The meaning of a word or phrase is what you know if and only if you know how it is used in the language. Given the *primacy of the sentence* this means that the meaning of a word or phrase, *W*, is what you know if and only if you understand how *W* contributes to the meaning of any sentence containing it. It follows that two words, *X* and *Y*, mean the same if and only if they make the same contribution to the meaning of every sentence.

Frege asked us to compare *F* with

G: The morning star is the morning star.

He pointed out that *G*, unlike *F*, *is* a sentence that you know is true just because you know what the words mean. It follows from the componentiality thesis that if the meaning of "the morning star" is just what it refers to, then, since it refers to the same thing as "the evening star" does, *F* and *G* must mean the same. Since they plainly do not mean the same, this is a *reductio* of the claim that the meaning of a name is its reference.

Frege's explanation of why *F* and *G* differ in meaning is that "the morning star" and "the evening star," though they have the same reference, differ in "the mode of presentation" of what they refer to, and he calls the mode of presentation associated with a word its **sense**.

We can see what Frege means by a "mode of presentation," and thus by a "sense," in the case we have been considering. To know the sense of "the morning star" you have to know that it refers to the heavenly body that often appears at a certain point on the horizon in the morning. To know the sense of "the evening star" you have to know that it refers to the heavenly body that often appears at a certain point on the horizon in the evening. In other words, for a name, a *sense* is a way of identifying the referent. If you know the sense of a name, you know what determines whether any object is the reference of that name. It is very important, as we shall see later, that a sense is defined as something you have to *know* in order to understand its use in sentences. This follows, of course, from Frege's basic idea that meaning is what you have to know in order to understand words.

Proper names are, of course, only one class among many classes of expressions that a theory of meaning has to explain. As we should expect, Frege, who discovered the primacy of the sentence, now asks whether we can apply similar notions to whole sentences.

> We now inquire concerning the sense and reference for an entire declarative sentence. Such a sentence contains a thought. Is this thought, now, to be regarded as its sense or its reference? Let us assume for the time being that a sentence has a reference. If we now replace one word of the sentence by another having the same reference, but a different sense, this can have no bearing upon the reference of the sentence. Yet we can see that in such a case the thought changes; since, e.g., the thought in the sentence "The morning star is a body illuminated by the Sun" differs from that in the sentence "The evening star is a body illuminated by the Sun." Anybody who did not know that the evening star is the morning star might hold the one thought to be true, the other false. The thought, accordingly, cannot be the reference of the sentence, but must rather be considered as the sense.

Frege says that by a "thought" he means "not the subjective performance of thinking but its objective content, which is capable of being the common property of several thinkers." So his claim is that the sense of the sentence "The morning star is a body illuminated by the Sun" is the content of the belief shared by two people who both believe that the morning star is a body illuminated by the Sun. This shared content is what philosophers have usually meant by the word **proposition**. We often say that a sentence *expresses a proposition*, which means that it has a certain content.

Notice that in this passage Frege applies something like the componentiality thesis to references when he says that "if we . . . replace one word of the sentence by another having the same reference, but a different sense, this can have no bearing upon the reference of the sentence." In other words he is assuming that the reference of a sentence is determined exclusively by the references of the component words or phrases. If we can discover a property of a sentence that is determined exclusively by the references of the words that make it up, we shall have discovered, according to Frege, what the references of sentences are.

So far we only know what the sense and reference of proper names are. We call two names with the same reference **co-referential**. So the question we must ask is: What property of sentences is always preserved if we replace the names in them by other co-referential names? Frege's answer is that the property that is preserved is what he calls the **truth value**. "By the truth value of a sentence I understand the circumstance that it is true or false. There are no further truth values." Frege's point is that if we substitute one name for another co-referential name in any sentence, then we shall not affect whether that sentence is true or false.

Thus, since "the morning star" and "the evening star" are co-referential, we should be able to replace one by the other in any true sentence and get a sentence that is true; and we should likewise be able to replace one by the other in any false sentence and get a sentence that is false. Let us accept, for the moment, that this is correct.

If the reference of a sentence is a truth value, then just as the sense of a name is a mode of presentation of the reference, so the sense of a sentence should be a mode of presentation of a truth value. And just as the sense of a name is a way of identifying the object it refers to, so the sense of a sentence will be a way of identifying whether or not the sentence is true. If you know the sense of a sentence, you know what determines whether that sentence is true or false.

If you know what determines whether a sentence is true or false, we say that you know its **truth conditions**. So that Frege's theory of meaning says that the meaning of a sentence is its truth conditions. Since, on Frege's view, every sentence that is not true is false, if you know when a sentence would be true, you know its truth conditions. For in any circumstance where it was not true, it would be false.

We have now reached a point where another major reason for philosophical interest in language becomes clear. Language is the medium in which we express truths. From the very beginning of Western philosophy, the nature of truth has been regarded as a crucial philosophical question. The theory of meaning provides one route to an answer. For looking at how sentences express truth and falsehood helps us to understand the nature of truth. In Frege's theory, where there is this close connection between meaning and truth, this traditional problem is central to philosophical semantics.

3.5 Predicates and open sentences

Once Frege has an explanation of the sense and reference of sentences he can explain the sense and reference of other words and phrases, relying always on the componentiality thesis, applied now both to sense and to reference. The sense of a word or phrase will be a property that determines the truth conditions – the sense – of a sentence in which it occurs; the reference will be a property that determines the truth value – the reference. To explain the rest of his theory, however, we shall need to introduce a little more terminology.

In traditional grammar, sentences were said to consist of a subject and a predicate. Thus, the sentence "Susan is in Canada" was said to consist of the subject, "Susan," and the predicate " – is in Canada." The **subject** – in this case a name – fixed what the sentence was about, and the **predicate** fixed what was being said about it. Suppose we are trying to determine what is the reference of " – is in Canada." Since Canada is the largest country on the North American continent, any sentence that says that something or somebody is in the largest country on the North American continent will have the same truth value as a sentence that says that somebody is in Canada. Using the componentiality thesis for reference, we can say that the property that the predicate " – is in Canada" shares with the predicate " – is in the largest country on the North American continent" is their common reference.

That shared reference, on Frege's theory, was *the class of things in Canada*. So, just as a name refers to an object, a predicate refers to a class of objects: and that class is called the **extension** of the predicate. If you want to find out if something is in the extension of a predicate, you simply make a sentence with the name of that thing followed by the predicate and see if that sentence is true. So if you want to know if something – call it X – is in the extension of the predicate "– is in Canada," you simply see if the sentence "X is in Canada" is true. If it *is* true, we say that X **satisfies** the predicate "– is in Canada."

Now we know what the reference of a predicate is. We can apply the general rule that the sense of a word or phrase is a mode of presentation of the reference. "– is in Canada" and "– is in the largest country on the North American continent" are different modes of presentation of the same class of objects: the class, namely, of things in the country whose capital is Ottawa. The sense of a predicate is sometimes referred to as its **intension**. As we shall see in 3.8, however, this terminology could lead to confusion, so I'll stick to talking of "senses."

Now Frege knew that not all sentences fitted the simple subject-predicate pattern. After all, is the sentence

S: John and Mary, who are friends of Peter's, sat in the garden and ate strawberries

about John or Mary or something called "John and Mary" or even something called "John and Mary, who are friends of Peter's"? So Frege suggested that we should replace the traditional notion of a predicate with the notion of what is called an **open sentence**. To get an open sentence from S, you simply remove one or several of the names. Thus

S_1: —— and Mary, who are friends of Peter's, sat in the garden and ate strawberries

and

S_2: —— and Mary, who are friends of ——'s, sat in the garden and ate strawberries

are both open sentences.

CHAPTER 3

We can easily see how to apply Frege's suggestion to S_1. If S is true, then John satisfies the open sentence S_1. So the extension of S_1 is the class of things that satisfy this open sentence, the class of things whose names produce a true sentence when they are put in the blank.

Frege suggested that the reference of S_2 was the class of ordered *pairs* of things such that if you put the name of the first member of the pair in the first blank, and the name of the second member in the second blank, you got a true sentence. An **ordered pair** is just a pair of things taken in a particular order. Obviously, it can be true that

John and Mary, who are friends of Peter's, sat in the garden and ate strawberries

when it is false that

Peter and Mary, who are friends of John's, sat in the garden and ate strawberries.

So which name you put in which blank is important, and that is why the pair has to be ordered. It is clear that this idea can be generalized: if you took out three names, then the open sentence would be satisfied not by ordered pairs but by ordered triples, and so on. However complex a sentence is, and however many names it contains, Frege's theory can say what the reference and the sense are of the open sentence produced by removing all the names.

In Chapter 1, you will remember, I introduced the idea of a **variable** to explain the Ramsey-sentences that functionalists use to set up their theory of the mind. There is a simple connection between variables and these open sentences. When you create an open sentence, you introduce one variable for each name you remove. So instead of writing the open sentence

— sat in the garden and ate strawberries

you write

X sat in the garden and ate strawberries.

(If you remove the same name more than once from a sentence, you can replace it each time with the same variable.) Frege showed that using this device, you could then explain how the words "some" and "all" – and related words like "somebody" and "everybody" – which are called **quantifiers**, worked in English. (Or rather, how the equivalent words work in German!) For "somebody" the story is that "Somebody sat in the garden and ate strawberries" is true if there is any person who satisfies this open sentence. For "Everybody" the story is that "Everybody sat in the garden and ate strawberries" is true if every person satisfies this open sentence; in other words, if any name you substitute for the X will produce a true sentence. For this reason, we sometimes write, instead of "Everybody sat in the garden and ate strawberries,"

For all *X*, *X* sat in the garden and ate strawberries;

and for "Somebody sat in the garden and ate strawberries,"

There exists an *X*, such that *X* sat in the garden and ate strawberries,

which is what we did with the Ramsey-sentences. "For all *X*, *X* . . ." is the **universal quantifier**; we use it to make the claim that everything – in the *universe!* – satisfies an open sentence. "There exists an *X*, such that *X* . . ." is the **existential quantifier**; we use it to make claims about the existence of something that satisfies an open sentence. Given the way we dealt with open sentences with two blanks just now, you can see how Frege could have gone on to handle sentences with more than one quantifier, in just the way we did in the Ramsey-sentences of Chapter 1.

3.6 Problems of intensionality

I have been assuming, as I said, that if we replace one co-referential term by another in a sentence, we should get a true sentence if the original sentence was true, and a false sentence if the original sentence was false. I have been assuming, that is, that the componentiality thesis applies to references as well as to senses. But Frege pointed out that this did not seem on the face of it to be correct.

Consider the two sentences "I believe that the morning star is Venus" and "I believe that the evening star is Venus." As we have seen, one of these could be true and the other false. Yet the one sentence is produced from the other by substituting co-referential expressions. We might conclude that it is just wrong to suppose that substitution of co-referring expressions preserves truth value.

What Frege argued, however, was that we have "the right to conclude only that 'morning star' does not *always* stand for the planet Venus." If, in the sentence "I believe that the morning star is Venus," the name "the morning star" does not refer to Venus, then, of course, it does not count as a counterexample to the componentiality thesis for reference. But this reply should only satisfy us if we have an explanation both of *when* it does not refer to Venus and *why* it does not. I will try and offer such an explanation at the end of this section and in the next. Before I do that, let me describe the way Frege set about solving this problem.

In the sentence

F: The morning star is the evening star

which we considered earlier, substitution of co-referential expressions, as we saw, preserves truth value. This means that the open sentence

F₁: — is the evening star

will produce a sentence with the same truth value as *F*, provided we substitute into the blank a word, such as "Venus," that has the same reference as "the morning star." An open sentence like this, that produces a sentence with the same truth value whenever we substitute an expression with the same reference for the blank, is called an **extensional context**. (Remember, the reference of a predicate was called its *extension*.)

On the other hand, the open sentence

I believe that the — is Venus

is not an extensional context, as we have seen. If we want to provide terms whose substitution into this blank will preserve truth value, they must be terms with the same sense. Since, as I have said, the sense of a predicate is sometimes called its intension, these are called **intensional contexts**. Frege's solution to the problems raised for his basic theory by intensional contexts was very simple. He proposed that in intensional contexts, words and phrases referred not to their normal references, but to their senses.

Though this is a very simple solution, it is also rather hard to get a grip on. It follows from this theory, after all, that "the morning star" in "I believe that the morning star is Venus" refers to the sense of "the morning star." So the sense of "the morning star" in this sentence is the mode of presentation of the sense that "the morning star" has in extensional contexts. It is the sense of a sense.

Put this way, Frege's proposal is not very easily understood; but we can put Frege's theory in another way, which makes it easier to grasp what he is getting at. He is saying that the contribution that the words "the morning star" in "I believe that the morning star is Venus" make to determining whether or not that sentence is true depends not only on their reference, but on their sense. And this is surely right. For whether or not I do believe that the morning star is Venus depends, in part, on whether I know that the star that sometimes appears at a certain point on the horizon at dawn is Venus; whether I believe it, then, depends on the mode of presentation that I associate with the words "the morning star."

In fact, Frege can offer a general explanation of why "I believe that — is Venus" should create intensional contexts. The effect of interchanging co-referential terms in the blank here is equivalent to interchanging co-referential sentences in the blank of the open sentence "I believe that —." According to Frege, the content of a sentence, the thought it expresses, is its sense. Two sentences with different contents express different beliefs. It is natural, therefore, that interchanging sentences with the same reference but different sense in the context "I believe that —" will sometimes lead us from truth to falsehood.

Many intensional contexts that involve the attitudes of people to propositions can be explained in this way. Peoples' attitudes to them depend on the thought and not simply on whether it is true. Thus, "I doubt that —," "I hope that —," "I fear that —," "I know that —," "I suppose that —," and so on, are all intensional contexts for this reason. These sorts of expressions are the names of what are called **sentential** or **propositional attitudes**, because what fills the blank is a sentence, which expresses a proposition. So Frege's proposal that we should treat the reference of an expression in an intensional context as its sense is a reasonable way of dealing, in the terms of his theory, with intensional contexts involving many of the sentential attitudes.

Unfortunately, however, not all intensional contexts involve sentential attitudes. If, for example, we replace the sentence "It is or is not raining" in "It is necessary that it is or is not raining" with a sentence with the same reference – i.e. truth value – we will not always get a sentence that is also true. Thus "I like celery" is true, but it is not necessarily true. So we must see, now, if we can explain why "It is necessary that —" creates intensional contexts.

3.7 Truth conditions and possible worlds

To answer this question, I am going to use a theory about necessity that has been developed in recent years, which starts from an idea of the eighteenth-century German philosopher Gottfried Wilhelm Leibnitz. That idea was the idea of a **possible world**. By a possible world Leibnitz meant *a way the universe might have been.* (Bear in mind that a possible world is not a way the *Earth* might have been, but a way the whole universe might have been.) Thus, we all believe President Kennedy might not have been assassinated. So, in Leibnitz's way of thinking, there is a possible world that is exactly like our universe until the moment that Kennedy was shot, and then differs from it in all sorts of ways. In fact, there are infinitely many such possible worlds. In some of them Kennedy dies of old age, in others he is assassinated later, and so on. There are infinitely many worlds, because there are infinitely many such things that might have turned out differently.

Leibnitz was able to use the idea of possible worlds to answer a number of important philosophical questions. In particular, he was able to say what it was for a sentence to be necessarily true. His explanation was that a sentence was necessarily true if it was *true in every possible world.* There is no way the universe could have been in which a necessary sentence was not true. Thus, "2 and 2 is 4" is true in every possible world.

Leibnitz believed that God, at the Creation, had chosen among all the possible worlds and chosen the best one. (It is from Leibnitz that we get the expression "the best of all possible worlds.") Since he thought that there were no possible worlds in which "2 and 2 is 4" is false, he held that even God could not have created a world in which two and two did not make four. Naturally enough, Leibnitz called the universe God in fact created the **actual world**.

We shall examine some other problems we can treat in terms of possible worlds in the chapter on science. But we can use Leibnitz's idea of a possible world here to build on Frege's theory of meaning. Frege said the meaning of a sentence was its truth conditions. We could formulate his theory as saying that what a sentence meant was determined by what the universe would have to be like if it were true. So we might propose, in Leibnitz's terminology, that the meaning of a sentence is determined by which possible worlds it is true and false in. How would this theory work out?

Leibnitz, as we have seen, thought that all the possible worlds, all the ways the universe might have been, really existed; and some other philosophers in recent times have also held this view. It is a difficult question whether possible worlds do exist, and certainly most people find the idea rather counter-intuitive. But whether or not you believe in the existence of possible worlds (apart from the actual one), Leibnitz's idea provides a very useful way of thinking about reference. For we can translate Frege's theory about reference very easily into Leibnitz's imagery.

Take names. Frege said the reference of "Bucephalus" was the horse it referred to. Well, that horse exists in many possible worlds. (Remember what this means: it means that the universe could have been different in many ways, while still containing that horse.) In some of those possible worlds it is ridden by Alexander; in others, Alexander doesn't ride it, but gives it instead to his teacher, Aristotle.

Take a simple predicate, like "– was ridden." Frege said that the reference of this predicate was its extension, the class of things that were ridden. In this world, Bucephalus is in that extension. But if he had stayed wild on the plains of Macedonia, he would not have been. So there is a possible world in which Bucephalus is not in the extension of "– was ridden" and in that possible world the sentence "Bucephalus was ridden" is false. In fact there are many possible worlds in which Bucephalus was not ridden. In some he stays in Macedonia, in others he gallops off into Russia.

The general idea of explaining reference in terms of possible worlds is simple: a subject-predicate sentence is true in a world if and only if the referent of the subject is in the extension of the predicate in that world. For a sentence to be true in the actual world – in other words for it to be simply true – the referent of the subject must be in the extension of the predicate in this universe.

Using the idea of possible worlds in this way to understand reference and meaning is called **possible-world semantics**. Given this possible-world semantics for reference, we can understand at once why "It is necessary that –" produces an intensional context. For this semantics says that

N: It is necessary that 2 and 2 is 4

is true if and only if

S: 2 and 2 is 4

is true in every possible world. If we substitute for *S* another sentence with the same reference, then we are simply substituting a sentence that is true in the actual world. So there is no guarantee that, in this context, substituting co-referring expressions will preserve the truth of *N*.

So far as reference is concerned, then, the possible-world semantics is easy. But what about sense? We have already seen that it is natural to say that the meaning of a sentence is determined by which possible worlds it is true and false in. Put another way, this means that the meaning of a sentence is determined by what its reference is in every possible world. For since the reference of a sentence is a truth value, once we know whether or not a sentence is true in a world, we know what its reference is in that world. It seems that the natural way, therefore, of treating the senses of words and phrases is to say that their senses are determined by what their references are in each possible world. I am going to follow this idea through for a moment. But, as we shall see in the next section, it turns out that it is not quite right to say that the sense of an expression is determined by its reference in every possible world.

To know the meaning of "Bucephalus," on this theory, would be to know what the reference of "Bucephalus" was in every possible world. So to determine the meaning of "Bucephalus" would be to identify the referent of "Bucephalus" in the actual world and its referent in every other world as well. To know the meaning of "– was ridden" would be to know what the extension of that predicate was in every possible world: to know that in any world the class of things that was ridden was the extension of the predicate "– was ridden." So to determine the meaning of "– was ridden" is to identify the extension of "– was ridden" in this world along with the extension of "– was ridden" in every other world.

Though this is, indeed, a natural way to apply possible-world thinking to Frege's theory of meaning, it turns out that this way of thinking about sense and reference is not equivalent to Frege's. For this reason, I shall say that the possible-world explanation gives words and sentences not senses but **intensions**, using what has now come to be the standard term. The intension of a word is determined once we fix its reference in every possible world. Intensions, unlike senses, are not meanings, which is why I said earlier it is confusing that the sense of a predicate is sometimes called its intension. To understand the distinction between senses and intensions, we must return to Leibnitz's answer to the question: What is it for a sentence to be necessarily true?

3.8 Analytic-synthetic and necessary-contingent

As we saw, Leibnitz said that a sentence was necessarily true if it was true in every possible world. We can use this fact as a basis for a *reductio* of the idea that intensions are meanings. According to the proposal that intensions are meanings, the meaning of a name is fixed once we know what it refers to in every possible world.

Let's consider, then, what the intension of "the morning star" is. Well, it turns out that in every possible world "the morning star" refers to the evening star. If we consider a way the universe might have been in which the morning star is in various ways different, that is the same thing as considering a way the universe might have been in which the evening star is different.

You might think that this was wrong. Surely it is possible, you might say, that the morning star should not have been the evening star? But think about it for a moment. Since the evening star is the morning star, *what* is it that you are supposing might not have been the evening star? Of course, the evening star might not have been visible on the horizon at dawn. So there is a possible world in which the evening star doesn't appear on the horizon at dawn. But that is a possible world in which the morning star doesn't appear on the horizon at dawn, either. In that world, the evening star might never have come to be called "the morning star." Because there is such a possible world, the sentence

The morning star might not have been called "the morning star"

is true. But in our language, in this world, the morning star *is* called "the morning star." And the thing that our expression "the morning star" refers to is the same thing in every possible world as the thing that "the evening star" refers to. It follows, of course, that the sentence

F: The morning star is the evening star

is true in every possible world, and thus necessary. The fact that true identity statements between names are all necessarily true is called the **necessity of identity**. It is the necessity of identity that leads to the conclusion that intensions are not meanings.

For, remember, the meaning of a sentence is what you have to know in order to understand it. If intensions were meanings, therefore, anyone who knew the meaning of the names in a language would be in a position to know the truth of every identity statement involving names. But, as Frege pointed out, *F*, which is an identity statement involving names, is not a piece of semantic knowledge, but a great astronomical discovery. This argument provides a *reductio* of the claim that intensions are meanings.

There is another important reason why this theory is wrong. If intensions were meanings, then the meaning of a sentence would be determined by the class of possible worlds in which it was true. So any sentences that were true in just the same possible worlds would have the same meaning.

This would have very bizarre consequences. It would mean, for one thing, that every necessarily true sentence had the same meaning. So "2 and 2 is 4" would mean the same as "16 and 16 is 32." More than this, any two contingent sentences that were true in just the same possible worlds would have the same meaning. Thus, not only would "The evening star is often visible on the horizon at dusk" mean the same as "Venus is often visible on the horizon at dusk," but "John is a bachelor" would mean the same as "John is a bachelor and 2 and 2 is 4"!

These are the two main sorts of reasons why we have to distinguish between senses and intensions. In 3.4 I said it was going to prove important that sense was defined as what you had to *know* to understand a sentence. Sense, Frege insisted, is a cognitive idea. ("Cognitive" just means "having to do with knowledge.") If two names, *a* and *b*, have the same sense, then anyone who *knows* their senses – anyone who understands how those names function in the language – will *know* that "*a* is *b*" is true. But an intension is not a cognitive idea. From the fact that two names, *a* and *b*, have the same intension, it does not follow that people who understand the language will *know* that "*a* is *b*" is true.

What is true in every possible world, then, is what is **necessary**. And we use the word **contingent** to refer to things that are true in only some possible worlds. Thus, it is a contingent fact that cucumbers are green, because they might not have been green. That is equivalent to saying that the universe could have been different in such a way that cucumbers were some other color; and thus, also, to saying that there are possible worlds in which cucumbers aren't green.

It is crucially important to notice that whether a sentence is necessary is *not* the same question as whether anyone who knows the meaning must know that that sentence is true. For this reason we need another word to describe sentences whose truth does follow, in this way, from their meaning. We call such sentences **analytic**, using a word that the great German philosopher, Immanuel Kant, introduced with this meaning. A true sentence that is not *analytic* is called a **synthetic** truth.

We have already seen that there are necessary truths – "The morning star is the evening star," for example – that are not analytic. But it is also true that there are contingent truths that *are* analytic. Thus, everybody who knows English and understands what "centigrade" means, in particular, knows that "Water freezes at sea-level at zero degrees centigrade" is true, because zero degrees on the centigrade scale is *defined* as the freezing point of water at sea-level. But it isn't necessarily true that water freezes at zero degrees centigrade: there are possible worlds in which it freezes at a higher temperature.

In the last chapter I said that rationalists thought that we could know necessary truths, because we could come to know them by reasoning, which is the only source of certainty. But, as we have now seen, this is not true. What we *can* find out by reasoning are analytic truths; but not all necessary truths are analytic and not all analytic truths are necessary. We use the Latin expression *a priori* to refer to truths that can be known by reason alone. In a sense, they can be known *prior* to any particular experience. *A posteriori* truths are those that require more than reason to discover. In a sense, they can only be known after (that is, *posterior* to) experience. The rationalists assumed that all necessary truths were *a priori* and all *a priori* truths were necessary.

Because the meaning of a sentence is known to everybody who understands it, anybody who understands a sentence that is analytic can work out that it is true. So, provided you understand an analytic sentence, its truth, for you, is an *a priori* matter. Whether every *a priori* truth is analytic is a disputed question.

It is essential, therefore, as I said a little earlier, to keep distinct questions about whether truths are analytic or *a priori*, on the one hand, from questions about whether they are necessary, on the other. That is one reason I have taken such trouble to use possible worlds to explain the relations between them. But there is another reason. Though we cannot use possible worlds in this way to explain the meanings of words, we *can* use them for another highly important philosophical task that has to do with language. And that task is understanding the nature of arguments.

3.9 Natural language and logical form

The study of arguments is **logic**, and beginning with the work of Frege very great strides have been made in this subject. In the work of philosophers after Frege, the excitement that followed their logical discoveries led them to find – like Aristotle more than two millennia before – that the nature and status of logical truths is a topic of intrinsic interest. Building on their theories, we can deepen our understanding of how arguments work.

Here, then, are some of the basic ideas of logic. An **argument** is a sequence of declarative sentences that leads us to a final sentence, which is the **conclusion**. The other sentences, the **premises**, are supposed to support the conclusion. An argument is **valid** when the conclusion must be true if the premises are true. If an argument is valid, we say that the conclusion *follows from* – or is a (deductive) **consequence** of – the premises. Logicians are especially interested in arguments that are **formally valid**. These are arguments where a *sentence with the form of the conclusion* must be true if a class of *sentences with the forms of the premises* are true. Such arguments are also said to have a **valid form**. The idea of the **form** of a sentence is thus crucial to an understanding of logical theory; and in order to explain what form is, I shall now make explicit an idea that we have been using implicitly throughout this chapter.

When I was discussing Frege's semantic theory, I talked about names and predicates and sentences, which are linguistic items, and discussed their connection with objects and properties and truths, which are things in the world. When we talk about the words and expressions that make up the sentence and the order in which they occur, we are talking about **syntax**. So among the syntactic properties of the sentence "Snow is white" are

(a) that its first word is "snow",
(b) that the predicate is "– is white", and
(c) that it is three words long.

The idea of form is essentially the idea of syntax.

In logic what we seek to do, then, is to identify those arguments that are reliable because of the *syntax* of the premises and the conclusion. So we want to identify patterns of argument that will work, whatever the particular content of the sentences. Just as we used variables earlier to stand in for names, so we can use **sentential variables** to stand in for sentences in order to make generalizations about arguments. Thus, using S and T to stand for sentences, we can say that an argument from a sentence of the form "S and T" to the conclusion S is reliable because it is not possible for "S and T" to be true when S is false. It is because we are interested in the form, the shape, of valid arguments, not in the particular contents of the sentences that make them up, that logic is sometimes called **formal** logic.

So far I have been talking about the **natural languages** that human cultures have developed for communication. But in order to study the issues about argument that are central to logic, philosophers and linguists have developed various **artificial languages**. When I wrote "S and T" just now, I was already moving away from natural languages towards the sorts of artificial languages that logicians have developed to study arguments. The use of symbols like sentential variables has a number of advantages. One is that it allows us to see very clearly how the form of an argument affects its validity. Another is that it allows us to escape some of the vagueness and imprecision of natural languages. But to use the artificial languages of formal logic we have to start by being clear about what we are developing them *for*. And if we are to be clear about this, it is very important to be clear about what is meant by the form of an argument in natural language.

So let's consider an example. Take a sentence we've looked at before, and a conclusion we could draw from it.

Premise: *S*: John and Mary, who are friends of Peter's, sat in the garden and ate strawberries.
Conclusion: *T*: Somebody ate strawberries.

Here there is one premise and the conclusion certainly seems to follow. But it is also formally valid. According to the definition I just gave, this means that a sentence of the form of the conclusion must be true if a sentence of the form of the premise is. So what are the forms of these sentences?

One way to get a clearer picture of what is meant by the form of a sentence is to go back to considering Frege's open sentences. We get open sentences by removing the names from complete sentences. We can then say that the sentence is *composed from* the names and the open sentence. (As before, we label the blanks with variables, one for each name we remove.) *S*, the premise in this argument, is composed from the names "John," "Mary," and "Peter," and the open sentence

O: *X* and *Y*, who are friends of *Z*'s, sat in the garden and ate strawberries.

Using the variables as labels we can say that "John" is in the *X*-position, "Mary" in the *Y*-position and so on.

Now there is nothing to stop us from removing words other than names. Just as we can have variables for names, we could have variables for nouns and for any other words. Thus we could say that *S* is made up of the three names, the noun "friends" and the expression

X and *Y*, who are *F* of *Z*'s, sat in the garden and ate strawberries.

This time we can use the label *F* to say that, in *S*, "friends" is in the *F*-position of this formula. *F* is a noun-variable, just as *X* is a variable for names. So we can generalize the idea of an open sentence to mean anything produced by replacing words with variables.

Notice that when we remove a word from a sentence to replace it with a variable, the open sentence we are left with can be used to make a different sentence. So we could make

S_3: Peter and Mary, who are friends of John's, sat in the garden and ate strawberries

from O and the same names, if we just put the names in different variable positions. What S and S_3 have in common is the fact that they are composed from the open sentence, O. When we say that sentences share a certain form, we mean they can be composed from the same open sentence. In other words, we can use the idea of *being composed from the same open sentence* to describe aspects of the syntax that certain sentences share.

Among the less interesting facts about the form of S is the fact that it is a sentence; and this simply means that we could remove *all* the words and replace them with the single variable that we earlier called a *sentential variable.* All sentences share this formal feature: they can all be composed by replacing a string of blanks with a string of words. We can make an open sentence by removing all the words from a sentence of English and then make another sentence by putting in another lot of words; though, of course, the rules of English syntax determine which strings of words make meaningful sentences.

But sentences share more interesting aspects of form than the fact that they *are* sentences: for example, the formal property shared by all the sentences that can be made from O by replacing the variables with names.

We can now re-examine the argument from

S: John and Mary, who are friends of Peter's, sat in the garden and ate strawberries

to

T: Somebody ate strawberries

in the light of this discussion of form. What aspect of the form of the premise and the conclusion makes the argument valid? The most general answer is that it is an example of an inference from a sentence of the form

Premise: $X P$

to a sentence of the form

Conclusion: Somebody P

where P is a variable for a predicate (in this case "ate strawberries") and X is, as usual, a variable for a name. Now the reason why the argument is valid is that *every* argument of this form is valid. This allows us to record a very broad generalization about many possible arguments.

This is not the only way in which an argument of this form can be shown to be valid, however. Thus, any inference from a sentence of the form of

    O: *X* and *Y*, who are friends of *Z*'s, sat in the garden and ate strawberries,

to

    T: Somebody ate strawberries

is valid too. However we fill in the *X*, *Y*, and *Z* places, if the resulting sentence is true, the conclusion must be true also. So this is one way of making a narrower generalization about which arguments are valid. But logicians focus their interest on a special group of formal properties of sentences, and study how the presence of those formal properties affects the validity of arguments.

One example of this sort of study is **sentential** – or **propositional** – **logic**, which makes generalizations about how the presence of the words "and," "not," "or," and "if" in sentences affects arguments. To do this, sentential logic uses sentential variables of the sort I introduced just now; but it also moves further in the direction of a purely artificial language by replacing the English words *and, or* and *not* with the symbols &, V, and ~, and the words "*If . . ., then . . .*" with →. A typical (and not very exciting) claim of sentential logic is that every argument of the form

   Premises: $S \rightarrow T$
                 S
 Conclusion: T

is valid. This form of argument actually has a name. It's called *modus ponens*. Whatever sentences you replace *S* and *T* with, provided you follow this rule, if the premises are true, the conclusion must be. (If you replace *S* in the first premise with a sentence, you must replace it with the *same* sentence in the second premise and the conclusion.) "And," "or" and "if" are called **connectives**, because they are used to connect sentences to each other. "*S* and *T*" is called the **conjunction** of *S* and *T*; "*S* or *T*" is called the **disjunction** of *S* and *T*; and "If *S*, *T*" is called a **conditional** with *S* as **antecedent** and *T* as **consequent**.

"Not," of course, isn't a connective: it applies to one sentence at a time so there isn't a second sentence to connect. But it is a **sentence-forming operator on sentences**: if you put "not" into one sentence in the right place, thus *operating* on that sentence, you get another, different sentence. Thus, we can go from "It's snowing" to "It's not snowing." "It's not snowing" is called the **negation** of "It's snowing." Since, in English, you can get a sentence equivalent to the negation of any sentence, *S*, by writing "It is not true that –" in front of *S*, we often write "Not-*S*" as shorthand for the form of the negation of *S*. But, of course, in the artificial language of propositional logic we can simply write " ~ *S*."

Predicate logic builds on sentential logic. It studies the way in which the quantifiers "all" and "some" affect validity. Thus, the inference

Premise: *X P*
Conclusion: Somebody *P*,

which I mentioned just now, is an instance of a simple result in predicate logic. Here we have variables for names and for predicates, not for sentences, and the quantifier "somebody." We were using the ideas of predicate logic in chapter one, when we constructed the Ramsey-sentences, using the existential quantifier "There exists an *X*, such that *X* . . ."

Now, not every valid argument gives you a reason to believe the conclusion. For even if the argument is valid, it only gives you a reason to support the conclusion if the premises are true. A valid argument whose premises are true is called a **sound** argument. The task of logic, therefore, is to try to give a theory that will allow us to identify which arguments are valid. Once we know which arguments are valid, we can see then whether we should believe their conclusions by deciding if we have reason to believe the premises. If an argument is valid *and* sound, then it does offer good reason to believe its conclusion.

Notice that it follows that there is another way in which we can use valid forms of argument in arriving at new beliefs. In a valid argument, the premises can't be true and the conclusion false; so, if the conclusion is false, the premises can't be true. Sometimes, therefore, recognizing that a form of argument is valid and knowing that the conclusion is false, we can infer that at least one of the premises is false. This is the logical truth we have relied on whenever we have used *reductio* arguments.

I defined a valid argument as one where the conclusion must be true if the premises are. Another way of putting this would be to say that, in a valid argument, it is impossible for the premises to be true and the conclusion false. This is the very notion of possibility that we used in talking about possible worlds. So in terms of possible-world semantics we could say that a valid form of argument is one where a sentence of the form of the conclusion is true in every possible world where sentences of the forms of the premises are true.

If a sentence can be seen to be true simply because of its syntax, independently of the particular names and predicates it contains, we can say it is **formally** or **logically** true. Formally true sentences are always necessarily true as well. Thus, "Snow is white or snow isn't white" is logically true, because every sentence of the form "*S* or not-*S*" is true in every possible world. It follows from these definitions of validity and consequence that any string of sentences leading up to a logical truth is a valid argument; and that a logical truth is a consequence of any string of sentences at all. The reason is that, since a logical truth is true in every possible world, *whatever* premises we put in front of it in an argument, it will be true in every world where they are true. Logical truths, then, are necessary truths, which can be identified as true by their form.

Now we already know that some necessary truths cannot be identified by their form as true. For, as we saw, every true identity statement is necessary. But these truths cannot be seen to be true simply by looking at their syntax. They are necessary but not logically true. Some identity statements – say, "Mars is the evening star" – are false; some, like

"The morning star is Venus," are true. But there is no guarantee that you will know *which* such sentences are true and which false just because you both understand the language and know that they have the syntactic property of being identity statements between names.

As I have already said, logicians have concentrated on systems of logic, like sentential or predicate logic, which identify arguments that are valid because of the presence of certain words like "and" and "all." We can say that these logics examine the **logical properties** of such words. Of course, most words cannot be fully understood in terms simply of their logical properties. However much you knew about the logical properties of the word "red" for example, you wouldn't understand it if you didn't know what red things look like. To understand "red" you need to know the *sense* of the word. But there are words – like "all" and "and" – whose whole meaning can be given by specifying their logical properties. Such words are called **logical constants**, and logicians take a special interest in them.

But in recent years a great deal of new work in logic has focused on the logical properties of other words: **epistemic logic**, for example, looks at the logical properties of "know," and **modal logic** studies the logical properties of "necessary" and "possible." Thus, we can have modal sentential logic, which includes these words along with sentential variables, negation and the connectives; and modal predicate logic, where we add variables for names and predicates as well. Possible-world semantics is, of course, particularly useful for modal logic; but we shall also be using possible-world semantics in the next chapter to examine some issues about the necessity of laws of nature. (You might have thought that "necessary" and "possible" were logical constants, that they could be defined simply by looking at their role in arguments. But the existence of different kinds of necessity – including the kind we shall look at in the next chapter – means that modal logic is not all you need to explain the idea of necessity.)

Recent formal logic has increased our understanding of validity, necessity and logical truth. But the interest of these questions is not simply that we want to make valid arguments or find logical truths. Philosophers are interested in logic not just because they want to make valid arguments, but because they want to know what makes an argument valid; not just because they want to discover necessary truths, but because they want to understand the idea of necessity.

So far I have suggested three reasons why philosophers have been interested in language:

(a) because it is their primary tool,
(b) because, unlike thoughts and ideas, it is public, and
(c) because it is the medium in which we express truths.

But many of the ideas that we have discussed in this chapter will come up in later chapters, and some of them came up when we were discussing philosophy of mind and epistemology. That brings me to the last reason I want to suggest: that philosophers have found again and again that starting with questions about language can lead to new insights in every area of the subject.

3.10 Conventions of language

In the introduction I said that the questions philosophers ask often take us to fundamental issues that seem remote from the questions with which we begin. It happened in the first two chapters and it has happened here. We started by wondering what it would take to show that dolphins or chimpanzees had a language, and we have got to a point where we have discussed sense and reference, intensions and extensions, logic and possible-world semantics. One thing is certain. We have seen that what is involved in having a language is very complex. So it is not surprising that it is hard to see how we should find out if there really is a dolphin language or if Nim really understands American Sign Language. In order to answer these questions, we should have to be able to say, finally, how we can tell if someone or something is using words and sentences in such a way that they have such properties as reference, sense, and truth conditions.

Philosophers have argued that our language has these properties because we have certain *conventions*, certain shared assumptions about how we use words. If we remember Frege's discovery of the primacy of the sentence, we shall want to ask, first, what the convention is that gives sentences their truth conditions and their truth values. The natural answer is that the convention that gives sentences truth conditions is the convention that you should use declarative sentences to say what is true. The philosopher H.P. Grice has proposed that what this amounts to is that we all expect someone who understands a sentence, *S*, to use *S* to get other people to believe that *S* is true. Starting with this basic idea, you can go on to look at sentences that are not declarative: orders, for example, or questions.

In using declarative sentences we make **assertions**. In using imperative sentences, we make orders. In each case we are producing a complete meaningful utterance, we are performing what linguists call a **speech-act**, though the particular types of speech-act differ in their particular functions. Despite these differences, however, we can use the ideas of Frege's semantic theory – the ideas that we used to explain the utterance of declarative sentences in the speech-act of assertion – to explain the contents of other speech-acts as well. For every one of the central speech-acts – assertion, questioning and ordering – Frege's idea of the truth condition can be used.

We say that the truth conditions of a declarative sentence *hold* if the sentence is true. In assertion we try to get others to *believe* that the truth conditions of the sentence we assert hold; in ordering we try to get someone to *make* the truth conditions hold; in questioning, we try to get someone to *tell us what* truth conditions hold. In Chapter 5, I shall look in more detail at orders in the context of discussing the philosophical theory about moral language that is called **prescriptivism**.

So Grice's theory tells us what it is to understand sentences, as we use them in these many speech-acts. To know the meaning of a sentence is to understand how it is used in speech-acts. But if we combine it with Frege's discovery of the primacy of the sentence, Grice's theory can also tell us what it is to understand the meanings of words. To understand the meaning of a word is to know how it contributes to determining the meanings of sentences. So to understand a word, *W*, is to know how it contributes to fixing what speech-acts you can carry out with sentences that contain *W*.

Notice that Frege's theory and Grice's are thus not inconsistent with each other. In fact they are really complementary. Frege's theory says we have to know the sense of a word to understand it, and that knowing the sense of a word is just knowing how it determines the sense of a sentence. To know the sense of a sentence is to know what it would be for it to be true. But that is precisely what you have to know on Grice's theory. You could say that Frege tells us what the meanings of sentences are – namely, truth conditions – and Grice tells us what the truth conditions are for.

Thus, on Grice's theory, Nim Chimpsky understands the American Sign Language gestures that mean "It is raining" if he both

(a) uses the signs to try to get people to believe that the truth conditions of "It is raining" hold, and
(b) expects people to use signs to try to get him (and others) to believe those truth conditions hold also.

And, of course, to believe that the truth conditions of "It is raining" hold is just to believe that it is raining. As far as orders are concerned, Nim understands the signs that mean "Bring me a banana!" if he both

(a) uses those signs to try to get people to make that sentence's truth conditions hold, and
(b) expects people to use them to try to get him (and others) to make them hold.

To make those truth conditions hold, of course, is just to bring the speaker a banana.

If Grice is right, and this *is* what it takes, there is a good deal of evidence that Nim understands the language at least some of the time. If he does understand, this is one more reason for seeing ourselves as part of, and not separate from, the rest of the natural world. Functionalism, causal theories of knowledge and a Gricean theory of meaning fit together as part of a naturalist philosophy.

3.11   Conclusion

We have travelled in this chapter through some of the main highways of the philosophy of language and logic. Starting with Hobbes's Cartesian theory of language – which I showed was open to Wittgenstein's criticism of private languages – we moved on to Frege's theory of meaning. Using some of Frege's ideas we were then able to explore some of the basic questions of semantics; and we were able to connect these questions with the ideas of recent possible-world semantics. This led us to a consideration of some of the basic ideas of formal logic. Finally, I looked at the way Grice had suggested we could connect the ideas of semantic theory with the use of language in practical communication.

The last two chapters dealt with questions that arise because there are conscious beings in the universe, reflecting on their own situation, creatures with minds seeking to know the world they live in. They are questions which could be asked about any creatures whose minds were sufficiently complex; though, of course, there is no reason to suppose that they would be asked *by* every such creature. But the concerns of this chapter have focused on what is (so far as we know) a specifically *human* institution – language – even though, as I have argued, there is nothing in principle that rules out the use of languages by other animals. In a sense we have been focusing on questions that are more and more narrowly about our own cultural situation. Without minds, no knowledge; without knowledge (of meaning), no language. In the next chapter we shall consider an institution that is even more specific than language, one that occurs only in the modern era and only in certain cultures. That institution is science.

4 Science

What makes an explanation scientific?

How can we justify scientific theories?

What is a law of nature?

4.1 Introduction

Every day, in newspapers all around the world, astrologers tell people what life has in store for them. Under each of the star signs, which go with birth dates, there is a short message telling, say, Taureans to take special care in financial matters or Librans to expect progress in affairs of the heart. People make many kinds of criticism of these horoscopes: that they are vague, or that they are inaccurate, or that they make people fatalistic. All of these criticisms could have been made of astrological predictions any time in the last two and a half thousand years, any time since Socrates. But there is one kind of criticism that is relatively modern, and that is made very often nowadays. It is that astrology is *unscientific.*

It is an important fact that this criticism is relatively modern. Until the seventeenth century most intellectuals in the West thought that there was something to astrology, and even those who did not believe in it would not have criticized it in this way. Of course, there is a simple enough reason for this. Science, in the modern sense, has only developed since the seventeenth century. As a result, in the philosophy of science – unlike philosophical psychology, epistemology and the philosophy of language – most of the problems are less than three centuries old.

Though criticism of theories as unscientific has become relatively familiar in the last three hundred years, it is not obvious what the force of this criticism is. If, after all, a particular astrologer often makes true predictions, people who read the horoscope might not care very much whether the predictions were scientific. What they want of astrological predictions is not that they should be scientific but that they should be true. My friend, Peter, who believes that astrology works, worries more about the vagueness of predictions and about their accuracy; and Mary, who believes in them too, worries, because she is a Christian, about whether she *ought* to make use of them.

But people who criticize astrology as unscientific are not just saying that they don't believe these horoscopes, and they are not just saying that it is morally wrong to rely on them. Indeed, someone could criticize astrology as unscientific and still believe that a particular astrologer was very good at predicting stock-market prices. So, what *does* it mean to say that a theory is unscientific?

This question is one of the central problems of the philosophy of science, which I am going to discuss in this chapter. Indeed, it has received so much attention that it has a name. Karl Popper, one of the most influential philosophers of science of our century, has called this problem the **demarcation problem**. What is it that distinguishes between science and non-science? How are we to *demarcate* the boundary between them?

Though this is a central problem of the philosophy of science, there are many reasons why understanding the nature of science has been important to philosophers. Logic has led to new work in the sciences of mathematics and linguistics; and the philosophy of mind exists in intimate relation with the science of psychology. Functionalism was prompted by the development of computers and of computer science. As we shall see at the end of the chapter, these are not the only places where the interests of scientists and philosophers overlap; and computer science, linguistics, mathematics and psychology are not the only sciences that raise philosophical questions.

These philosophical issues about particular sciences are interesting and important. But there is a much more general reason why understanding science is important to philosophy. We saw in Chapter 2 that questions about what and how we know are a central philosophical concern. Philosophy has a general interest in science because it is an organized search for knowledge. After all, what better way to find out about knowledge than to examine the theories and institutions in our society that have made the greatest contribution to expanding our knowledge of the world?

4.2 Description and prescription

As we saw in earlier chapters, philosophers do not only try to understand concepts and theories, they also criticize many of our ordinary beliefs. Skeptics, for example, challenge our ordinary claims to knowledge, arguing that we know much less than we think, and Wittgenstein and the behaviorists challenged our ordinary unreflective belief that we might have Hobbesian "twinges." Philosophers not only try to understand what we *do* believe, but also argue about what we *should* believe. Claims about what we should say, or think, or do are **prescriptive**: they prescribe courses of thought and action. In the philosophy of science, too, description and prescription go hand in hand.

But in the philosophy of science, unlike the philosophy of mind or epistemology or the philosophy of language, the object of study is an institution – science – that developed in particular societies in the relatively recent past. All human societies have had minds and knowledge and languages, yet only recently have most societies come to have science. For this reason the descriptive task of trying to say what science is like is one that philosophers share with historians and sociologists of science. As philosophers, however, we want to ask the epistemological question whether science really does provide us with the knowledge it seems to, to address the prescriptive question whether we should accept some or any of the claims of scientific theories. If we do accept them, especially those that challenge our common-sense beliefs, then we want to have a proper understanding of them and to investigate their significance. But in order to make this sort of philosophical assessment of science, we must first try to see what it is really like.

This is why the philosophy of science and the history of science are often studied together – indeed, many universities have programs or departments of the history and philosophy of science, where the two kinds of study are carried out together. If we look at science in this historical way we can ask both, descriptively, how scientists construct their theories, and, prescriptively, how they should construct and seek support for them. Because this approach looks at the development of science through time, we can call it a **diachronic** approach.

Philosophers of science also discuss questions that have to do not with the way science develops, but with the theories of science at a particular stage in its development. On this approach, we ask, descriptively, about the structure of scientific theories and what they say about the world, and prescriptively, about what justifies our belief in them. This way of studying science we can call **synchronic**; it has to do with issues about the state of science at a particular time.

The logical positivists made an important distinction that runs in parallel with the distinction between diachronic and synchronic questions. Some issues, they said, have to do with the **context of discovery**. These are questions about how to set about deepening our scientific understanding of the world. Thus, questions about how we should design experiments – questions of experimental **methodology** – belong to the context of discovery. But there are other questions that arise, which have to do with how we organize the evidence, the data, we collect from experiment and observation in order to decide whether it supports our theories. The issue here is not how we develop our theories but how we defend and justify them, and such questions are said to belong to the **context of justification**.

We should not assume, in advance, that the answer to the demarcation problem will have to do only with synchronic matters or only with diachronic ones: it might require considerations of either or both kinds. Nor should we assume at the start that what makes a theory scientific is either how you set about developing it or how you justify it: perhaps solving the demarcation problem will involve considerations about both the context of discovery and the context of justification.

I didn't set out to introduce you to philosophy by trying to define "philosophy." And I'm not going to begin discussing science by trying to define "science" either. Rather, I want to begin by discussing some of the distinguishing features of scientific theories. This is most easily done in terms of a specific example. So I shall start out, now, with a simplified example of a scientific theory with which you may already be familiar. When we have spent some time discussing some of the characteristics of scientific theory, we shall be in a better position to return to the demarcation problem.

4.3   An example: Gregor Mendel's genetic theory

In the late nineteenth century, a Czech monk named Gregor Mendel developed a new theory of biological inheritance. Most biologists of his day believed that plants and animals inherited their characteristics from the germ cells of their parents, by a blending of genetic material, rather like the mixing of fluids. It was supposed, for example, that when the pollen from a white-flowering pea fertilized a red-flowering pea, the seeds would usually produce peas with pink flowers, because the material that made the flowers white in one plant blended with the material that made the other flowers red to produce this intermediate coloring.

Mendel suggested that this theory was quite wrong. He proposed that the genetic material that offspring inherited from their parents persisted unchanged in the next generation. To each of the characteristics of the offspring there corresponded, he said, units of heredity that came to be called *genes.* The characteristic appearance of an organism is called its *phenotype.* The genes that affect a particular phenotypic characteristic of an organism come, according to Mendel's theory, in various types. Genes that affect the same phenotypic characteristic are called *alleles.* On Mendel's theory, when a male and female mate, they each contribute one allele of each gene to their germ cells. These germ cells join to form the fertilized egg, which develops into the adult organism. So, while the germ cells have just one allele of each gene, the new organism has two alleles of each gene once more, one from each parent. The complete collection of all the genes of an organism is called its *genotype.*

Let's see how Mendel's theory would work out for the genetics of the flower color of peas, assuming a much simplified version of his theory of inheritance. Suppose peas with red flowers have two red-making alleles for petal color, and peas with white flowers have two white-making alleles. We'll call the red-making alleles R, and the white-making ones W. So, when these red- and white-flowering peas are crossed, each of their offspring will get one R and one W allele. Let's suppose that this is what makes them have pink flowers.

Organisms with two alleles of the same gene, like the red and the white peas, are called *homozygous.* The pink peas, with different alleles, are called *heterozygous.* If the blending theory had been correct, then crossing one of the heterozygous pink-flowering peas with a red-flowering pea should have produced offspring all of the same color. The pink-making genetic material would have blended with an equal quantity of the red-making material to produce a pea that was, say, a deeper, redder, shade of pink. But what actually happened, according to Mendel, if you did cross red and pink peas, was that you got two sorts of offspring. Some were pink, others were just as red as the red parent.

His theory explained this. For, if he was right, the original alleles, R and W, were still fully present in the pink peas; their genotype was RW. When they were crossed they gave one allele to each offspring, so that half of their offspring got R, and half got W. The red peas were homozygous; their genotype was RR. They could only give one R allele to each offspring. Half of the offspring of this cross between pink and red plants got two Rs and half got one R and one W. The offspring had exactly the same genetic constitution, so far as petal-color was concerned, as one or other of the parents. They were all either RR or RW.

In this case, the heterozygous plant was intermediate in phenotype between the parents. But Mendel also proposed that some alleles had a property called *dominance* over other alleles. One allele, A, was dominant over another, B, if its presence in the genotype made an organism have the same phenotype as a homozygote both of whose alleles were **A**. The other allele, **B**, was called the *recessive* member of the pair. Thus, suppose purple-making alleles, **P**, dominated **W** alleles, so that all the offspring of a cross between a purple pea with and a white pea would have purple flowers. Even where one allele was dominant and the other recessive, however, the recessive allele was still present. So, if you crossed two purple peas that were heterozygous and each had one **W** allele, those offspring that got a **W** allele from both parents would be white. In this case the cross between two purple-flowering peas, both with genotype **PW**, would produce some **WW** offspring, which would be white.

Mendel supported his theory of dominance with the results of some experiments. He showed, for example, that if you crossed purple peas with white ones, all the first generation was purple. What that meant in terms of the theory was that a cross between **PP** and **WW** could produce only **PW** offspring, and, since **P** dominates **W**, these all look like their **PP** parents. Then he crossed these first generation hybrids with each other and found that some of the offspring were purple and some were white. Translating once more into terms of Mendel's theory, we can say why this was. Crossing the **PW**s with each other would produce **PP**, **PW** and **WW** offspring. The first two genotypes would produce purple flowers; but the last one would produce white ones. So Mendel's theory got all of these cases right.

Every organism has many genes, according to Mendel's theory. Since the genes persist and do not blend, you should be able to predict all the possible phenotypes that could be produced by a cross, once you know the genotype of the parents. But Mendel wondered whether the genes that determined different characteristics were linked together, so that if a pea got a gene for white flowers it also got, say, the gene for hairy stems.

If the genes for different characteristics were not connected, then they would be assigned to offspring independently of each other. Suppose that the hairy-stem allele, **H**, dominated the smooth-stem allele, **S**, just as **P** dominates **W** in the gene for the color of the petals. Consider a pea that was heterozygous for both petal color and stem surface. It would have, say, one **W** and one **P** allele of the color gene; and one **H** and one **S** allele of the stem gene. If these genes were inherited independently of each other then this plant would be able to contribute four different combinations of genes to its offspring: **WH**, **WS**, **PH**, **PS**.

Suppose we crossed this plant with one that was homozygous for both white petals and smooth stems, so that all of its offspring got the combination **WS**. The resultant offspring would have one of the following four genotypes:

1. **WS WH**   2. **WS WS**
3. **WS PH**   4. **WS PS**

and these genotypes should come in roughly equal numbers. These four kinds of plant would have the phenotypes:

1. White petals, Hairy stems   2. White petals, Smooth stems
3. Purple petals, Hairy stems   4. Purple petals, Smooth stems.

If, on the other hand, **W** was linked somehow to **S**, genotype 1 would not exist: the cross would produce no white-flowering hairy-stemmed peas. Similarly, if **P** was linked to **H**, then genotype 4 would not exist; the cross would produce no purple-flowering smooth-stemmed peas.

In a series of experiments, Mendel showed that, in fact, for several pairs of characteristics you got all the four possible combinations. And so he proposed his laws of *independent assortment and recombination* of genes. These said that *both* when different genes in an organism separated to form the germ cells *and* when they joined together again, they did so independently. We can see what this means in practice if we consider an organism that is heterozygous for two genes. Suppose it is **Aa** for one gene and **Bb** for another. If allele **A** ends up in a germ cell, it is just as likely to be paired with **B** as with **b**. That is independent assortment. And if a male germ cell has allele **A**, it is just as likely to fertilize an egg with allele **B** of the other gene as it is to fertilize one with allele **b**. That is independent recombination.

Because the separation of alleles and their combination were basically random processes, Mendel's experiments were more complex than this. His results were statistical. And using very basic statistical ideas he was able to make rough predictions not only of the variety of phenotypes that could result from a cross, but also of their frequencies.

Let's summarize the main propositions of Mendel's theory of the gene.

1. Certain aspects of the phenotype of an organism are determined by its genes. (Let's call these the *genetically determined characteristics.*)
2. These genes may come in various types, called alleles, which differ in the consequences that their presence makes to the genetically determined characteristics.
3. Each of these genetically determined characteristics may exist in different forms – different colors of petals, for example, or textures of stem.
4. Genetically determined characteristics are produced by pairs of alleles of the gene that corresponds to them.
5. Every organism gets two alleles of each gene, one from each parent.
6. If an organism gets identical alleles from each of its parents it is homozygous for that allele, otherwise it is heterozygous.
7. If an organism is heterozygous for an allele, **A**, it has the genetically determined characteristic corresponding to **A**, which we call the **A** phenotype.
8. An allele, **A**, must exist in one of three relations to any other allele, **B**. **A** can either
   (a) be dominant with respect to **B**, or
   (b) be recessive with respect to **B**, or
   (c) interact with **B**.
9. If **A** is dominant with respect to **B**, then an organism that is heterozygous and has the genotype **AB** will have the **A** phenotype.

10. If **A** is recessive with respect to **B** then an organism that is heterozygous and has the genotype **AB** will have the **B** phenotype.

11. If **A** interacts with **B**, then an organism that is heterozygous and has the genotype **AB**, will have neither the **A** nor the **B** phenotype, but some other phenotype that is determined by **A** and **B** together.

Along with these claims about how genes behave go the *laws of independent assortment and recombination of genes*:

12. ASSORTMENT: When two different genes in an organism separate to form the germ cells they do so independently.

13. RECOMBINATION: When two different genes join together again to form the new genotype they do so independently.

4.4   Theory and observation

This simplified version of Mendelian genetic theory will allow us to examine many of the features of scientific theories that philosophers of science have discussed. The first important thing to say about Mendel's theory is that it was a great feat of creative imagination. He couldn't see (or touch or hear or taste) genes, so he had to **postulate** them in order to try to explain the results of his experiments. To postulate the existence of entities is to hypothesize that they exist.

What, exactly, was involved in hypothesizing that genes exist? Certainly Mendel had to do more than say that he thought there were things called "genes." What he had to do as well was to say what some of their properties were. We can see *why* he had to do this in terms of Frege's theory of meaning. For in order to understand a term like "gene" we have to give it a sense, which is, as you will remember, an associated *mode of presentation.* So he had to say what anything would have to be like in order to be a gene. You understand the name "the morning star" because you know that something is the morning star if and only if it is a heavenly body that usually appears at a certain point on the horizon in the morning. Mendel had to associate some such sense with his word "gene."

Because the word "gene" had no established sense associated with it, the outline of the theory I presented above is a sort of implicit definition of the word. To make it an explicit definition we have to remove the word "gene" from the theory as I summarized it above. We can then introduce the idea of a gene in a way that is equivalent to using a Ramsey-sentence, just like the one we used in chapter one to develop functionalism. Once more, we write out Mendel's theory as a single conjunction of the eleven claims and the laws: call this very long sentence *MG* (for "Mendelian genetics"). Then we replace the word "gene" throughout with a variable *X*, and other new terms like "allele" by other variables. Let's suppose that these were the only new terms. We can now define genes and alleles, quite simply, as the two kinds of thing that satisfy this complex open sentence, *MG'*.

Genes and alleles are, so to speak, any Xs and Ys that make all Mendel's thirteen propositions true at once. This way we can define the word "gene" in terms of notions that we already understand: notions like *phenotype* (which just means the visible characteristics of the organism), *organism* and *parent*. Of course, this isn't like an ordinary definition where we define one word only in terms of others we already understand. There is the other term – "allele" – that we don't already understand. But just as the Ramsey-sentence allowed us to interpret "pain", even though the definition involved the concept of "worry," so here we have replaced the words "allele" and "gene" by variables at the same time, and come to understand "allele" along with the term "gene." Mendel's theory that there are genes and alleles thus amounts to saying that there are two kinds of entity that together satisfy MG'.

Now the reason all of this is necessary is, of course, the fact that I mentioned at the beginning of this section: Mendel couldn't see or otherwise sense genes. They were not *observable*. Because of this he could not introduce the term "gene," in the way we *can* define the name "the evening star" or the predicate "– is red," by pointing to something. (This was what Wittgenstein meant by an **ostensive definition**.) That is why unobservable entities have to have their names introduced in terms of things that we can observe. For if we didn't connect their names in this way with things we could observe, we could never use the names. There would be no role for the names in our language, because there would be no circumstances in which experience would lead us to use them.

The term "gene" refers to something that Mendel couldn't observe, but it is also what is called a **theoretical term**. It is a theoretical term because it is introduced by way of a theory, in this case MG. Philosophers have sometimes thought that all unobservable things had to be referred to by theoretical terms. Whether this is true is partly a question of definition. If any set of propositions – such as 1 to 13 in MG – that plays the role of introducing a term can be called a "theory," then all names for things we can't observe will be theoretical terms, by definition. But if we restrict the word "theory" to relatively complex sets of propositions, or to propositions that we still regard as speculative, then some terms for unobservables won't be theoretical. Until we developed manned space-flight, for example, we couldn't see the other side of the moon. Some astronomer might have introduced the term "Moonback mountains" to refer to mountains on the other side of the moon. Thus "There is a Moonback mountain" would be explained by a simple Ramsey-sentence

MM: There exists an X, such that X is a mountain on the other side of the moon.

Moonback mountains would have been unobservable but, in one sense, their name wouldn't have been terribly theoretical. Normally, we call a term "theoretical" only when the sentence by which we introduce it is complicated or hypothetical. Is it a theory that the large circular source of light that we see in the sky is a large heavenly body that radiates light? If it is, "sun" is a theoretical term. If it isn't, "sun" isn't a theoretical term. It's as simple as that.

The issue is complicated by the fact that as we get used to using certain theories we are less and less aware that they are theories at all. When the earliest astronomers first proposed that the thing in the sky was a large spherical object, this was a theory. But gradually, over time, it has become part of common sense. Every child (in our society) learns that the sun is a large three-dimensional body and not just a disk in the sky.

The point is that even common-sense beliefs were often once new theories. Indeed, philosophers of science have tended to argue that common sense on any particular matter is just another theory. If we don't call the view that the sun is a heavenly body a theory, it is because we are not aware of the fact that this was once an exciting and original discovery. In ordinary life, we tend to use the word "theory" to refer to claims that we are still unsure about or that we know we were once unsure about. We tend not to use it for beliefs that we have come to take for granted. In this usage, the distinction between theoretical and non-theoretical terms belongs to the context of discovery: it has to do with how we came by the terms and how secure we have become in our use of them. But philosophers use the word "theory" to mean any set of beliefs about how the world is, even if those beliefs are relatively simple or obvious or familiar. The point about a theory is that it is a set of propositions that might or might not be true. The way philosophers think about the question, whether something is a theory is an issue about the context of justification.

Even if the question whether all terms for unobservable entities are theoretical is partly a definitional question, however, there is no doubt at all that some highly theoretical terms refer to things that are perfectly observable. The term "electron microscope" describes a perfectly observable thing. You can observe one in many physics and biology departments. But it is certainly a theoretical term. It can be understood only by way of a theory about electrons.

Many philosophers of science, especially since the logical positivists, assumed that all unobservable entities are referred to by theoretical terms, and all theoretical terms refer to unobservable entities. You can see why they might have been led to think this. If we are to refer to unobservable entities we have to introduce them by way of sentences like *MM*. Because of the way philosophers use the word "theory," they would say that it is a theory that there were mountains on the other side of the moon. That makes "Moonback mountain" a theoretical term. You should keep in mind that, on this usage, when I say that a term is theoretical I do not mean that it can be understood only in terms of an elaborate or complicated theory.

Because of this, the connection between the question whether a belief is theoretical and the epistemological concern that our beliefs be based on observation is not a simple one. It is simply a mistake to suppose that because a term was introduced by way of a theory the thing it referred to could not be observed. This mistake shows up in the case of Mendel's theory. Though Mendel couldn't see genes, when light microscopes and staining techniques improved in the early twentieth century, geneticists came to believe that they *could* see them. It turned out that some genes (in the salivary glands of fruit-flies, for example) were much bigger than others and could be stained so as to reflect light under a microscope. They looked like colored bands on the chromosome. This didn't make the term "gene" any less theoretical, but it did make genes observable.

Philosophers call things that we can observe *phenomena*. A **phenomenon** is something like a phenotype (which, as you may have guessed, shares part of its etymology – a Greek root meaning "show" or "appear" – with the word "phenomenon"). A phenomenon is something you can experience with your senses. As far as Mendel was concerned, the claims he made about genes were not just about phenomena, they were about unobservable reality.

Nevertheless, there is an important connection between theoretical terms and observability. As I said just now, if there were no connection between a theoretical term and observable things, we would have no way of using it to refer to things in the world. As the empiricists (whom we discussed in Chapter 2) argued, it is only through experience that we can justify our beliefs about the world.

When I began my discussion of empiricism in Chapter 2, I said that its rise came along with the rise of science. Because of this, empiricism has often been the unofficial philosophy of scientists. One of the reasons that philosophers of science have insisted on a connection between theoretical terms and the observable world is that they have mostly been empiricists who were impressed by the considerations that led to the development of foundationalist epistemologies. You will remember that I also said in Chapter 2 that foundationalist epistemologists insist

(a) that we must find some class of beliefs, of which we have secure knowledge; and
(b) that once we find this class, we can then honor some of our other beliefs with the special status of knowledge by showing that they are properly supported by the members of this class of *foundational beliefs*.

For empiricists, the foundational class of beliefs is beliefs about the observable world. That is why it is important for empiricists that we can introduce those theoretical terms that refer to things we *cannot* observe by way of Ramsey-sentences that connect them with objects and properties that we *can* observe. For then we have some prospect of being able to justify our theoretical beliefs by reference to observation, in exactly the way empiricism requires, even if our theoretical terms refer to unobservable entities. Connecting theoretical terms with observation offers empiricists the prospect that science can lead to genuine knowledge.

4.5   The received view of theories

Empiricists, then, place great importance on the thesis that the foundational class of beliefs, the class that justifies all our knowledge, is the class of observational beliefs. As a result, when they come to discuss the structure of scientific theories, they make a strong distinction between terms that are and terms that are not *observational*. This is a different – though related – distinction from the one that I have made between observable and unobservable entities. The example of the electron microscope shows why it is important to distinguish between the two questions:

(a) Is it observable?

(b) Do we use observational terms to refer to it?

Observability is an attribute of things and properties, not of terms. So empiricists need to give a definition of observational terms.

The obvious way to do this is to say that a term is **observational** if we can tell whether it applies simply by observation, without relying on any theory. Thus, "red" is an observational term because we can tell whether something is red just by looking and "loud" is an observational term because we can tell whether a sound is loud just by listening. The reason "electron microscope" isn't an observational term is not that we cannot observe electron microscopes. Rather it is that when we look at a piece of apparatus, we need some theory to interpret what we see, if we are to tell whether it is an electron microscope or not. To tell whether something is an electron microscope, you have to be able to find out whether it forms an image of an object by reflecting electrons to a detector; and to do this requires a good deal of theoretical knowledge. In other words, it looks as though the distinction between observational and non-observational terms is really the distinction between non-theoretical terms and theoretical ones.

I shall return to this issue again in the next section. For the moment, I am going to assume that we can make a distinction between observational terms, which we apply by using our senses alone, and theoretical terms, which we apply on the basis of observations *as interpreted by theory.*

Given a distinction between theoretical and observational terms we can divide all the terms in a theory into three: for along with observational terms and theoretical terms, we shall need logical terms, like the *connectives,* the *quantifiers* and, as we shall see, the *modal* terms, "necessary" and "possible." With these three kinds of terms we can build our theories; and the logical positivists (who called themselves, you remember, "consistent empiricists") developed an account of the structure of scientific theories that was based on these distinctions. That model has been so influential that Hilary Putnam, the American philosopher, once called it the **received view** of theories.

On the received view, a theory is stated in a language that contains, along with the logical terms, a vocabulary of observational terms and of theoretical terms. The **observation language** consists of sentences containing only observational and logical terms. The **theoretical language** contains only theoretical terms and logical terms. There will also be **mixed sentences**, containing both theoretical and observational terms.

The theory itself will contain two parts. One part, the **theoretical postulates**, will be stated entirely in the theoretical language, and will describe the relations between the entities and properties that the theory postulates. But if we are to use the theory we must be able to connect these theoretical postulates with observation. So we need as well some mixed sentences called **correspondence rules**, which will connect the entities postulated by the theory with things we are able to observe. These rules explain how theoretical sentences correspond to observational ones. Together, the theoretical postulates and the correspondence rules constitute the theory.

We can see how this model works in the case of *MG.* The theoretical postulates of *MG* will include, for example,

8. An allele, **A**, must exist in one of three relations to any other allele, **B. A** can either
   (a) be dominant with respect to **B**, or
   (b) be recessive with respect to **B**, or
   (c) interact with **B**.

This pair of propositions certainly is not one we can confirm simply by observation. To connect it with observation, we have to include correspondence rules such as:

9. If **A** is dominant with respect to **B**, then an organism that is heterozygous and has the genotype **AB** will have the **A** phenotype.

10 and 11 will obviously also be important correspondence rules if we want to apply 8. But even these will not be enough, by themselves, to apply the theory in any particular case. To do that, we would need to replace the variables **A** and **B** with the names of specific genes and phenotypes. So we could say

Flower color in peas is determined by a gene, which has alleles, **R**, **W** and **P**, that produce red, white and purple flowers in the heterozygous plant. **R** and **W** interact to produce pink flowers. **P** is dominant with respect to **W**. . .

and so on. Correspondence rules like these connect the theoretical postulates with observation, and make it possible to see what the theory says will happen in particular cases.

The empiricist philosophers of science who developed the received view spent a great deal of effort on trying to characterize the structure and functioning of theories. They did this because they were concerned with the epistemological problem of how we know about entities – like genes – that we cannot experience with our unaided senses. But they were interested in theories for another reason. Theories are one of science's most distinctive products. Of course, science has other important products as well. Airplanes and antibiotics, barometers and bazookas, cars and computers, the whole alphabet of modern technology depends for its development on the work of scientists. But we could imagine a (rather strange!) culture that pursued scientific research without much interest in its technological possibilities. What seems impossible is to conceive of science without theory. The development of theories about how different parts of the world work is what science is for. If you don't want scientific theories, you don't want science.

To understand how theories work is to understand a large part of what science is about. But why do scientists want to construct theories? What are they for?

One empiricist answer to this question is that we want theories in order to make reliable predictions. Our ordinary experience and the observations it yields do not always provide us with the ability to make predictions. You could go on breeding peas for years, noticing that crossing purple and white peas sometimes produced purple and sometimes produced white peas but never notice that there was the subtle pattern of results that Mendel discovered. Once you have the theory, however, you can set about predicting when the offspring will be white and when they will be purple: you can even predict the frequencies with which the two colors will result.

Now most people would say that the reason that Mendel's theory enables us to make these predictions is that it is *true*. There really are genes with alleles, which are transferred from parents to offspring. The reason that Mendelian genetics gets predictions of flower colors right is that it is part of the correct *explanation* of how flowers get their colors.

This view of theories is called the **realist** interpretation of theories. It says that the entities the theory talks about are real and the theoretical postulates and the correspondence rules of a good theory are as true as the sentences of the observation language. Of course, we can't observe the theoretical entities directly, so that it is harder to get to know about them than it is to get to know about observable things. But, because we have the correspondence rules that connect the theory with observation we can find out about theoretical entities in an indirect way. After all, doesn't the fact that Mendel's theory allowed us to predict the outcome of breeding experiments entitle us to think that genes exist? Or, to put the question another way, doesn't the success of Mendelian predictions give us reason to think that his theory gives the right explanation of how inheritance works?

The close connection between successful prediction and explanation has led to the received account of how theoretical explanation works in science. This account of explanation starts from the received view of theories. It's called the **deductive-nomological** model of explanation, or the "**DN** model" for short; and it was developed by another member of the school of logical positivism, Carl Hempel.

4.6 The deductive-nomological model of explanation

We can explain many sorts of things in terms of scientific theory. Mendel's theory explains particular events – this cross produced purple offspring – or general regularities – all the offspring of a red-white cross will be red or pink. Hempel's theory is meant to apply to explanations of both these kinds. He calls the sentence that describes the fact we are trying to explain the **explanandum** (which is Latin for "what is to be explained"). And the sentences that we use in making the explanation he calls the **explanans** (which is Latin for "what does the explaining").

Let's take, as our example, Mendel's explanation of the outcome of a particular cross.

EXPLANANDUM: We crossed a pink pea with a (homozygous) red one and the cross produced red and pink offspring.

The explanans will contain two sorts of sentences. One sort will state **antecedent** conditions, which describe the set-up in which the explanandum occurred. In this case, the antecedent conditions are just:

C: We crossed a pink pea with a homozygous red one.

The other sentences in the explanans represent general laws. I shall return to the issue of what makes a generalization into a law in a later section. For the moment, let's work with the definition that a law is a generalization that the theory says must be true. Thus, we have

L_1: A pea has pink flowers if and only if it has genotype RW.
L_2: A homozygous pea has red flowers if and only if it has genotype RR.

along with *MG* and the laws of independent assortment and recombination. So the explanans consists of C, L_1 and L_2, along with Mendel's theory and its laws. These laws allow us to deduce that

L_3: A cross between RR and RW must produce some offspring that are RR and some that are RW.

Together C, L_1, L_2 and L_3 allow us to deduce

E: The cross must produce red and pink offspring.

And from C and E we can deduce

EXPLANANDUM: We crossed a pink pea with a (homozygous) red one and the cross produced both red and pink offspring.

(In this deduction we first draw from E the consequence

E': The cross produced red and pink offspring,

using the law of modal logic that says that if something must be so, it is so, and then draw the explanandum as a consequence by using the elementary law of sentential logic that says from two sentences [C and E] you can deduce their conjunction.)

Hempel says that this explanation is sound if it satisfies three conditions.

    I. *Logical conditions of adequacy*
       (*R1*) The explanandum must be a logical consequence of the explanans.
       (*R2*) The explanans must contain general laws.
    II. *Empirical condition of adequacy*
       The sentences constituting the explanans must be true.

Hempel summarizes his view in the following diagram:

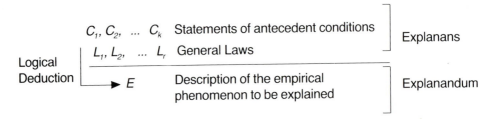

Now you can see why this is called the **deductive-nomological** model. "Nomological" comes from the Greek word *nomos*, meaning law. Hempel thinks that the explanation is correct if you can *deduce* the explanandum from the *laws* of the theory.

I said that we can explain not only particular events but also general truths and that Hempel's theory takes account of this. There is a variety of general truths we might want to explain, among them some laws. There are observational laws, for example, which are generalizations that the theory says must be true, but which are stated in the observation language.

Purple and white peas, when crossed, give rise to purple and white peas

is an observational law. This, too, can be derived logically from *MG*, along with the two laws and correspondence rules, which tell us that **P** is dominant to **W**. We can deduce laws in the mixed language, such as the law that

Homozygous red peas crossed with white peas will have only pink offspring.

Finally, of course, we can deduce theoretical laws from *MG*, such as that

Two homozygous genotypes of distinct alleles will produce only heterozygous geno-types in the first generation.

The fact that we can explain generalizations on this model is of very great significance for the received view: it allows us to tell a story about how science can develop. One of the striking features of the history of science is the way in which earlier theories get superseded by later ones. Sometimes, of course, we just discover the old theory was wrong. It makes false predictions. But sometimes we discover that we can keep much or all of the old theory, while the new theory develops, because the new theory explains the old theory.

Something like this happened in the history of genetic theory. It was discovered that genes were in fact segments of the chromosomes – the bodies in the nuclei of cells that carry hereditary information. It was possible, therefore, to explain why all of the first eleven of Mendel's claims were true. They were true because small portions of the chromosome obeyed these eleven principles. For example, every cell of the organism, except the germ cells, had two chromosomes of each type, and that was why there were two genes of each type in each cell. Thus, according to the DN model, these eleven claims of Mendel's theory could be explained by the chromosome theory, because they could be derived logically from it.

But some genes failed to obey the laws of independent assortment and recombination. They were not inherited independently. This was because, if two genes were on the same chromosome, when the chromosomes came to be divided between the germ cells, the genes were bound together and so were inherited together. If the genes for stem-texture and flower-color had been like this, for example, then, as we saw, Mendel might have got only two out of the four theoretically possible kinds of offspring.

Nevertheless, where genes were on different chromosomes, they *did* obey the laws of independent assortment and recombination. So, as it turned out, these laws, which were one of the most significant parts of Mendel's theory, were in fact only true in special cases: the cases where the genes were on different chromosomes.

Thus, when chromosomes were discovered, genetic theory was able to build on Mendel's theory. On the received view of theories, we can see how science can be *progressive*. When we make new discoveries we do not always have to start all over again; and the new theories actually make it possible to explain why the old ones worked, when they worked.

The process of showing that an old theory can be derived from a new one as a special case is called **theory reduction**. We can derive the old theory from a new one, using the special conditions under which the old theory works as the antecedent conditions of the explanation. On the DN model the successes of the old theory are, thereby, explained. Thus, in the case of genetics, the fact that Mendel's theory was superseded by the chromosome theory didn't mean that all the explanations it had made possible had to be given up. The old explanations were still adequate in all those cases that didn't depend on the laws of assortment and recombination, just because all the other laws were still true. And even those Mendelian explanations that presupposed the laws of assortment and recombination could easily be salvaged, in any case that involved only pairs of genes on different chromosomes.

This view of theoretical progress also accounts for an important fact about the many so-called "crucial experiments" in scientific history – those experiments that play a decisive role in the changeover from one theory to another. On this view of scientific progress, such crucial experiments play the role of showing where an old theory breaks down. But, just because the old theory usually works in many cases, the circumstances of the crucial experiment are important in defining the antecedent conditions under which the old theory *does* work. The crucial experiment contributes to the progress of science not simply by getting us to jettison the old theory, but by showing something about its limitations. Thus the experiments that demonstrated that not all genes were independent showed that Mendel's theory was limited in its applications, a fact that the chromosome theory was able to explain.

The received view of explanation and of theory-reduction was realist. It assumed that the theoretical entities of an explanatory theory really existed. Hempel's realism came out in the empirical condition of adequacy, which requires that the laws be actually true. If Mendel's theory, including its laws, is true, then genes exist. But other empiricists were so impressed with the way in which theories make prediction possible that they suggested this was *all* they were for. If they were right, then a good theory was one that made reliable predictions and a bad one was one that made unreliable ones. The theoretical entities did not have to exist for the theory to give good explanations. In short, the theory doesn't have to be true, it just has to make the right observational predictions.

This view of theories is called **instrumentalism**. Instrumentalism, then, holds that theories are just *instruments* that allow us to predict phenomena. But instrumentalism, though it is quite consistent with the fact that scientific theories have led to a great increase in our capacity to predict (and thus control) what happens in our world, certainly doesn't seem to capture what most scientists think they are doing. After all, according to the instrumentalist view, Mendel's theory wasn't really about unobservable entities called genes at all. The only part of Mendel's theory that matters for the instrumentalist is the observation language. Indeed, any theory that made had exactly the same predictions as *MG* in the observation language would be just as good. That's because the instrumentalist gives up the empirical condition of adequacy for explanations.

One of the major arguments for instrumentalism is epistemological. Instrumentalists, like logical positivists, are radical empiricists. They want to say that beliefs are justified only if they have empirical support, only if there are observations that lead you to believe them. We can see why this might lead you to think that you ought not to believe in unobservable entities.

Consider any theory, such as *MG*, that refers to unobservable things. The instrumentalist can say that whatever evidence you have for *MG* is exactly as good as the evidence for a different theory: the theory that says that the world appears to behave *as if* there were genes. Call this theory the *instrumentalist alternative to MG.* The instrumentalist alternative to *MG* makes exactly the same claims in the observation language as *MG* does. But you cannot possibly get evidence that favors *MG* over the instrumentalist alternative to *MG*: the only difference between them is in what they say about things that cannot be experienced.

This epistemological argument for instrumentalism amounts to a challenge: the instrumentalist wants us to show why we should care about matters to which no possible evidence is relevant. That most of us *do* care is obvious enough. It is one thing to suggest that *we* can only use terms that connect with things we can observe, which is what the received view says, and another to say, with the instrumentalists, that we have no reason to believe that there are things we could not, under any circumstances, observe. Indeed – we can respond to the instrumentalist's challenge – surely, whether or not *we* can observe a thing is just a fact about us. And why should the furniture of the universe depend on us? The issue here is essentially the one that came up in the private language argument and in the argument for verificationism. Wittgenstein said that we must be able to check that we are referring to a thing properly if it is to exist. The verificationist says we must be able to know about something if it is to exist. And the instrumentalist says we must be able to observe a thing if it is to exist. All these views are to some extent **idealist**: they hold, in opposition to **realism**, that the existence of things depends in some way on their relationship to our minds.

Not only is instrumentalism idealist, its consequences are in other ways counter-intuitive. If instrumentalism were right, for example, the astrologer who makes success-ful predictions of how the stock market will move would have to be regarded as giving a good scientific explanation of why the prices move the way they do. And, surely, even if such an astrologer were always right, we could still doubt that the theory gave the correct explanation of why the stock market behaves as it does. But the instrumentalist could reply that the reason why we reject this explanation is that astrology also makes other predictions that are not true. If astrologers could limit their theory so that it only made predictions about the stock market, and provided those *predictions* were correct, the instrumentalist would be happy to say that their *explanations* were correct, too. I shall argue in a moment that there is another objection to instrumentalism, an objection that will then lead us to a serious argument against the received view.

4.7 Theory-ladenness

Instrumentalists believe only in the existence of observable things and their observable properties. But the distinction between what we can and cannot observe is relative. As the philosopher of science Grover Maxwell has written:

> There is, in principle, a continuous series beginning with looking through a vacuum and containing these as members: looking through a win-dowpane, looking through glasses, looking through binoculars, looking through a low-powered microscope, looking through a high-power micro-scope, etc., in the order given. The important consequence is that, so far, we are left without criteria which would enable us to draw a non-arbitrary line between "observation" and "theory."

This continuum is not very worrying in itself. But it is rather troubling to suppose, as the instrumentalists do, that whether we should say that something exists depend on the apparently arbitrary question of where in this continuum we draw the line.

This objection to instrumentalism is one of the reasons that many philosophers have given it up. But a much more basic objection than this has been developed in recent years, one that grows out of the work of the American philosopher Russ Hanson. His objection, put at its simplest, is that there is no such thing as an observation-language! If Hanson was right, then the idea that we should regard only the sentences of the observation language as true would have the consequence that we would have to regard *all* theories as untrue. And that would, surely, be a *reductio* of the instrumentalist position.

To understand Hanson's view, we must remember how we defined the distinction between observational and theoretical terms. An observational term, I said, is one that we can apply by using our senses without the help of theory. A theoretical term is one that we apply on the basis of observations, but observations that we need theories to interpret. But suppose that every statement we made on the basis of observation, however simple and easy it was to make, in fact depended on theory. Then this distinction would break down. Russ Hanson argued that this was in fact the case. According to him, every empirical statement that says anything about the world depends on theory.

To see why Hanson thought this it helps to begin by noticing that whenever we see something we also see *that* something. When I see a ripe apple, I see *that* there is a ripe apple before me. You cannot observe something without observing that a certain state of affairs obtains. But when I see that something is an apple, this commits me to believing something beyond what I have actually observed. It commits me to believing that, if I stretch out my hand, I will be able to touch it, for example; it also commits me to believing that it grew on an apple tree. (You might like to consider how this fact is connected with Frege's discovery of the primacy of the sentence. We can't use names except in sentences; we can't experience the referents of names except in the context of facts.)

Now though we would not normally say that

Things that look like this apple are ripe apples and grow on trees

is a *theory*, it *is* a theory in the philosopher's sense. It says something about the world; something that might or might not be true. To make the observation statement "This is a ripe apple," on the basis of this experience, you have to suppose that this little theory is correct.

The instrumentalists might argue, at this point, that I have cheated. What they have in mind as an observation statement, is, by definition, something that you can make without theory. All I have done is to show that "This is a ripe apple" isn't an observation statement. But surely, they will insist, there are *some* observation statements, in this sense. To suppose that there are some such observation statements is to espouse what the American philosopher Wilfred Sellars has called the **myth of the given**, the idea that there must be some experiences that give us knowledge independently of any theory at all.

Sellars has attacked the myth of the given, and his arguments are very powerful. But even if they were not, there is an overwhelming reason not to accept them as the basis for your philosophy of science. For even if there were things we could know on the basis of no theory at all, they would not be the sorts of things that science is concerned about. To see why this is, consider a sentence, S, which is supposed to be one that we can make on the basis of observation without any theory at all. Suppose that you are having the experience that justifies you in believing S is true. Since S commits you to no theory at all, it cannot commit you to believing that other people will gain evidence for the truth of S if they make observations. But then, whatever S is like, it cannot be part of the public world of things that science is supposed to be about. For if a public object exists, then other people can come to experience it. (If you remember the private language argument, you will be able to see that we could use it to argue that there could be no such sentence as S; and, in fact, that is exactly one of argument against the myth of the given that philosophers have made.)

Hanson's view that every observation statement depends on some theory, however simple it is and however convinced we are that it is true, is called the view that observation is **theory-laden**. Observation is theory-laden, because whenever we make a judgment on the basis of our sensory experience, the judgment commits us to the existence of objects, events or properties that go beyond that evidence. This fact, that evidence always leads us to make claims beyond the evidence, is called the **underdetermination of empirical theory**. The contents of our empirical beliefs are not fully determined by the evidence we have for them. There is an obvious connection between the underdetermination of empirical theory and the defeasibility that we noticed (in Chapter 2) as a characteristic of our judgments about the world. Just because our empirical claims always go beyond the evidence, they could always turn out later to be wrong. The "sight" of an (illusory) apple could fail to be followed by the "feel" of an apple, when you stretch out a hand.

The theory-ladenness of observation threatens the received view because the received view depends on making a distinction between the observation language, and the theoretical language. If there is no such distinction, the received view cannot be maintained. Notice, however, that the fact that observation is theory-laden doesn't threaten the idea that we need to be able to connect our theories with experience if we are to have a use for them. Even if we have to have theories to make any observations at all, we still need to be able to have grounds for believing theoretical propositions, and, if empiricism is right, such grounds are provided by experience. What is threatened is not the empiricist view that theory needs to be connected with observation, but the received view that observation is possible without theory. Thus, we can simply reconstruct the received view, without relying on an absolute distinction between an observation language and a theoretical language. We won't worry exactly about where we draw the boundary. All we will insist on is a practical distinction between sentences that we are able in practice to check fairly easily by using our senses, on the one hand, and sentences that require more time or apparatus or calculation to decide about, on the other. We'll call the first sort of sentence *observational*, and the second *theoretical*, wherever we draw the boundary, and it will still be true that we need to be able to connect theoretical sentences with observational ones, if we want to put a theory to use.

But Hanson made a more radical suggestion than this one. He suggested that even those sentences whose truth-value we can decide easily by using our senses change their *meaning* when we use them in connection with new theories. I suggested that terms like "gene" get their meaning from something like a Ramsey-sentence, that their meaning is fixed by their relationships with terms for things that we can observe. Hanson suggested that the converse holds: what observational terms mean depends on their connections with theoretical terms also. Whenever there is a change of theory, *all* terms, including relatively observational ones, change their meaning. Thus, he suggested that when Copernicus realized that the Earth went round the Sun, and not *vice versa*, the word "Sun" changed its meaning. This view is called the **meaning-variance hypothesis**.

The meaning-variance hypothesis, if true, would threaten the DN model of theory-reduction. For example, when we came to use the chromosome theory to derive, say, an observational law of *MG*, we would be trying to derive a sentence that used "pea" to mean one thing from a theory that used "pea" to mean something different! And, obviously, in a valid deduction you have to keep the meanings of words constant throughout the argument. It would follow that we could not give the rather natural explanation of how science progresses that went with the received view.

Fortunately, there are serious problems with the meaning-variance hypothesis. The main objection to the meaning-variance view is that Hanson offers no grounds for thinking that *every* term must change its meaning with a change in our theories about that thing. If this were right, then every time we changed our beliefs about anything, that would involve changing the meanings of all the sentences about that thing. Someone who came to believe that water is H_2O would have to mean something different by "I'd like a glass of water, please" from someone who didn't believe it. But this is a *reductio* of Hanson's position. For it follows from his view that you and I would mean different things by most of the words we use, since we certainly differ in some of our views on almost every subject.

Nevertheless, Hanson's position does make us conscious of the possibility that as our theories change, some of our words *do* change their meanings. Mendel may have meant the laws of independent assortment and recombination to be part of the definition of a gene. If that is so, then his theory is not true of what we call "genes." For, on our meaning of the word "gene," some genes do not obey these laws. We would have to say that Mendel's views were about genes on different chromosomes. But we could still say both that the chromosome theory was an addition to the knowledge acquired by Mendel and that the chromosome theory explained his theory's successes. For, if we said that his word "gene" referred to what we call "genes on different chromosomes," we would be able to derive his laws from our theory.

4.8 Justifying theories I: The problem of induction

The problems I have been discussing about the structure of theories and the logic of explanation are central to the philosophy of science. But, as you will quickly see, they do not settle the issue of what makes a theory scientific. They do not settle the demarcation problem. The reason is simple. That a theory satisfies all the conditions of the received view and is used to make explanations according to the DN model doesn't by itself make it scientific. Suppose Jim turned up with a theory of the gene exactly like Mendel's. If he had no evidence to support it and felt, in fact, that it didn't need experimental support, we would be impressed, no doubt. But we would hardly regard him as a scientist.

What would have made this theory scientific would have been the way he set about justifying and developing the theory. Mendel's theory is not scientific just because it is true. After all, it *isn't* true! Nor is it scientific just because it can be stated in terms of the received view (modified to take account of theory-ladenness) – for, as we have just seen, someone could offer Mendel's theory in a way that wasn't scientific. It looks as though the answer to the demarcation problem is going to depend not on the structure of the theories but on the way we develop or support them. These are issues in the **context of discovery and justification**.

So how do we develop and justify our scientific theories? The obvious answer is that scientists support their theories by gathering evidence in exactly the sort of way Mendel did. We then use the theory to make predictions and then we see, through experiment and observation, whether those predictions come out right.

The process of gathering evidence and using it to justify general propositions is called **induction**. And in the early days of modern science, the eighteenth-century Scottish philosopher David Hume argued that there was a serious difficulty in justifying induction. He posed what we now call the **problem of induction**.

To see the force of the problem it helps to begin with a simple picture of how you might go about supporting a scientific generalization. How, for example, would you go about supporting the generalization that purple genes dominate white ones in peas? The answer seems obvious. You would see whether purple genes dominated white ones in a whole series of crosses. The general idea, then, is that to find out if the generalization "All *A*s are *B*s" is true, you must look at a lot of *A*s and see if they are *B*s. If you find that they are, that supports the generalization. This process of arguing from many instances of *A*s that are *B*s to the conclusion that all *A*s are *B*s is called **enumerative induction**. It is the most basic kind of inductive argument. An *A* that is a *B* is an *instance* of the law "All *A*s are *B*s." And if the existence of something gives us grounds for believing a sentence, we can say that it *supports* the sentence. So we can say that the view that we develop and justify laws by enumerative induction is the view that laws are supported by their instances. The position that science does and should develop in this way is called **inductivism**.

Here is a passage from Hume's *Enquiry Concerning Human Understanding* where he argues that enumerative induction is unjustified. He considers the problem of how we should confirm the generalization that bread provides nourishment.

> From a body of like color and consistence with bread, we expect like nourishment and support. But this surely is a step or progress of the mind, which wants to be explained. When a man says, *I have found, in all past instances, such sensible qualities conjoined with such secret powers*: And when he says, *similar sensible qualities will always be joined with similar secret powers*; he is not guilty of a tautology, nor are these propositions in any respect the same. You say that the one proposition is an inference from the other. But you must confess that the inference is not intuitive; neither is it demonstrative: Of what nature is it then? To say it is

experimental, is begging the question. For all inferences from experience suppose, as their foundation, that the future will resemble the past, and that similar powers will be conjoined with similar sensible qualities. If there be any suspicion, that the course of nature may change, and that the past may be no rule for the future, all experience becomes useless . . .

Hume's question is what justifies the inference, the "step or progress of the mind":

> I have found, in all past instances, such sensible qualities conjoined with such secret powers
> So: Similar sensible qualities will always be joined with similar secret powers.

He says that it isn't a **tautology** – by which he means that it isn't an analytic truth – that these two sentences are equivalent, so that the inference is not logically valid or "demonstrative." That is certainly true. For there are possible worlds where bread is nourishing until today and then not nourishing tomorrow, because, for example, all of us lose the enzymes for digesting the carbohydrates in bread because the Earth is irradiated by intense cosmic rays. And he says that it isn't intuitive: we don't know that it is true by intuition.

But, as he points out, it looks as though it would be a valid inference if we added a further premise:

UNIFORMITY: The future will resemble the past.

That is, it looks as though, if we add this **principle of the uniformity of nature**, we can reason like this:

> INDUCTION: In the past bread was nourishing.
> The future will resemble the past.
> So: In the future bread will be nourishing.

Hume thought that the problem of induction was that the principle of the uniformity of nature was neither a logical truth nor intuitive and that there was therefore no obvious reason why we should believe it. After all, it is itself a generalization. If the only way to justify a generalization is to use an argument of this form, we would have to argue for the principle of the uniformity of nature like this:

> In the past the future resembled the past.
> The future will resemble the past.
> So: The future will resemble the past.

But this is obviously a question-begging argument. It has its conclusion as one of its premises. Nobody who wasn't already convinced that nature was uniform could be persuaded by this argument.

The major problem with the sort of inference that is involved in INDUCTION is that, unlike deductive inferences, which are logically valid, the conclusion says more than the premises. We call such inferences **ampliative**; they *amplify* or go beyond the premises. One way of seeing that the inductive inference, INDUCTION, is ampliative is to notice that the conclusion is not true in all of the possible worlds where the premises are. As we saw in the last chapter, in a logically valid inference, the conclusion *is* true in every possible world where the premises are true. So in a deductive inference we can reliably draw the conclusion because it is true in *all* of the worlds where the conclusion is true. But in an inductive inference, we start with premises that show we are in a certain class of worlds and draw a conclusion that is true in only *some* of those worlds. Since the information in the conclusion is more than the information in the premises, we seem to have manufactured some information out of thin air!

In a sense, the problem of induction is the first problem in epistemology that was raised by the development of science. For making empirical generalizations – some of them, like Newton's theory of gravitation, generalizations about the whole universe – is absolutely central to the natural sciences.

Many attempts have been made since Hume's day to say what justifies induction as a form of ampliative inference. Some of them have relied on a principle of the uniformity of nature. But all these suggestions were shown to be unhelpful when the American philosopher Nelson Goodman showed in 1955 that even if the principle of the uniformity of nature were correct, it would not solve the problem of justifying these inferences. Goodman's work thus poses what he called the **new riddle of induction**.

Any solution to Hume's problem that requires a principle of the uniformity of nature supposes that we understand what it means for the future to be like the past. Goodman's new riddle shows that this is not such a clear idea. The problem, remember, is how to justify conclusions of the form "All *As* are *Bs*" on the basis of lots of evidence of the form "This *A* is a *B*." Goodman produced examples where we had lots of evidence of the form "This *A* is a *B*" but we would certainly not think that the conclusion that all such *As* were *Bs* was reasonable.

Here is his most famous example. Suppose all the emeralds in the world that have been examined up until now have been green. Since we have discovered that each emerald we have observed is green at each time we have looked at it, we are entitled to infer by enumerative induction that

All emeralds are always (i.e. at all times) green.

Consider, now, the invented predicate "– is grue". We define it as follows:

GRUE: Something is grue if and only if it has been examined before January 1st 2000 and is green, or has not been examined before January 1st 2000 and is blue.

You will notice that it follows from this definition that all the emeralds observed so far are grue. The time is before January 2000 and all the ones we have observed so far have been green each time we have looked at them. So we are entitled by the same argument to infer that

All emeralds are always grue.

So far there may seem to be no problem. But what will happen on New Year's Day 2000? If all the emeralds we find after then are blue, then they will indeed have been grue all along; but if they aren't, then they were never grue. In that case enumerative induction will have led us badly astray. If they *are* all blue, then enumerative induction will not have led us astray by getting us to infer that emeralds are always grue, but it will have led us astray by getting us to infer that they are always green. Either way, then, enumerative induction will have led us astray.

Goodman's own suggestion for dealing with the new riddle of induction is that we should only rely on enumerative induction in certain cases, cases where the predicates involved, unlike "– is grue", are what he calls **entrenched**. A predicate is entrenched if it has frequently and successfully been used in other inductions. He says that predicates that are well entrenched are **projectible**; we can rely on them when we project them into the future.

The difficulty with this answer is that it looks as though it begs the question in exactly the way that Hume originally pointed out. For Goodman seems to be recommending that we project those predicates that we have successfully projected in the past. But that seems to rely on the inference:

This predicate has been successfully projected in the past.
So: This predicate will be successfully projected in the future.

And that is just another enumerative induction!

4.9 Justifying theories II: Popper and falsification

The problem of induction arose because we supposed that scientific generalizations were supported by their instances. But Karl Popper, who, like many of the twentieth-century philosophers I have mentioned, was associated with the Vienna Circle, argued that this was a mistake. Hume, Popper argued, was absolutely right. Laws are not supported by their instances. What happens in the sciences is that people like Mendel creatively invent hypotheses. They then set out to examine their instances, not because the instances support the laws, but because, if they don't support the laws, they know that the hypotheses are false. Science, in Popper's view, does not proceed by induction and the *verification* of true theories. Rather, we go on with the hypotheses we make until they are **falsified**, until, that is, experience shows that they are *not* true.

POPPER

Karl Popper (b. 1902) was born in Vienna, Austria, and studied mathematics, philosophy, and physics at the University there. He was associated with – but never a member of – the Vienna Circle, the influential group of philosophers who founded logical positivism. In 1937, Popper moved to New Zealand to escape the threat of the Nazi occupation of Austria, and he taught there until his appointment at the London School of Economics in 1945. Popper has written influential work in both political philosophy and the philosophy of science; but his major reputation is based on *The Logic of Scientific Discovery*, published in 1935. Unlike the positivists, who placed great emphasis on verification, Popper's leading idea was that of falsification: for him what distinguished science from other kinds of intellectual inquiry was that its claims could potentially be shown to be false by experimentation or observation. Because of this Popper placed great emphasis on the importance of subjecting theories to intense criticism, in order to eliminate those theories that were false. Only by eliminating false theories could science

progress. Popper's work in political philosophy, especially in his famous work *The Open Society and its Enemies*, which put forward a vigorous critique of political dogmatism, essentially applies the theory of knowledge developed in *The Logic of Scientific Discovery* to society. He argues that society – like science – can only progress in an atmosphere of free criticism.

Popper relies here on a simple logical fact, a fact about predicate logic. The problem of induction arises, in his view, because for the law that "All *A*s are *B*s" to be true, there must not be one single *A* that is not a *B*. It follows that until we have examined every single *A*, we cannot be sure that the law is true. But, by the same token, we only have to find *one A* that is not a *B* in order to show that a law is false. So, while we can never be sure that a law is true, we can certainly be sure that a law is false.

Popper, then, doesn't *solve* the problem of induction, but, as he says, he *dissolves* it, by showing there never was such a problem. There is no problem of induction in science because scientists do not proceed by induction. Rather they proceed by **conjecture** – that is, imaginatively inventing new theories – and then make observations and do experiments that may lead, in the end, to **refutation**. Then they try out new theories, and another cycle of conjecture and refutation begins.

Popper's rejection of inductivism is radical. He denies that we are *ever* justified in believing that scientific theories are true. We may *accept* them until they are falsified; but *accepting* a theory, for Popper, is not the same as believing it to be true. To accept a theory is to keep using it provisionally in the knowledge that at any moment observation or experiment may force us to give it up. One way of putting Popper's view is to say that he takes fallibilism very seriously.

Because Popper places such emphasis on the fact that scientists give up theories that are false, rather than insisting, as classical empiricism did, on trying to find theories that are true, his position is called **falsificationism**. Indeed, Popper's answer to the demarcation problem is that what makes a statement scientific is that it is possible to falsify it.

Popper's position has won a good deal of support among scientists. For they have the experience all the time of having to give up theories because experiments show them wrong. They probably also find flattering the fact that Popper insists on the importance of the creative process of conjecture! No amount of hard work collecting instances will lead to a new theory, in Popper's view, without the original creative act of the human mind. Popper's claim is, in essence, that we are justified in using theories not because we have evidence that they are true, but until we have evidence that they are false.

Despite its popularity among scientists, there are certainly problems with Popper's view. To begin with, the simple logical point I made just now is really not so simple as it seems. It is true that whenever we have evidence that one *A* is not a *B*, that shows that it is false that all *A*s are *B*s. But in order to find out that one *A* is not a *B*, we always have to rely on other generalizations. To find a homozygous purple pea that does not produce purple offspring when crossed with a homozygous white pea, I have to rely on such generalizations as the (rather elementary) law that white peas look white. If I am not entitled to assume that this law is true, then I am not entitled to believe that I have found a white offspring of such a cross.

Of course, this particular law is one that we are rather sure of. But in many crucial experiments we rely on a whole lot of highly theoretical laws in order to show that an old theory was wrong. Many of the experiments that showed that Mendel's laws of independent assortment and segregation were wrong involved theoretical assumptions about what was going on in particular crosses.

Moreover, Popper's theory makes it difficult to understand why science seems to progress. On the DN theory of explanation, old theories are often reduced to new ones, so that we show that the old theory is a special case of the new one. But on Popper's view, all that we are entitled to keep from the old theory are the instances where it succeeded and not any of the laws. Once the old conjecture is falsified we are free to make any new conjecture that is consistent with the existing data; and the claim that this is how science actually proceeds – throwing out the old theories and starting again from scratch – is hardly consistent with the historical evidence.

A final difficulty with Popper's view is that it is highly counter-intuitive to say that we never have any reason to think that theories are true. For the Popperian, the relevance of experimental evidence is not that it confirms the truth of our theories. Indeed, Popper explicitly rejects all inductivist talk of scientists confirming theories. Rather evidence is relevant because theories that have survived rigorous testing are what Popper calls *better corroborated* than those that have not. But if corroboration provides no reason for thinking a theory is true, why is it a reason for accepting it at all?

This question is especially urgent because for any well-corroborated theory – any theory, that is, that has survived rigorous testing – there are infinite numbers of different and incompatible theories that have *not* been tested, but that are also consistent with all the existing evidence. Of course, no one has even thought of most of them, and many of them are likely to seem just silly. But the point is that so far as Popper is concerned, they have just the same chance of being true as the well-corroborated theory. If the evidence of experiments does not give us reason to think that our theories are true, why should we prefer theories that have survived experimental testing to other as-yet-unfalsified theories that have not?

This question is a very serious challenge to Popper's philosophy of science. Nevertheless, without a solution to the problem of induction, Popper's theory at least provides a way of explaining what we do in science that does not depend on a form of argument, induction, which seems to be unjustifiable.

Popper's theory and inductivism each offer an answer to the demarcation problem. Inductivists say that theories are scientific if they are based on inductive evidence. This means that the criterion of demarcation belongs to the context of discovery. It has to do with how we come to believe the theory. An inductivist would say that the astrological beliefs I mentioned at the start are unscientific because they were not properly derived from and supported by inductive evidence.

But Popper's view is that how we came to believe our laws has nothing to do with what makes them scientific. Rather, what makes them scientific is that they are always open to falsification. For Popper, astrologers are unscientific because their theories are so vaguely formulated and so hedged-about with qualifications that they could never be shown to be false. So Popper's demarcation criterion belongs to the context of justification.

4.10   Laws and causation

We have seen that the crucial issues in the justification of scientific theory have to do with how to justify the generalizations that theories make. This remains an active topic in the philosophy of science in the study of **confirmation theory**. But I have so far said very little about the contents of the generalizations that science makes and, in particular, about what is meant by a scientific *law*. The aim of science, as we have seen, includes the creation of theories that contain laws; laws that, when true, we call *laws of nature*.

I have been assuming that natural laws say simply that all *A*s of some kind are *B*s. But, as Hume realized, scientific laws say more than that. You will remember that when he introduced the problem of induction he talked about the "secret powers" of bread. What he meant by this was that to say that bread is nutritious is not just to say something about what it does, but also to say something about what it *can* do. To have a power is to have the ability to do something.

Hume is pointing out that the law that bread nourishes us is not simply the generalization that

GENERALIZATION: All people who eat bread are nourished by it.

It also has the consequence

LAW: Anyone who ate bread would be nourished by it.

We can bring out the difference between these propositions by considering, once more, the idea of a possible world. The generalization says only that all the people who eat bread in the actual world gain nourishment from it. But the law says that all the people who eat bread in other possible worlds are nourished as well; even people who don't exist in this world; even those who do, but are not bread-eaters.

Of course, the law doesn't mean that people who eat bread in *every* possible world are nourished. There are worlds where the law does not hold, otherwise it would be a necessary truth that bread nourishes. Nevertheless, in all the worlds where the law does hold, all the bread-eaters are nourished. The class of worlds where natural laws hold is called the class of **nomically possible worlds**. ("Nomically" means "having to do with laws", and comes, like "nomologically," from the Greek word for law.)

The key fact, then, is the *necessity* of laws. Just as metaphysically necessary truths are true in every possible world, so natural laws are true in every nomically possible world. One thing that you cannot explain without a sense of the *necessity* of laws is the fact that because it is a law of nature that hot air rises, a body of air *would have risen* if heated, even if, in fact, it *wasn't* heated.

This fact has serious epistemological consequences. The problem of induction shows that it is hard to justify going from the fact that some of the *A*s in the actual world are *B*s to the belief that all of them are. But, to justify the law that all *A*s are *B*s, we have to show not only that all the *A*s in the actual world are *B*s, but that all of the *A*s in the nomically possible worlds are *B*s also. When Mendel claimed that it was a law of nature that purple alleles dominated white ones, he was committed not just to a view about the outcomes of all actual crosses, but also to a view about what the outcomes would have been of crosses nobody ever made. If there is a problem about justifying the former inference, there must be more of a problem about justifying the latter.

We can consider the problem at its clearest in a simple case. Consider some cross that Mendel never made, between a particular homozygous purple pea-plant and a particular homozygous white one. Mendel was committed to this proposition:

If I had made that cross, the offspring would all have been purple.

A sentence like this is called a **contrary-to-fact conditional** or a **counterfactual**. It says what would have happened if something that didn't happen *had* happened.

Counterfactuals are extremely important to science, for two reasons. First of all, one way of describing the difference between generalizations and laws is to say that generalizations don't and laws do support counterfactuals. The true generalization "All the coins in my pocket are silver" is not a law; which is reflected in the fact that it is not true that if this penny were in my pocket it would be silver. Generalizations, like this, that are not lawlike are called **accidental generalizations**. They do not support counterfactuals. Laws, on the other hand, do support counterfactuals, as we have seen.

The second reason that counterfactuals are important is that when we say, for example, that having two purple alleles *causes* a pea to be purple, we are committed, among other things, to the counterfactual

If this pea had had two purple alleles, it would have been purple.

We can understand what this counterfactual means in possible-worlds terms: it says that in all the nomically possible worlds where the pea has two purple alleles, it has purple flowers. All causal sentences entail counterfactuals in this way. And much of natural science is about causality. Justifying the claim that science gives us knowledge requires that we are justified in having such counterfactual beliefs. The issue of how these beliefs are to be understood and justified is also a topic of current concern in logic and the philosophy of science.

4.11 Conclusion

In this chapter, we have seen how philosophers have approached some of the central questions about science. What is a theory? How do we explain the events that happen in our world? How do we justify scientific claims? What is a law of nature? And, finally, what do we mean when we say that *A* causes *B*? Of course, there are many important questions in the philosophy of science that I have not discussed, and starting from the work we have done in this chapter you can go on to look at some of these questions.

Whichever questions you choose to follow up, you will find again and again, as we have seen once more in this chapter, that questions in one area of philosophy impinge on another. The private language argument of Chapter 1 is relevant to the myth of the given; foundationalist epistemology, from Chapter 2, came to be relevant to the theory-observation distinction; Frege's theory of meaning, from Chapter 3, helped explain why theoretical terms have to be introduced by something like a Ramsey-sentence.

But I want to end this chapter by making a point about the continuity not just between different parts of philosophy, but between philosophy and science. To make this point, I need to say a little more about causation.

Causation is important, in part, because the kind of understanding science offers us is an understanding of the causes of events in our universe. To know what caused an event is to know why it happened, and that is to understand the event. Indeed, it has been suggested that what it means to understand an event scientifically *is* to understand its causes. Many philosophers of science up to our own century held that every event had its causes and that the task of science was to find out what they were. The thesis that every event is caused is called **determinism**. If determinism is true, then once the universe started, everything that happened afterwards was determined by natural laws. Many philosophers of science in the past believed that because determinism was true, if we discovered the true laws of nature we would be able, in principle, to understand every event that happened.

But scientists have argued in this century that determinism is not true. Quantum theory, which is the theory that most physicists now believe, says that there are some events that do not have causes. If understanding an event scientifically means knowing what caused it, then this means that scientists believe they have evidence that some things cannot be scientifically understood. Thus quantum theory denies the philosophical thesis that reality can be fully understood. It does look as though, just as we cannot isolate one branch of philosophy from the others, so we cannot isolate philosophy from our scientific beliefs.

5 Morality

What do moral judgments mean?

How can we tell what is right?

When, if ever, is it right to kill someone?

5.1 Introduction

Suppose I asked you to pick one kind of action that was clearly and obviously wrong. You might well suggest, as an uncontroversial example, *killing an innocent person.* One reason why terrorism in the modern world is so shocking is that its victims are usually ordinary, apparently innocent people. There is no reason to believe they are responsible for the wrongs that terrorists claim they are trying to put right. Most people share this reaction. Most would agree, at least to begin with, that killing innocent people is clearly and obviously wrong. But by now you have done enough philosophy to know that this obvious answer to an apparently straightforward question hides many difficulties. Let us consider just two of those difficulties for the principle:

K: Killing innocent people is wrong.

First: what do we mean when we say that someone is "innocent"? The very same people who will agree that killing innocent people is wrong will often agree that it is not wrong for an airman to bomb a military target in wartime, even when he knows that there is a good chance that civilians will be killed as a result. Some of those civilians might well be opposed to the war, or to the government of their country, and might, therefore, be playing no part in military action against the airman's country. If you believe K, but also think that the airman is right, you have to argue that these civilians are not innocent. If that is so, you have to decide *why* they are not innocent. Many answers have been given to this complex question, a question that has become especially urgent for us because we have weapons of warfare that we know are bound, if we were ever forced to use them, to kill enormous numbers of civilians. We thought it was clearly wrong to kill innocent people, but that depends on believing that it is clear who is innocent. Reflecting on the question of killing in warfare can easily lead you to wonder whether this is, indeed, so clear.

But there is a second kind of difficulty with the proposition that it is wrong to kill innocent people. It is that some morally serious, caring people have felt that there is at least one sort of case where killing clearly innocent people is not only *not* wrong and *not* undesirable but actually desirable and right. That case is when a seriously ill person, in great pain, asks us to kill them. Killing someone in these cases is called *euthanasia*, which comes from a Greek word meaning "a good death." Reflection on euthanasia can easily lead you to wonder whether it is always wrong to kill even the innocent.

The two kinds of difficulties with the principle, *K*, exemplify two of the major kinds of issue that are central to **ethics**, which is the name we give to philosophical reflection on morality. The first problem had to do with the analysis of a concept – innocence – that we make use of in forming our moral decisions. It was a question that forced us to try and define the concept clearly. The second question had to do not with understanding and defining a concept but with whether a particular moral belief, *K*, was true. Obviously we should want to have a good understanding of the concept of innocence before we decided whether *K* was correct, so that the questions of definition are prior to questions about truth. But even once the questions of definition are settled, the substantial questions remain.

Whether or not *K* is true is a very important question and people have very strong feelings about it. It is surely right to feel strongly about such questions. But because they are so important, we should try not to let our feelings get in the way of deciding about them. Precisely because we care deeply about human life, it would be a tragedy to let the strength of our feeling lead us into error.

How, then, should we try to settle these questions? In the case of scientific questions, as we saw in the last chapter, we set about developing theories and look to see whether, by experiment and observation, we can find reasons for thinking they are true – or, if we follow Popper, no reasons at least for thinking they are false. But observation and experiment are not, by themselves, likely to allow us to settle whether it is ever right to kill the innocent. Only a moral monster would want to test the claim that innocent people should not be killed by killing some innocent people to "see if it was wrong!"

Even if such a monster did carry out this horrible "test," however, that would obviously not settle the matter. What are we supposed to look for when we see an innocent person dying that will show us that the killing is wrong? Even if seeing such a thing convinced *you* that it was wrong, there seems to be nothing about the killing that you can observe, which you could point to in order to persuade someone else that the killing was wrong. If, on the other hand, someone could not see that the outcome of a Mendelian crossing experiment was that some of the peas were purple and some white, we could conclude that there was something wrong with their eyes. But a psychopath who did not believe that a killing was wrong would not need to have anything wrong with his or her senses.

More than this, we do not need to experience actual killings to judge that they are wrong. Simply thinking about a possible killing of an innocent person would lead most of us to judge that we should not carry it out. Someone who carried out this sort of test would display a serious misunderstanding of the status of moral claims, because such tests are simply not relevant. Moral claims seem to be, in this respect, like formal ones: we decide them not by experience but by thought.

Notice that we have been led from thinking about *whether an action is right or wrong* to thinking about *how we should decide whether an action is right or wrong.* We are now

CHAPTER 5

asking questions about the *status* of moral judgments, as well as about *which* judgments we should assent to.

Questions about what is right and wrong, good and bad, we call **first-order** moral questions. They are questions about which moral beliefs we should accept. Questions about the nature, structure, and status of first-order moral views, on the other hand, we call **meta-ethical**. They are questions about our first-order moral views. This distinction is crucial in the philosophical discussion of moral questions. People who have very different meta-ethical theories can agree about which actions are wrong; and people who share the same meta-ethical theories can disagree about it. Nevertheless, as we shall see, there are many occasions where our meta-ethics and our morals interact.

5.2   Facts and values

We have already come across an important meta-ethical discovery. Whatever your moral beliefs, settling moral questions has to involve something over and above the kind of observation that is so central to science. But, though beliefs about moral question are in this way like *a priori* beliefs, we cannot settle moral questions simply by logic, either. For even if I offer you a proof that killing innocent people is wrong, you may be able to follow every step in the argument and still disagree with my conclusion. You may reject my conclusion simply because you do not accept the premises of my argument. Furthermore, I shall not be able to show you that my premises are true without other premises, and there is no guarantee that you will accept these either. As we saw in Chapter 3, *a priori* truths, like

If John is eating strawberries, then someone is eating strawberries

can be established, in a sense, without relying on any premises at all. Just as they differ from empirical judgments, moral truths are not, in this crucial epistemological respect, like *a priori* truths.

The kinds of questions that observation and experiment or proof alone can help us to settle are *factual* questions. There is a matter of fact about whether they are true or not, and logic and experience are ways of finding out what is true. But moral questions are matters of *value*; and matters of value do not seem to be settled by experience or logic alone.

This is not to say that logic and experience are irrelevant to moral decisions. If I were trying to decide whether to help my mortally sick friend by killing him, I would need to know whether he really wanted to die and whether he was really in great pain. To find that out I would need some empirical evidence. And, as we shall see again later in this chapter, logic plays an important role in moral thought, because our moral beliefs need to be consistent. It was because it was *inconsistent* to hold both

Killing innocent people is always wrong

and

Killing innocent civilians in warfare is sometimes right

that the case of the airman raised a problem for our moral beliefs.

One way of making the distinction between factual and evaluative questions is to point out that when you accept an evaluative claim it commits you to certain courses of action. You cannot reasonably both accept that killing innocent people is wrong and go ahead and kill an innocent person. When you judge that something is the right thing for you to do, you are committed to thinking that you ought to do it. On many occasions, therefore, "I ought to do it" commits you to a course of action.

I say "on many occasions" because we sometimes say "I ought to do it" in the course of discussing reasons *for* doing something and then go on to give other reasons *against* doing it. Thus, if I have promised my godchild, Liza, to take her to the zoo, I might say

I ought to take Liza to the zoo because I promised her I would.

but then go on to add that, unfortunately, I cannot take her, because I have to attend an important meeting. But when all of the relevant reasons for and against acting have been considered, and I say

All things considered, I ought to go to the meeting

that commits me to a course of action. This kind of "all things considered" *ought* is central to our moral thinking.

David Hume, the eighteenth-century Scottish philosopher who invented the problem of induction, was also one of the first people to put the difference between factual and evaluative questions in terms of the distinction between questions about what *is* so and those about what *ought* to be so. In the following famous passage from his *Treatise of Human Nature* he argues that once we recognize this distinction, we shall have to reject all the "vulgar" – that is, common or ordinary – "systems of morality."

> I cannot forbear adding to these reasonings an observation, which may, perhaps, be found of some importance. In every system of morality, which I have hitherto met with, I have always remarked, that the author proceeds for some time in the ordinary way of reasoning and establishes the being of God, or makes observations concerning human affairs; when of a sudden I am surprised to find, that instead of the usual copulations of propositions, *is*, and *is not*, I meet with no proposition that is not connected with an *ought*, or an *ought not*. This change is imperceptible; but it is, however, of the last consequence. For as this *ought*, or *ought not*, expresses some new relation or affirmation, 'tis necessary that it should be observed and explained; and at the same time that a reason should be given for what seems altogether inconceivable, how this new relation can be a deduction from others which are entirely different from it. But as authors do not commonly use this precaution, I shall presume to recommend it to the readers and am persuaded, that this small attention could subvert all the vulgar systems of morality, and let us see, that the distinction of vice and virtue is founded not merely on the relations of objects, nor is perceived by reason.

CHAPTER 5

The conclusion of this passage is just Hume's way of saying that moral questions are not questions of fact. For he thought that all empirical truths were about "relations of objects" and all logical truths could be "perceived by reason." (In traditional logic the subject, *S*, and the predicate, *P*, were said to be connected by the **copula** "is" or "is not" to produce a sentence that said "*S* is *P*" or "*S* is not *P*"; which is why Hume calls these the "usual copulations.")

The distinction between *fact* and *value* is central to all discussion of meta-ethics since Hume's day; and his argument in this passage has been summarized in a famous slogan: you can't derive an "ought" from an "is." One reason this distinction is so important is that it is relevant to both of the two great questions in meta-ethics: What do moral judgments mean? and What justifies them? Let us call the first of these the **moral content question**. To answer the second question, we have to do some **moral epistemology**. Once we accept the fact-value distinction, we are committed to the view that the meaning of moral judgments has to be explained in such a way that moral claims cannot be derived from factual ones alone. And we are also committed to finding a moral epistemology that shows that moral beliefs are justified in different ways from factual ones.

5.3 Realism and emotivism

The moral content question is, of course, a question in philosophical semantics. As we saw in Chapter 3, one plausible way to say what a sentence means is to say what the world would have to be like for it to be true; to give its truth conditions. So a first stab at an account of the meaning of moral judgments would be to say what their truth conditions are. When I judge, say, that

> *K*: Killing innocent people is wrong
> or I ought not go about killing innocent people

the words "killing innocent people" have the same sense and reference as they do in the factual sentences

> Killing innocent people is common
> or I have seen someone killing innocent people.

The new questions, therefore, are about the meaning of "I ought not to" and "is wrong." Let's try to see what a truthconditional semantics for "is wrong" might look like.

Our explanation of what a predicate like "– is red" meant involved saying what it *referred* to. We said that its reference was its extension, which was a class of objects. Since *K* is equivalent to

> *K'*: Every action that is a killing of an innocent person is wrong

the class of things in the extension of "is wrong" is a class of actions. So far, so good.

But we then went on to give the *sense* of "– is red" by saying that it was a way of determining that reference. How are we to determine which acts are in the extension of "is right"?

Anyone who believes that the way this extension, in particular, and the truth-values of moral claims, in general, are determined is not importantly different from the way the truth-values of factual claims are determined, we call a **moral realist**. Moral realists think that, just as there are ordinary facts "out there" in the real world that determine whether factual claims are true or false, so there are moral facts in the world that determine the truth-values of moral claims.

One major difficulty for the moral realist arises because moral beliefs commit us to action in a way that factual ones do not. It is instructive to examine this difference in a little more detail.

We certainly *do* act on the basis of factual beliefs: and, in Chapter 1, I suggested a functionalist theory of beliefs that explained why that was. But when we act on the basis of a factual belief we do so because we already have preferences or desires that make the belief relevant to deciding what to do. If I want to eat a strawberry, then I need to find out where there are strawberries, which is a matter of fact, before I can set about the action of eating them. But believing that there are strawberries in the kitchen doesn't commit me to going there to eat them. What does commit me to that action is the combination of the belief that there are strawberries in the kitchen and the desire to get strawberries to eat.

If, however, for some bizarre reason, I decided that I *ought*, all things considered, to eat the strawberries in the kitchen, then I would be committed to doing so *whether I wanted to or not*. Whereas factual beliefs commit us to action only in conjunction with our preferences or desires, moral beliefs commit us to action whatever our preferences or desires. The terminology I shall use to mark this difference is that moral beliefs are **action-guiding**, while factual beliefs are not. Always remember, however, that beliefs guide action, too, but in a different way. The moral realist's view – that there's no difference between the way the truth-values of factual and of moral beliefs are determined – has to explain why there is, nevertheless, this important difference between them.

Immanuel Kant, the great German philosopher of the Enlightenment, was one of the first people to identify this sort of action-guiding "ought"; and he called it a **categorical imperative**. He contrasted categorical imperatives with what he called **hypothetical imperatives**; such as the "ought" in the sentence

If you want to get there quickly, you ought not to walk but to take a taxi.

This "ought" is hypothetical because it depends on a *hypothesis* about what you want. Even if someone just said:

You should not walk. You ought to take a taxi.

the "ought" would still be hypothetical because it would still be based on this hypothesis

KANT

Immanuel Kant (1724-1804) was born in Königsberg in East Prussia (now Kaliningrad in the USSR), and went to high school and university there. He worked as a private tutor while pursuing his studies until, in 1755, he got his master's degree; and he then began to teach at the University of Königsberg, where he taught for the rest of his career. Thus, unlike Descartes and Plato, who travelled widely, Kant never left the region in which he was born. His first works were in the natural sciences and geography and it was not until he was nearly forty that he began to concentrate exclusively on philosophy. The writing of his most famous work, *The Critique of Pure Reason*, occupied the bulk of his middle years and it was finally published in 1781. This so-called "first" *Critique*, which dealt with metaphysics, was followed, in 1788, by a "second", *The Critique of Practical Reason*, which dealt with ethics, and the "third," *The Critique of Judgment*, in 1790, which dealt with aesthetics. Kant was the first modern philosopher to spend most of his life as an academic, teaching and writing philosophy in a university, and he developed a particularly technical vocabulary for his philosophical work, modelled, in part, on the technical language of the sciences.

This has the effect of making much of his writing formidably difficult to read. Nevertheless, *The Critique of Pure Reason* and the *Groundwork of the Metaphysic of Morals*, published in 1785, are among the most important and influential works in metaphysics and ethics of the modern era. The ideas of the "analytic" and "synthetic" from *The Critique*, as well as the distinction between categorical and hypothetical imperatives from *The Groundwork*, are but a portion of the large Kantian legacy that still informs philosophical inquiry today.

---

about your wants. So you cannot identify a hypothetical imperative simply by seeing whether it is preceded by "If you want to . . ." Instead you must consider whether the speaker would withdraw the "ought"-sentence if you said that you didn't have the desires he or she seemed to be supposing you to have. If someone would still say you ought to do something whatever you said your wants and desires were, then their "ought" would be categorical.

We can express one challenge for moral realism simply by asking how it is to explain the categorical nature of moral imperatives. The force of this challenge becomes clearer if we recall the way in which we connected the idea of a truth condition with the idea of communication at the end of Chapter 3. Because of the connection between the truth conditions of sentences and the contents of beliefs, we were able to say that we use the speech-act of assertion to communicate our beliefs. Thus, we said that someone who understands "It is raining" uses it to get other people to believe that the truth conditions of the sentence hold.

In the normal case of the speech-act of assertion, I get you to believe that it is raining because you think that I believe it and that I am in a position to know. That is why we call Mary's asserting that it is raining the *expression of her belief* that it is raining: for she gets us to believe it by giving us reason to think that she does. The moral realist, then, regards the assertion of *K* as a way of expressing the belief that killing innocent people is wrong. The problem is that, if it is an ordinary belief that is being expressed, it is hard to see how it can also be action-guiding: beliefs, as I said, guide action only in concert with desires.

So the fact that moral assertion commits us directly to action might lead you to suppose that moral sentences do not express beliefs but feelings, preferences or desires. For, unlike having factual beliefs, having feelings, preferences or desires can lead directly to action. As the English philosopher Elizabeth Anscombe once said: "The primitive sign of wanting is trying to get"!

The view that moral sentences express not beliefs but feelings, preferences or desires, I shall call **emotivism**. Strictly, as the term suggests, emotivism would be the view that moral sentences express feelings or *emotions.* But the view that moral sentences express action-guiding states of mind rather than beliefs is the core of emotivism even in this stricter sense. I shall call action-guiding mental states that dispose you towards doing something **pro-attitudes**. Those that dispose you against some action, I shall call **con-attitudes**. Pro-attitudes and con-attitudes together I shall call just **attitudes**.

Moral realism and emotivism represent the extreme poles of views on the moral content question, and these views tend to produce polar positions in moral epistemology. The moral realist will say that since moral sentences express beliefs that can be true or false, and since they can be justified or unjustified, moral beliefs are candidates for knowledge. The emotivist, on the other hand, will say that, since moral sentences express attitudes, which cannot be true or false, they are not candidates. So realism and emotivism, as views about the moral content issue, tend respectively to go with **cognitivism** – the view that we can have moral knowledge – and **non-cognitivism** – the view that we cannot – in moral epistemology.

In Chapter 3, we saw that issues about the sense of words and sentences were cognitive: they had to do with knowledge. So it is not surprising that different views about the content of moral judgments are associated with different views about moral epistemology. Now we have characterized the range of view on the moral content question, we can look in more detail at the views about moral epistemology that are associated with them.

5.4 Intuitionism

Moral realists, then, tend to be cognitivists; but they do not *have* to be cognitivists. The reason is that even if moral beliefs can be true and justified, whether that is sufficient for knowledge will depend on your view of knowledge. In Chapter 2, you will remember, I suggested that we might want to defend a view of knowledge in which it is true belief produced by a reliable method. Now, *production* is a causal process, and if moral properties are not causal properties, then, on this causal theory of knowledge, you could be a moral realist and a non-cognitivist as well.

But the best known recent realist position is that of the English philosopher G.E. Moore. Moore combined moral realism on the content issue with cognitivism in his moral epistemology. His particular form of cognitivism is called **intuitionism**. An *intuitionist* in ethics holds that we have a *faculty* that allows us to perceive moral qualities, just as we have the faculty of vision that allows us to see colors. That faculty is called **moral intuition**. For the intuitionist, then, we justify our moral beliefs in the way we justify all our beliefs: by evidence and reasoning from it.

In his book *Principia Ethica* Moore took as the basic moral concept not rightness but goodness. According to Moore an action is right "if it will cause more good to exist in the universe than any other possible kind of alternative." The central problem of moral epistemology for Moore is to discover how we can know which of the possible consequences of our actions are good.

Moore held that "goodness" is what he called an **unanalyzable** property. It is unanalyzable because you cannot explain what "good" means in terms of any other concepts. Moore pointed out that some philosophers – the **hedonists** – had identified goodness with the property of *making people happy.* But, he said, even if the extension of the predicate "– is good" is the same as the extension of the predicate "– makes people happy," these two predicates have different meanings. Moore claimed that an objection like this could be made for any proposed definition, which said that something was good if and only if it was *P.* He thought that, provided *P* was not itself a moral predicate, you could always intelligibly ask

But are all *P* things *really* good?

The fact that "good" was in this sense unanalyzable was one of the reasons why Moore thought there was a strong similarity between seeing something was yellow and seeing it was good. For even if a physicist were to tell us that

– is yellow

and

– emits or reflects light in wavelength *W*

were co-extensive predicates, so that something was yellow if and only if it emitted or reflected light of that wavelength, we could still understand the question

But are all things that emit in wavelength *W* really yellow?

To understand what "yellow" means you need to know more than the wavelength of light that causes yellow sensations. You need to know what it is like to have a yellow sensation: and no definition in words can tell you that.

Goodness, then, for Moore, is a property of people, things and events that we cannot define in terms of any other notions. We experience the nature of goodness by moral intuition as we experience the nature of yellowness directly by the faculty of vision. But Moore also recognized that there was a difference between yellowness, which he called a **natural** property, and goodness, which he said was a **non-natural** property.

It is not entirely clear what Moore meant by this term, but he certainly thought of natural properties as being the sorts of properties, like yellowness, which could be studied by natural scientists. Not surprisingly, many people have taken the distinction between natural and non-natural properties to be another way of making the distinction between facts and values. Certainly, at least one thing that Moore held to follow from the non-naturalness of goodness was that you could not derive a claim that something was good from claims about its possessing other natural properties, like color or shape or even the capacity to give people pleasure. In other words, one thing he meant by saying that goodness was non-natural was that, just as you cannot derive an "ought" from an "is", so you cannot identify "good" with any natural property. Moore said that any attempt to identify a natural and a non-natural property committed the **naturalistic fallacy**; and this term is now often used to refer to any attempt to derive an "ought" from an "is."

The hedonists held that, once we knew something gave people pleasure, we could infer that it was good. Their moral epistemology, then, required us to be able to tell what would give pleasure. Hedonists think we find out about goodness *indirectly*, by finding what gives pleasure. But, according to Moore, we know what is good *directly* by moral intuition, just as we know what is yellow by vision; and that, for Moore, is all there is to moral epistemology.

This may seem to be an attractive position. After all, it gives a simple answer to the basic question "How do you justify moral beliefs?" But there are certainly many differences between the perception of colors and the perception of, say, the goodness of friendship.

One difference comes out when we remember that moral beliefs are fundamentally action-guiding. This means that we need to decide on the moral properties of actions before we carry them out. The fact that Anne experiences the rightness of an action, *A*, can hardly be supposed to *cause* her perception of its rightness and her consequent decision to do *A*; for *A* cannot cause anything until it exists. In general, in fact, since moral beliefs are action-guiding, we need to have a clear grasp of the properties actions would have if we carried them out *before we decide what to do.*

The intuitionist can argue, however, that what we learn from experience is that actions with certain properties are right, and that we judge that an action is right, because we have grounds for thinking it will have those properties. Thus, the intuitionist might say, experience shows us that causing people pain is wrong. Our moral faculty allows us to recognize, through experience, the wrongness of such actions. This judgment is confirmed every time we carry out an action, *A*, intended to avoid causing pain, and discover, through moral intuition, that *A* is right.

But there are serious problems with this view of moral experience. First of all, as I have

CHAPTER 5

already mentioned, the way we actually make our moral decisions is to reflect on the outcomes of the actions that are within our power. In trying to decide whether I should go to the meeting or let my godchild down, I think about her disappointment, her loss of confidence in my promises, and the fact that I shall be weakening her understanding of the importance of keeping your word. The fact that these consequences would – if they were likely to occur – be relevant reasons for not letting her down is not something I learn by experiencing her disappointment or loss of confidence, but by *imagining* them. In imagination we do not experience real events, rather we contemplate possible events. If moral intuition is like experience at all, it is not like perception of happenings in the actual world, but like perception of happenings in other possible worlds.

But talk of perception of other possible worlds is at best a metaphor. Perception is a causal process, in which things in the world interact with our sense-organs to give rise to beliefs. For something to be perceived it must actually exist: and the only things that actually exist are things in the actual world. If talk of a faculty of moral intuition is to be taken seriously, we have to suppose that we really can intuit the moral properties of actual objects by exercising the faculty.

There are two major objections to this view of moral intuition. One is a straight rejection of the idea of moral perception, because it comes without a proper account of how moral perception would work. Moore claims that seeing that something is good is like seeing that it is yellow. But there are lots of ways in which this is simply false. Unlike yellowness, for example, goodness is not something we can just recognize again once we have experienced an instance of it. I can't tell a French speaker what "good" means simply by showing them a few good deeds. In the perception of a yellow thing – to give another difference – the yellowness causes us to have certain experiences that are the basis for judgment; things can "look yellow." But it is doubtful that my judgment that someone is a good person is simply caused by my sensing their goodness; and doubtful, too, that there is any particular experience that is produced in us by good acts and good people. An intuitionist, who speaks of moral perception, owes us an explanation of these significant epistemological differences.

The second objection to Moore's view of moral intuition have been well put by another British philosopher, Alasdair MacIntyre. MacIntyre argues that Moore's view fails to explain the action-guiding character of moral judgment.

> Moore's account leaves it entirely unexplained and inexplicable why something's being good should ever furnish us with a reason for action. The analogy with yellow is as much a difficulty for his thesis at this point as it is an aid to him elsewhere. One can imagine a connoisseur with a special taste for yellow objects to whom something's being yellow would furnish him with a reason for acquiring it; but something's being "good" can hardly furnish a reason for action only to those with a connoisseur's interest in goodness. Any account of *good* that is to be adequate must connect it intimately with action, and explain why to call something good is always to provide a reason for acting in respect of it in one way rather than another.

MacIntyre's point is that Moore cannot explain why the moral "ought" is categorical. For the imagined moral connoisseur is someone who happens to have wants and desires that turn their desire to do good into a hypothetical imperative.

If you want to be good, you ought to do this

would certainly appeal to the connoisseur as a reason to act. But it would not be a recognizably *moral* reason, since the imperative here is hypothetical.

5.5 Emotivism

Emotivists, by contrast, face neither of these objections. The action-guiding character of pro-attitudes means that they have an automatic answer to the second objection. The reason why moral demands are categorical is that they express attitudes. So you do not have to have desires over and above those attitudes in order for them to be action-guiding: they are action-guiding in themselves already. Nor can we object to emotivism on the basis of its views about moral perception, since emotivists do not think that there is any such thing. Indeed, the major difficulty for emotivists is precisely that they do not have very much to say about moral epistemology. On the simplest emotivist view, knowing what you think on a moral question is simply a matter of finding out what you really feel.

Emotivism is often associated with moral **relativism**, the view that what is good depends on who you are (or in what culture or when you live). For if moral sentences are expressions of attitudes and not of beliefs, then which moral beliefs you assent to will depend on what attitudes you (or your community) happen to have.

It is not obvious, however, that an emotivist *has* to be a relativist. It is indeed natural to suppose, to begin with, that what you feel is simply up to you. How you feel about swimming in cold water does indeed depend on you and your circumstances, and it doesn't usually make much sense to suppose that it is either correct or incorrect to have the feelings one has on this topic. But, on the other hand, there is a whole range of feelings where an assessment of their correctness *does* make sense. And if it does make sense to justify or criticize feelings, then emotivism might have scope for being non-relativist, even if it didn't justify feelings in the way we justify our beliefs. We normally justify beliefs about matters of fact by finding perceptual evidence in their favor. But some feelings can be justified by means other than finding evidence for them; and this is a reason to hope that there could be similar ways of justifying moral beliefs other than by finding evidence for them. This argument would be circular if the only feelings we normally sought to justify were moral feelings; but they aren't.

There are, in fact, two sorts of criticism of desires that we can make. One way to criticize desires is to show that the desire is based on false beliefs. My desire to take my godchild to the zoo can be criticized by pointing out that she hates animals. I want to take her to the zoo in order to give her an enjoyable afternoon. But if she hates animals, she won't enjoy the visit. This sort of criticism involves only the assessment of the truth-value of the belief on which the desire is based. The possibility of criticizing desires in this way does not help answer the relativist, however. For moral attitudes are categorical imperatives: they do not depend, in this way, on beliefs.

Some non-moral desires, however, do not depend in this way on beliefs, either. My desire to give my godchild an enjoyable afternoon is not based on beliefs. Whereas taking Liza to the zoo is a *means* to the *end* of giving her an enjoyable afternoon, giving her an enjoyable afternoon is something I want to do for its own sake. (And even those who would claim that the desire to give a child some fun was in some sense a moral desire would surely admit that there need be nothing moral in Liza's craving for chocolate!) So a second way to criticize desires is to say, not that they depend on false beliefs about the means to some end, but that the ends themselves are irrational. Let us call a desire that is not dependent in this way on a belief a *basic desire*. People who are pleased when they are offered buckets of mud for which they have no use are likely to be criticized as irrational. We would naturally be inclined to suppose that someone with a basic desire for buckets of mud needs not tolerance but treatment. Indeed, such a desire might seem to be evidence that they did not know how to reason. One way to resist relativism, then, is just to hold that some attitudes – even though logically consistent – are irrational. As we shall see, this was Kant's view.

But many philosophers have felt that rejecting attitudes or desires that we don't share by calling them "irrational" is simply an expression of a prejudice. Unless we can say *why* it is irrational to want useless buckets of mud, rejecting such a desire may just be a reaction to the fact that we do not share it.

How else might we combine the view that moral sentences express not beliefs but attitudes with the claim that morality is not simply a matter of what you happen to feel? Perhaps we should begin with a more sophisticated version of emotivism, which gives a richer view of the content of moral judgments.

In a more sophisticated emotivism we need to say more exactly what sorts of pro-attitudes are expressed by saying "Doing A is right". One influential answer to this question was developed under the name "emotivism" by the American philosopher C.L. Stevenson.

Stevenson saw that if you said that people who made moral claims were just expressing their feelings, then two people who made apparently opposed moral claims would not be disagreeing with each other. If I say

T: Tom ought to be kinder to his dog

and Cynthia says

Not-*T:* It's not true that Tom ought to be kinder to his dog,

then if *T* is simply a fancy way of saying

T': I don't like the way Tom treats his dog

and Not-*T* is simply a fancy way of saying

Not-*T'*: I don't mind the way Tom treats his dog

then Cynthia and I are not really disagreeing. *T* and Not-*T* look as though one is the negation of the other, so they cannot both be *true*. But *T'* and Not-*T'* are just the expression of two different attitudes. Of course, the *same* person could not agree to both *T'* and Not-*T'*, because one person cannot both approve and disapprove of the same acts. Two different people *can* assent to them at the same time, however, without there being any inconsistency between their utterances. In fact, people very generally differ in what they like and dislike.

Of course, Cynthia and I might utter Not-*T* and *T* respectively because we were in disagreement about the facts. Perhaps she had not seen Tom dragging his dog on its chain or heard the dog howling when Tom forgot to feed it. But even if we were agreed on all the facts, she could still continue saying Not-*T* and I could go on saying *T*. At this point, if *T* meant *T'* and Not-*T* meant Not-*T'*, our "disagreement" would amount simply to the fact that we had different attitudes.

But Stevenson suggested that there was more to it than that. When I say *T*, I am not simply expressing my feelings. What I mean is not so much *T'* as

T": I don't like the way Tom treats his dog and I want everybody else to adopt the same attitude.

My objection to Cynthia's position is based on the fact that when I make a moral claim I am expressing an attitude that I want everybody to share. So, whereas, on the simple emotivist view that moral sentences express our attitudes to things, Cynthia and I are disagreeing only in the sense that we have incompatible attitudes, on Stevenson's view we are disagreeing in a more fundamental way. For Stevenson, what Cynthia says means

T": I don't mind the way Tom treats his dog and I want everybody else to adopt the same attitude

and the second conjunct here expresses a desire that I want her – and everybody else – not to have. Though my moral judgment is not inconsistent with hers, her having the judgment is itself something I am opposed to.

This element of universality, the desire that everyone should share our moral attitudes, is what differentiates moral sentences, on Stevenson's view, from simple expressions of feeling. And it also means that someone who is a meta-ethical emotivist need not be a moral relativist. For meta-ethical emotivists can say that their own moral claims make demands on other people, whatever those people happen to feel and wherever

CHAPTER 5

they live. Thus, when I say "Kindness is good," according to the sophisticated emotivist I am saying that I have a pro-attitude to kindness and that I want everyone else to have that pro-attitude. I am not saying, as the relativist would require, that I only want every one who happens to share my feelings (or my culture) to have this attitude.

Many people hold, however, that even sophisticated emotivism makes it very difficult to resist relativism. Of course you can tell people that you want them to share your attitudes; but why should the mere fact that you want this give them a reason to come to share them? And if it gives them no reason to agree with you, then even if you are not a relativist, you will still have to accept that whether people will agree with you will depend on what attitudes, pro and con, they happen to have. You will have to accept that what principles people hold *does* depend on what they feel, even if, not being a relativist, you do not think that it *ought* to depend on what they feel.

Now Stevenson in fact argued that we utter moral sentences in order to try to get other people to share our attitudes, just as we utter factual sentences in order to get them to share our beliefs. So that, on his view,

A is the right thing for X to do

is not so much equivalent to

I want X to do A and I want everybody else to want it too

but to

I want X to do A. Please want it too.

Moral remarks are not so much expressions of my feelings as attempts to get others to feel the same.

This aspect of Stevenson's theory is much less satisfactory than his basic recognition of the universality of moral claims. For it still leaves the major challenge of relativism unanswered: why should the mere fact that I ask you to share my attitude lead you to come to share it? When I express my factual belief that something is yellow, you have a reason to come to believe it too, provided that

(a) you have grounds for thinking that I am in a position to know – because, for example, I have seen it – and
(b) you have grounds for thinking that I don't want to deceive you.

But when I ask or order you to share my feelings, you can have no analogous reasons for coming to share my attitude. On Stevenson's view, there is no such thing as knowing that something is right or wrong, and so you cannot have a reason like (a). Nor can you have a reason like (b), in his view, since deceiving someone is getting them to believe something false, and he has no way of explaining how moral statements could have truth-values.

Nevertheless, as I say, the recognition of the claim to universality of moral sentences is a very important insight about the content of moral judgments. It was central to the moral philosophy of Immanuel Kant, who suggested that moral claims had two distinguishing marks:

(a) they were action-guiding – in fact they were categorical imperatives – and
(b) they were in a very specific way addressed universally to all rational people.

This second mark of the moral claim is expressed in the **principle of universalizability**, which we shall discuss next.

5.6 Kant's universalizability principle

We have already seen that Kant held that it was a distinguishing mark of moral propositions that they were categorical imperatives. This is an observation about the *form* of moral judgments, since it doesn't tell us anything about the content of morality, about which particular categorical imperatives we should accept. Kant's universalizability principle was intended to allow us to test any moral judgment by the use of our reason and decide whether we should assent to it. It was a way of using reason to give the *content* of morality.

According to Kant, the universalizability principle that allows us to give content to morality is this categorical imperative:

UNIVERSALIZABILITY: You ought to act only on maxims that you can at the same time wish to be universal laws of nature.

In fact, Kant argued in the *Groundwork of the Metaphysic of Morals* that this was the only categorical imperative, from which all of the principles of morality derived. It is important, therefore, to understand what Kant means by this principle. To see what it means, we can consider how Kant applies it in a particular case.

He considers a man who is in desperate need of money and is deciding whether he should take a loan. This person knows that he will not be able to pay the loan back. He knows, Kant says, that acting in this way is "perhaps quite compatible with my own entire future welfare." But he then applies the test of universalizability. This leads him to see that he cannot act morally this way. For in so acting, he is following the maxim:

Whenever I believe myself short of money, I will borrow money and promise to pay it back, though I know this will never be done.

And if this maxim became a universal law of nature and everybody followed it then no one would ever believe in promises "but would laugh at utterances of this kind as empty shams."

The crucial idea of the universalizability test, then, is this. When deciding what to do you consider what your general reason is for acting in this particular way. That is what is meant by discovering the **maxim of your action**. Then you see what would happen if this maxim became a law of nature. Now we saw in the previous chapter that a law of nature is a generalization that *must* be true. So that if your maxim became a law of nature, everybody would have to act on it. If our reasons allow us to accept this possibility, then we may act according to the maxim. Otherwise, we may not.

There is one central idea here, which is crucial to the way Kant thought about morality. It is that the principles of morality should be impersonal: they should apply to everybody. Of course, since a maxim will generally be of the form

When conditions C obtain, you ought to do this

it may never apply to me because I never get to be in those conditions. But moral rules, according to Kant, apply to us all equally. In any possible world where you are in the conditions that make the maxim operative, you ought to obey it.

This idea is one that fits very well with the ideas we all have about morality. You may disagree with me about whether a principle is morally correct; but, if you agree with me on the principle, you have to accept that it governs both of us.

Kant's moral philosophy is extremely complex and connects very closely with his views on the nature of the mind and the role of reason in our lives. The universalizability principle, which is, perhaps, his most famous contribution to moral philosophy, has built into it a very important role for reason in our moral thought. For, according to Kant, applying the universalizability principle involves the exercise only of our capacity to reason.

Though the universalizability principle certainly does capture a feature of our moral thought, the claim that it derives solely from reason is not easy to accept. For the principle refers to what you can will. And it is not obvious that there has to be anything wrong with the *reason* of someone who accepts that moral principles have to be universalizable but disagrees with our normal moral ideas, because they are willing to accept consequences we are not. The case which Kant gives to exemplify his principle's application is, in this way, rather misleading. For the institution of promising is, in the context of human social life, one that everyone can benefit from, whatever they happen to want. Perhaps only someone who couldn't reason properly would be unable to recognize this.

But consider a rather different principle, from which some of us can expect to benefit more than others; the principle that

It is wrong to kill innocent people against their will simply because it pleases you.

Consider someone who is a certain kind of psychopath. He is strong and well-armed and enjoys killing people. Call him "Attila the Hun." Attila the Hun might be willing that it should become a universal law that you may kill innocent people for fun, because he is quite sure that no one is likely to be able to kill him. He could say that he is quite happy to accept the possibility that other people would try and kill him for fun, if the maxim became a law of nature, but, he would add: "Just let them try."

The only way Kant can get round the fact that Attila the Hun does not see that his proposed maxim is morally unacceptable is to say that he is being unreasonable: to say that no reasonable person could will that that maxim should become a universal law. To get any moral substance out of the universalizability principle, in other words, you not only have to make assumptions about human life – that promising is something we can all benefit from, for example – but you also have to suppose that there are constraints, beyond consistency, placed by reason on what you can will to become a law of nature.

Kant's derivation of content for moral principles, then, requires both

(a) that we make substantial assumptions about human life, and
(b) that we rule out as unreasonable some things that a person could will to become a law of nature.

The first requirement, (a), is not too troublesome. It makes morality depend on contingent facts about how the world happens to be. But Kant does not need to be worried by this. For it is surely reasonable that human morality should be tailored to the needs of human life. It is because he does not explicitly recognize this fact that he can regard the moral principles he derives both as *a priori* – knowable by reason alone – and yet synthetic – not true simply as a matter of meaning. For, in fact, like other synthetic truths, the moral principles depend on empirical assumptions and are thus not really *a priori* at all. Indeed, because of (b), the moral principles Kant derives depend also on an assumption about what a reasonable person can will: so that, for this reason also, the content of the moral rules depends on more than facts about meanings. But, even if Kant's theory did not face these problems, it would also face another serious difficulty.

In order to apply the universalizability principle, you have first to identify the maxim of your action. But someone who is both uncaring about others and sufficiently ingenious can always describe the maxim of their action in such a way that they would be willing to universalize it. Consider a Nazi, like Hitler, who thinks it is all right to kill members of what he regards as inferior races. Hitler, who regards himself as an "Aryan," could agree that he was not willing to universalize the principle

You may kill innocent people if it suits you

but simply add that he *was* willing to universalize the principle

You may kill innocent people if it suits you, provided they are not Aryans.

Even if we think it is unreasonable for Hitler to universalize the first principle, because it would put his own life unnecessarily at risk, it is hard to see that it is unreasonable – as opposed to just plain wrong – to universalize the second one. He might even agree that, if he had been a Gypsy, a Jew, or an African, it would be quite permissible to kill him if it suited you.

Despite first appearances, then, Kant's rather abstract universalizability principle is not going to be enough to get us a content for morality. It will certainly rule out, as a matter of pure reason, any maxims whose universalization will lead to inconsistency. Thus Kant will be able to explain why you cannot *both* accept the maxim that killing innocent people is wrong *and* allow that it is all right to engage in indiscriminate bombing in warfare. If we are to give a philosophical foundation to our moral beliefs, consistency will be a very important beginning. But we need more than that if we are to have principles with substantial moral content. Just to apply Kant's principle we need to know some general facts about human life; and even people who agree with us about these facts might be able to get round the universalizability principle by gerrymandering the maxims on which they acted.

5.7   Dealing with relativism

I said that the fundamental challenge of relativism to the emotivist was that there seemed to be no reason why the mere fact that I recommended a certain attitude should lead someone else to accept it. Kant tried, in effect, to face this problem by saying that, provided the attitudes I recommended were ones that appealed simply to reason, any reasonable person would accept them. But, as we have seen, the universalizability principle requires more than reason to lead to substantial moral principles. Now Kant thought, in fact, that you could derive from the universalizability principle a version of the **Golden Rule** that we find in many moral systems around the world; the rule that we should "do unto others as we would have them do unto us." In a sense, Hitler could be said to be following this rule, if he was willing to say that you would have been entitled to kill him if he hadn't been Aryan. But that is not, of course, what the Golden Rule means. What it means is that you shouldn't treat *anybody* in a way you would not like to be treated, whatever their race (or sex or age, and so on). A principle that treats people who belong to one race differently from the way it treats others is not an acceptable moral principle. To explain why, however, we have to say something other than that it cannot be universalized.

One of the most important recent moral philosophers, the British philosopher R.M. Hare, has taken up this challenge. He starts, like Kant, with the recognition that moral claims are categorical imperatives and that they must be universalizable. But he also recognizes that these two formal demands on moral principles need to be added to, if we are to end up with a really substantial moral view. And he deals with the problems raised both by Attila the Hun and by Hitler, in two different ways.

Hare's way of dealing with the problems raised by someone like Hitler is to restrict the kinds of features of actions and situations that we are allowed to take into account in universalizing our categorical imperatives. In particular, he says, we should consider "the likely effects of possible actions in those situations on people (ourselves and others); that is to say, on their experiences." And he goes on to suggest that we should also consider the effects on other sentient beings: creatures that are capable, like us, of having experiences.

The idea that we should treat everybody equally, and the idea that we should consider the consequences for them of what we do, rule out the principles of racists like Hitler as moral principles. These basic ideas are the parts of the Golden Rule that the universalizability principle leaves out. Hare sometimes suggests that we should not call a principle that discriminates, as Hitler's did, between different kinds of people a "moral principle." Given the way most of us use the word "moral," this is probably right. But even if we would not *call* it a moral principle (but, perhaps, an immoral one), this doesn't really get to the heart of the problem. The heart of the problem is that even if we wouldn't call this principle "moral," the mere fact that Hitler espoused the principle does not show that he had a defective reason. So that we are still left with the problem of relativism: the problem that we don't seem to have any reason to expect Hitler to come to agree with us simply because we announce our con-attitude to racial discrimination.

In other words, even though Hitler himself was wrong about the facts – Jewish people did not cause Germany's problems – and probably not a very sound reasoner, neither of these deficiencies seems to account for his moral errors. I shall get back to the question of how we should react to this fact in a moment. For now, let us return to Attila the Hun and see what Hare has to say about him.

Hare calls someone like Attila the Hun a **fanatic**. Fanatics are people who are willing to universalize maxims that allow them to do things to other people that they would not like done to themselves. Hare says that someone like this is not engaging in successful moral thinking; that, in fact, there is something wrong with the fanatic's imagination. The argument goes like this.

In order to decide whether you can universalize a maxim, you should consider what the effects would be of the maxim's being universalized to apply equally to everybody. Suppose the consequences of your act would be that some people would suffer terribly and nobody would derive much benefit. Then, if you really exercise your imagination and consider what it would be like for you to suffer terribly, you are bound to come to prefer that this should not occur; and that means that you cannot consistently will that the maxim should be universalized, for if it were universalized you would have to be willing to accept that the same thing should be done to you.

This argument is really quite convincing: once we get Attila the Hun to universalize in the right way, he would have to be most unreasonable to accept that it was all right for people to do to him what he was willing to do to others.

Some philosophers have insisted that a problem remains: how, they ask, should we react to the fact that Attila the Hun and Hitler will not universalize in the right way? But why, exactly, is this a problem? When I introduced the idea of relativism I said that a relativist held that what was good depended on who you were or what society you lived in. But, as we have seen, if the sophisticated emotivist account of moral content is correct, when I say "Kindness is good," I am saying that I have a pro-attitude to kindness and that I want everyone else to have that pro-attitude. I am not just saying, as the relativist would require, that I want every one who shares my feelings or my culture to have this attitude. It does not follow from the fact that people who disagree with us morally need not be wrong about the empirical facts and may not be incapable of reasoning that we have to accept their moral claims. What does follow is that, just as we have to give factual grounds for rejecting factual mistakes, and logical grounds for rejecting errors of reasoning, so we have to give moral grounds for rejecting their moral errors. What is wrong with Attila the Hun and Hitler is that they are wicked; they lack sympathy for others and they do not have a pro-attitude to treating people equally. The fact that these are errors neither of reasoning nor of fact does not make them any the less wrong.

Why, then, do so many people think that the fact that moral judgments express attitudes means that whether you should accept them depends on where you live or who you happen to be? The answer is, in part, that they confuse two different senses in which judgments can be *subjective*. The view that moral judgments express attitudes means that they are, in one sense, subjective. Which judgments you will agree to depends on what attitudes you have, which is a fact about you. But, in this sense, factual judgments are subjective also. Which ones you will accept depends on what beliefs you have. From the fact that they are subjective in this sense, therefore, it does not follow that they are subjective in the sense that you are entitled to make any judgments you like.

Once we have seen this, we can answer what I called the real challenge of relativism: to explain why you should expect someone to share your pro-attitudes. The answer to this question is simply that if someone does not have the right pro-attitudes then they may well *not* come to agree with you, however many facts you show them or arguments you make. The error is to react to this fact by supposing that it obliges us to give up either the universality or the categorical nature of our moral claims. Someone who reacts in this way is trying to derive an "ought" – You ought not to make universal or categorical claims – from an "is" – No amount of argument will force someone to share your pro-attitudes.

5.8   Prescriptivism and supervenience

Hare calls his account of moral contents a version of **prescriptivism**. This is because he holds that the meaning of moral terms is never equivalent to any descriptive or factual terms. Moral sentences *prescribe* rather than *describe*. The reason this is so, he claims, is that in saying something has a certain moral property we are expressing not just beliefs but attitudes. Someone like Hitler or Attila the Hun can share all our descriptive beliefs and disagree, nevertheless, with our moral ones because they do not share our attitudes. But Hare also points out that, though two people can share all their descriptive beliefs and still not share their moral judgments, they cannot share all their moral beliefs and not share their factual ones. The technical way of expressing this fact is to say that moral properties are **supervenient** on non-moral ones: two actions or situations that are identical in their non-moral features must, as a matter of logical fact, share their moral ones. Many kinds of properties are, in this way, supervenient on properties in other classes. Chemical properties, for example, are supervenient on physical ones. No two things that have all the same physical properties can differ in their chemical ones.

This important fact about moral judgments is one that prescriptivists are in a very good position to explain. For an attitude, whether pro or con, is, by definition, a state that disposes you for or against action. Because it is a universalizable attitude, a moral judgment always has the form:

M: In circumstance C, I and everyone else ought (or ought not) to do A.

Now the term C, which specifies the circumstances, has to be a factual term: it has to characterize states of the world. Suppose, for the purposes of *reductio*, that it did not characterize a factual state of affairs. Then it could not lead you to do anything at all. For in order to apply M, you must be able to discover whether, in fact, C obtains.

All my moral judgments, then, will be of the form of M. Given that I have these moral judgments, what I believe I and others ought and ought not to do is determined by what I believe the facts to be. This is precisely the respect in which our moral judgments are like our desires: given our desires, what we want to do is also determined by what we believe the facts to be.

5.9 Problems of utilitarianism I: Defining utility

So far we have largely discussed meta-ethical questions. But Hare's work provides a natural transition from purely meta-ethical questions to moral questions *and* the application of meta-ethical theory to them. For Hare is not only a meta-ethical prescriptivist but someone who has the substantive moral view that is called **utilitarianism**. Indeed, he argues that, if you first

(a) consider what maxims you are willing to universalize, and then,
(b) make sure they meet the conditions
    (i) that we treat everybody equally and
    (ii) that we take into account the consequences of our actions for sentient beings,

you will find that you are drawn to accept utilitarian principles. Hare's meta-ethics thus leads him to his first-order moral principles.

Utilitarianism is composed of two basic claims. One is what is called **consequentialism**: this is the view that an act should be assessed purely by its consequences. Its opposite is moral **absolutism**, for absolutists hold that certain kinds of acts are wrong and right, whatever the consequences. Consequentialism does not yield substantial moral principles, however, until it says both *which* consequences you should consider and *how* they should affect your actions.

The first utilitarians, nineteenth-century British philosophers like Jeremy Bentham and James Mill, believed that the consequences you should consider were simply the happiness or unhappiness that your actions would cause. They thought you should seek to *maximize* the amount of happiness – which means they were hedonists – hence their famous slogan: "The greatest happiness of the greatest number." They thought we should act in such a way that as many people as possible were as happy as possible.

This certainly looks like a very generous-hearted principle. But this form of utilitarianism immediately has to answer a question. Suppose you have the choice between making some people a little happy, on the one hand, or a few people very happy, on the other hand, which should you choose? In order to answer this question we need to be able to have some sort of way of measuring happiness. The measure the utilitarians suggested they called **utility** – hence the name of their view. They held that it made sense to say such things as

U: Sarah would get twice as much utility as James from eating this bar of chocolate.

Because of this, they felt they could answer the problem. All you had to do was to add up the amount of utility each person affected would get from each of the actions you were able to perform, and choose the action that created the most utility.

It soon emerged, however, that this view of utility faced a number of very difficult problems. First of all, is it really clear that we know what it means to say that James gets half the amount of utility that Sarah gets? We may sometimes have a sense that one person is happier than another; but we do not know how to tell in general which of any two people is happier, and we certainly do not normally think, even when we *do* know who is happier, that it makes sense to suppose that the difference in their happiness can be measured precisely.

Because of their interest in measuring utility, the utilitarians made important contributions to economics. For classical economics sought to explain how economies worked by supposing that every individual was trying to maximize his or her own utility. Indeed, the problem of measuring utility has been central to economics ever since the utilitarians. Since "happiness" is a rather vague notion, they tried to make the idea of utility rather more precise; and they did this essentially by defining utility as a measure of the satisfaction of your desires. Roughly speaking, what they suggested was that the stronger your desires the more utility you got from their satisfaction. If you wanted coffee twice as much as you wanted tea, then you got twice as much utility from a cup of coffee as from a cup of tea.

If we remind ourselves of the discussions of the first chapter, we shall see why it is a very challenging problem to develop a scientific theory of utility. Such a theory must allow us to measure desires precisely enough to make it possible to apply the utilitarian principle that you should seek to maximize human utility. The reason why this is a challenging problem, of course, is that utility is a mental state that has all the epistemological problems that come under the heading of the problem of other minds.

Because of this, economists attempted to find, first, behaviorist and, later, functionalist accounts of utility. (In fact, Ramsey, who invented functionalism about mental states, also made important contributions to the foundations of economics, for just this reason.)

But it turned out to be very difficult – some would say, impossible – to find a functionalist account of utility that made sense of claims like *U*. You could give a functionalist account of desire and belief that made sense of the idea of Sarah wanting, say, coffee twice as much as she wanted tea, though such measurements only made sense given some rather arbitrary-looking assumptions. But you could not develop a theory that made sense of Sarah wanting coffee twice as much as James did.

This problem of the **interpersonal comparison of utility** is very important to the philosophy of economics, and to utilitarian morality: but it requires a good deal of technical apparatus to discuss it. Suffice it to say here that unless interpersonal comparisons of utility are possible, utilitarianism cannot be applied.

5.10 Problems of utilitarianism II: Consequentialism versus absolutism

But this basic problem of defining and measuring utilities is by no means the only challenge that faces the utilitarian. Let us put to one side the question of how to measure utility and simply suppose that it can be solved. There are still two major sorts of objection to utilitarianism. One sort of objection starts with hunches about what people's utilities might be and shows that utilitarianism recommends actions that seem quite plainly immoral.

But how are we to judge whether what seems immoral really is immoral? In developing our moral views in a philosophical way, we take into account our meta-ethical views. But, as we have seen, meta-ethics does not, by itself, settle substantial moral questions. When we consider a substantive moral theory such as utilitarianism, we have to require not only that it be consistent with our meta-ethics, but also that it be consistent with our existing basic moral beliefs. No amount of philosophical argument is likely to persuade us to give up our deepest moral beliefs. We might find ourselves changing *some* of our moral views as a result of reflection, not merely in order to make them logically consistent, but because, for example, we see that certain principles that we have held in the past would lead, once universalized, to horrible consequences. But, in the end, there will be a kind of movement back and forth between the moral beliefs we start with, and moral theory. I shall discuss this process in a little more detail in the next chapter. For the moment, let us just proceed in this way.

Consider the simple and familiar moral principle that one should not lie. Utilitarians, because they are consequentialists, are not likely to accept this principle. For, they will say, sometimes telling a lie may have better consequences for human utility than telling the truth. We should consider in each case what the consequences will be and act accordingly. Provided it has the best consequences for human happiness, lying may sometimes be the right thing to do.

An absolutist will say, on the other hand, that lying is always wrong. It does not follow that the absolutist will never tell a lie. For, an absolutist can say, though lying is always wrong, some things are a good deal worse than lying. Thus, suppose Theresa lives in a totalitarian state. She is helping to hide an opponent of the regime, who risks being tortured if he is caught, though all he has done is to speak out against torture and oppression. Suppose, now, a police officer comes to the door asking whether she is hiding that person. Even if Theresa is an absolutist about lying, she does not have to tell the truth. To do this would not only be a betrayal of the trust, but it would lead to the suffering of a noble individual.

Theresa will not say that lying, in these circumstances, is *right*, but that it is *the lesser of two evils.* Fate has dealt her a choice between principles. Her view, as a moral agent, is that lying in this situation is obviously the lesser evil.

But what is the content of Theresa's judgment that it is wrong to lie even in this case? She would certainly agree that, in this case, she ought, all things considered, to lie. The difference between Theresa and the consequentialist here is not in the actions they do, but in the attitude they take to them. Theresa will regret having to lie. The utilitarian will not. In this sort of case, many people will agree with the utilitarian that Theresa has the wrong response. She simply has nothing to regret, they will say. If Theresa agrees with this, we shall have no answer to the question what the content is of her judgment that the act was wrong.

It is because many people believe that it is simply right to lie in such cases that they find the consequentialist position very plausible in the case of lying. But the consequentialist surely owes us some explanation of why we all have the intuition that there is something wrong about lying. The answer will be that

(a) the practice of truth-telling contributes to human happiness in most cases – which is why we all begin by thinking of it as wrong; but also,
(b) individual lies are justified if telling the truth would lead to more harm than good.

Indeed, a consequentialist can argue that feelings of regret, such as Theresa may feel, can themselves be given a consequentialist justification. Hare says

> Nobody who actually uses moral language in his practical life will be content with a mere dismissal of the paradox that we can feel guilty for doing what we think we ought to do.

And he suggests a number of reasons why a consequentialist should actually want us to have such reactions. First of all, he takes it for granted, surely correctly, that such feelings help us keep to our principles. Without them, many of us would be constantly slipping into doing what we believed was wrong. So the feelings are essential. Now we could try to develop a sophisticated set of feelings that went exactly with our moral beliefs. But to do that, we should have to attach the feelings, so to speak, to very complex principles. Once we start on this process with our principles, Hare argues, we will end up with moral principles of tremendous complexity. We start with a principle that says "One ought never to do an act which is *G*" (where *G* is, say, "a lie"); then we consider Theresa's problem. So, as Hare says, we modify our principle.

> Instead of reading "One ought never to do an act which is *G*," it now reads "One ought never to do an act which is *G*, unless it is necessary to avoid an act which is *F*."

Here *F* might be "the betrayal of a noble individual." Reflection on other cases will soon have us adding that even if it is necessary to do *G* to avoid *F*, we should not do so in circumstances *H*; unless – as another case might make us think – it is also *I*. And so on.

But once we get to principles of this complexity, it is hard to get our feelings attached to them in the right way. Hare's point, then, is that our moral feelings must, as a matter of psychological fact, attach to manageable principles, and that having the feelings is itself something that has a consequentialist justification. What is right and wrong is determined by the utilitarian principle, but our moral feelings cannot run precisely in parallel with them. So it is better overall to have the feelings, even if they sometimes lead us astray.

Nevertheless there are cases where most people think that consequentialism about lying is simply wrong. Suppose, for example, Ben is dying of a rare disease. Someday soon he will just drop dead, and nothing he or anyone else does can change that. Jane, a utilitarian doctor, might well feel that she should just not tell him, because it will only make him unhappy. Yet many of us think that, in these circumstances, Ben would have a right to know that he was going to die.

This sort of case is a more challenging problem for the utilitarian because it suggests not only that our moral feelings do not fit utilitarian principles, but that our moral judgments do not fit them either. We can give a utilitarian explanation of why we might want to have non-utilitarian feelings, but it would be just inconsistent to give a utilitarian explanation of why utilitarian principles were wrong.

The intuition that we cannot accept consequentialism as a moral theory is even stronger in cases where more is obviously at stake: in cases, for example, which involve killing people against their will. Jonathan Glover, a British philosopher, has suggested just such a case. He asks us to consider a man in prison.

> His life in prison is not a happy one, and I have every reason to think that over the years it will get worse. In my view, he will most of the time have a quality of life some way below the point at which life is worth living. I tell him this, and offer to kill him. He, irrationally as I think, says that he wants to go on living. I know that he would be too cowardly to kill himself even if he eventually came to want to die, so my offer is probably his last chance of death. I believe that in the future his backward-looking preference for having been killed will be stronger than his present preference for going on living.

This case constitutes an objection to utilitarianism, indeed to most forms of consequentialism. It looks as though the consequentialist will here have to agree that I should kill the prisoner. For the consequences of doing so will be better for him. But Glover suggests that the consequentialist might argue that drawing this conclusion ignores two important considerations.

First, such a killing may have many side-effects that have so far not been mentioned. Thus, for example, the man's family might regret his death, even if they knew that his life would have been unpleasant. And, for another example, if it came to be known what you had done, this would have a terrible effect on the morale of other prisoners in the prison. They might well fear that you would make such a judgment about them. This is especially likely to worry them because of the second consideration that the consequentialist may say we have ignored: namely, that it is not, in fact, very easy to predict what the future course of a person's mental states will be. As Glover says: "If a man wants to go on living, although this does not force me to accept that his life is worth living, I would have to be very optimistic about my own judgement to be sure that he is wrong."

But drawing attention to these considerations does not really allow us to accept the utilitarian's claims. For we can simply construct a case where these considerations do not apply. Suppose we were sure that no one would find out; sure that the prisoner had no family; and sure about his current and future mental states. The utilitarian would then have to accept that it is right to kill the prisoner. Yet many of us would think that it was still quite wrong to kill him against his will.

The view that it would be quite wrong to kill the prisoner will be defended by any philosopher who believes that it is a central moral principle that we should respect a person's autonomy. Respecting people's autonomy means placing a very great deal of weight in our decisions about them on what they themselves judge to be important. Kant expressed this idea when he said that it followed from his universalizability principle that we should never treat people as means but always as ends. To kill the prisoner is to regard his utility as more important than his wishes, and thus, in a sense, to treat him as a means to the end of maximizing utility.

If Kant was right, and we must respect people's autonomy, then consequentialism – the claim that we should always judge actions simply by their consequences – must be wrong. Even if we think that it is generally a good thing to maximize utility, the application of this principle must be subject to constraints. In particular, we may maximize people's utility only in contexts where this is consistent with respecting their autonomy. In the end, consequentialists cannot explain why many of us regard respect for other people's autonomy as important.

5.11 Rights

I have been discussing moral issues largely from the standpoint of someone who has to decide what to do. So I have been focussing on the question of what principles we should use in making these decisions. Approaching moral issues this way, you are bound to begin by focusing on the question: which acts are right and which ones are wrong? Utilitarianism provides a simple answer to this question. But it is an answer that is inconsistent with some very basic features of our moral thinking.

What it leaves out of account is the fact that we think of people as having rights that should be respected, as well as having the capacity for happiness, pleasure and pain. Respect for a person's autonomy, which explained why the prisoner's feelings mattered, derives from the view that he has a right to that respect. And it is respect for autonomy that also explains why many people believe that euthanasia is sometimes morally right in cases where a rational person has asked to be killed.

The notion of a right is thus central to much of our moral thinking. Recently moral philosophers have clarified the nature and status of rights a good deal. The term "right" is used in two main sorts of cases. In the first sort of case, which involves what we call **negative rights**, I have a right to do something if I am morally free to do it, and other people have the obligation not to hinder me if I do choose to do it. This is the sense in which we speak of the right of free speech. When we say that people have a right to speak freely, we mean not only that they may do so, but that it would be wrong to stop them.

On the other hand, we also speak of rights where people not only have a negative obligation not to hinder me in doing something, but a positive duty to help me. This is the sense in which people sometimes speak of a right to an education. For they mean that everybody is free to pursue an education and someone – often the government – has a duty to help them if they make that choice. In cases such as this we speak of **positive rights**.

Each kind of right entails corresponding duties. Sometimes, especially with positive rights, these are duties for specific people: children have the right to be fed and clothed by their parents or guardians. Sometimes, and especially with negative rights, these duties are duties for everyone. Everybody is obliged not to hinder me in the free expression of my opinions.

Once we reject consequentialism as the basis for morality, it is natural to start thinking about rights, just because, where a right imposes a duty upon us, we cannot ignore that duty and look simply to the consequences of our actions. Because the prisoner had a right to have his autonomy respected, we could not kill him, even though we thought that he would be much better off dead. His autonomy requires us positively to take into account what he says.

Many people would claim that there is a much more basic bar to killing this prisoner. They would say that people have a right to life; a negative right which creates a corresponding duty in all of us not to kill them. Such people are absolutists about killing. They would say that this is the basis of the widespread belief, with which I started the chapter, that

K: Killing innocent people is wrong.

You will recall, from my discussion of Theresa, the absolutist about lying, that the fact that an absolutist thinks something is wrong does not mean that they will never think they ought, all things considered, to do it. So my argument about the airman need not worry an absolutist who thinks that people have a right to life. The absolutist can say that, though it is, indeed, wrong to kill innocent civilians in warfare, it may be even worse not to fight for your country in a just cause.

Because rights and duties can conflict in this way, we will need not only to know what rights and duties there are, but which ones are most important. And, just as the utilitarians faced problems with measuring utility in order to find a common currency for trading one person's happiness against another's, so rights-theorists face problems in

CHAPTER 5

finding a way of adjudicating between competing rights and duties. These issues are complex: but they reflect the complexity of our moral lives, and they are central to the philosophical consideration of morality. In the next two chapters I will consider some more specific rights and duties, in the context of political philosophy and the philosophy of law. We shall see that in politics and law, consequentialism does not fit with our basic conceptions of right and wrong.

5.12 Conclusion

In this chapter, I have only scratched the surface of ethics. But I have tried to give an overview both of the main areas of meta-ethics – the question of the meaning of moral judgments and the problem of moral epistemology – and of some philosophical approaches to first-order moral questions. I argued that these questions were not independent, that the main themes of meta-ethics interact with some issues in first-order morality. Thus, for example, the basic difference between factual and evaluative beliefs – that the latter but not the former are action-guiding – seems to raise the issue of relativism, the possibility that the truth of a moral belief depends essentially on whose it is.

I have suggested that the route to relativism depends on confusing two different issues. One is the moral-content issue, which divides emotivists and prescriptivists, on the one hand, from moral realists, on the other. On this question I sided with the prescriptivists. I argued that people who do not share our basic moral attitudes cannot be offered reasons and evidence that is bound to lead them to agree with us. But the other issue is not an issue about moral content, it is a substantive moral dispute: a dispute between those – the relativists – who think that we cannot say that people who disagree with us about basic moral questions are just wrong, and those – non-relativists – who hold that we can. And here I sided with the non-relativists. To argue from prescriptivism to moral relativism, I suggested, is to confuse two different senses in which moral judgments could be said to be subjective.

I then turned to a debate about first-order morals between those consequentialists who think that whether an act is right and wrong should be decided by looking only to its results, and those absolutists who believe that the fact that something has consequences that are good overall does not always mean that it is right. As I said a little while ago, I shall follow up this question in the next two chapters.

But I have not discussed some of the central concepts of our moral thought: freedom and responsibility, for example, or praise and blame. What I have tried to do is to give you a sense of a range of views on what moral judgments mean and on how we should decide which judgments to accept. Clarity about these questions is an important first step in making up your mind about morality. But it is *only* the first step.

6 Politics

What is a state?

Do governments have a right to be obeyed?

What is justice?

6.1 Introduction

In the forests of Eastern Zaire, right at the heart of Africa, lives a pygmy people called the Mbuti. They move about the forest in small groups of several families, gathering honey and hunting antelope, and sometimes joining together with other groups for a communal hunt. The Mbuti think of themselves as belonging to bands that are defined by the territories in which they were born. But they do not necessarily live with the band to which they "belong," and they move freely, when they marry, to live with other small groups of families. The Mbuti have religious and moral ideas, ideas about marriage and hunting, beliefs about the forest they live in and the other people – whether pygmies or not – who share the forest with them. They co-operate in hunting and in building the small houses they set up each time they settle for a period in a particular part of the forest.

There is no doubt, then, that we can speak of the Mbuti as forming a society. Their language, customs, and beliefs bind them together and make their culture distinctive. Yet what is extraordinary about this society, for us and for people from most other societies, is that the Mbuti have no political organization. They have no chiefs or kings, no laws or courts, no government of any kind: in short, the Mbuti have no politics.

Since political philosophy examines the concepts we use to think about politics, it may seem strange to begin this chapter by discussing the Mbuti. But their society, like other "stateless societies," provides us with the occasion to ask what it is that turns a group of people into a state. Because political life is the life of people organized in states, we need to answer this question if we are to define the scope of political philosophy.

Why, then, does Mbuti society not constitute a small state? They clearly have social conventions (including those of language); and they are able to settle disputes and regulate their common life. So we cannot say that a state is just any collection of people, with shared conventions, organized in such a way that they are able to regulate their lives together. Rather, the key distinction between the Mbuti and societies organized into states has to do with the *way* they settle disputes and organize their common life.

Mbuti methods of hunting require the cooperation of many individuals; and without the hunting they would not be able to feed themselves adequately. When one of them behaves anti-socially, therefore, by disrupting a hunt or failing to play his or her part in it, something needs to be done to get them to change their behavior. In many societies, this would be done by the state. If you or I fail to carry out our duties as citizens, we may first be ordered to obey the law by police officers or other officials, and then tried in courts and punished if we refuse. In most earlier societies, a chief or a king or queen could have ordered you to carry out your duty, and would have ordered you to be punished if you disobeyed. But the Mbuti gain each other's cooperation in a way that is much more like the way we persuade our friends to help us. Sometimes, for example, they tease those who fail to live up to their obligations. On other occasions, they try to persuade anti-social men and women by reminding them of the obligations that all Mbuti acknowledge; or they point out how important cooperation is if they are to survive. What they cannot do, because they do not have the necessary institutions, is punish someone – by locking them up or executing them or ordering them to do community service.

The key difference between Mbuti society and a state, therefore, is that among the Mbuti there is *no single recognized person (or group) with the authority to gain compliance with its rulings through the use of force.*

It was the great German sociologist Max Weber who had the fundamental insight that it is the monopoly of the authority to use force that distinguishes the state. In order to understand the full significance of Weber's view, we need to understand the notion of *authority* that is involved here. And the first thing we must recognize is that having authority involves meeting both factual and evaluative conditions.

Let us take the factual conditions first. If you are to have authority, as some monarchs and the assemblies of democracies do, you need both to be able to enforce rulings – to have the capacity to police them – and to have fairly widespread acceptance, within the society, of the exercise of that capacity. However much we feel that leaders who have been removed by an illegitimate military *coup d'état* ought to be regarded as having the authority to govern a country, if they are simply unable to enforce any rulings, we would not say that they have authority in that country. To have authority you need to have some degree of power.

That, then, is the factual condition for having authority. But if a group of bandits takes over an area, and is able to enforce its rulings by the simple threat of force, that does not constitute an exercise of authority. To call such control the exercise of authority, we would need also to believe that the bandits had the *right* to exercise it. People may disagree substantially on what gives someone the right to exercise control over others; they may dispute the moral basis of authority. They may also disagree about who has that right in a particular case, even if they agree about its moral basis. But unless a person has some right to be obeyed, what they have is not authority but bare power.

It follows that Mbuti society would not turn into a state simply because someone was able to control the actions of the Mbuti by threat of force. A bandit leader who could control the Mbuti would satisfy the factual condition for authority without satisfying the evaluative condition. So that the primary conceptual question of political philosophy – What is a state? – leads immediately to the primary *moral* question of political philosophy – Under what circumstances does a person or group have the right to control a society? This is the question of the **justification of political authority**.

6.2 Hobbes: Escaping the state of nature

One obvious answer to this question is simply: "Under no circumstances." The view that control of a society by a government is never morally justifiable is **anarchism**: the claim that the state never has legitimate authority. As we shall see towards the end of the chapter, anarchists can certainly raise arguments for their position; but it has never been widely supported among philosophers.

One of the best-known answers to the question of justification of authority was given by Thomas Hobbes, the English philosopher whose work I have mentioned already, in his classic book *Leviathan*; and, unlike anarchism, Hobbes's answer is one that many philosophers have found compelling.

Hobbes began by considering what life would be like if we didn't recognize any authority, and he derived his answer from his view of human nature. Because he was concerned with the basic question of why we need states, Hobbes needed to consider those aspects of human nature that most affect our social lives. So he divided his attention, in effect, between the human tendencies that work for cooperation and those that work for conflict.

On the one hand, Hobbes said, human beings have a "desire of Ease, and sensual Delight" and a "fear of death, and wounds," which, along with a "desire of Knowledge, and Arts of Peace," make us want to cooperate together socially. But, on the other hand, we have tendencies, which Hobbes plainly thought more significant, that make us work against each other. These tendencies derive from the circumstances of human life.

Hobbes's consideration of the circumstances of human life began with the claim that human beings are very close to being equal in their physical and mental capacities.

> Though there be found one man sometimes manifestly stronger in body, or of quicker mind than another; yet, when all is reckoned together, the difference between man, and man, is not so considerable, as that one man can thereupon claim to himself any benefit, to which another may not pretend, as well as he. For as to the strength of body, the weakest has strength enough to kill the strongest, either by secret machination, or by confederacy with others . . .

Because of this rough equality of capacities, all of us have more or less the same chances of achieving our goals; and, Hobbes said, since our goals conflict – sometimes I want something you want and we can't share it – we become enemies. We become enemies because we have to "destroy or subdue one another" if we are to get what we want. Since this is so, we have every reason to be suspicious of each other – and this is a second source of conflict. Finally, Hobbes says, we all want to be respected by others (Hobbes calls this the desire for glory), yet people often undervalue or even despise others. These three factors – competition for scarce resources, the mistrust which follows from it, and our desire to be respected – are what Hobbes calls the "principal causes of quarrel." Competition leads us to use violence to get what we want; mistrust leads us to use violence to protect what we fear others want; and the desire for "glory" leads us to use violence against those who do not respect us.

HOBBES

Thomas Hobbes (1588-1679) was born prematurely in Malmesbury, Wiltshire, in England, as a result of his mother's shock on hearing that the Spanish Armada was sailing to attack England. In a Latin verse autobiography, written in later life, he joked that, as a result, "fear and I were born twins." Hobbes went to Oxford University at the then normal age of 14 and graduated five years later in 1608. On graduation he became tutor to the son of William Cavendish, later the second Earl of Devonshire. He thus had access to a great library and to foreign travel. This travel took him, in 1610, to Europe, where he discovered that the Aristotelian philosophy he had learned at Oxford was now in disrepute. When he returned he took up the translation of the Greek historian Thucydides, which he hoped would persuade his compatriots of the dangers of democracy that would follow if the conflict between Charles I and Parliament led – as it finally though temporarily did lead – to the end of the monarchy. His anti-democratic views put him at risk when the King's

disagreements with parliament began the lead-up to the English Civil War. In 1640, he fled into exile in France. After the Civil War he returned to England, where *Leviathan*, the first great work of modern political philosophy, was published in 1641. Hobbes published a great deal on a wide range of topics – from optics to history – even publishing, at the age of 86, a translation of the *Iliad* and the *Odyssey*.

Because we are involved in a struggle against others, all of us have

> a perpetual and restless desire of Power after power, that ceaseth only in Death. And the cause of this, is not always that a man hopes for more intensive delight, than he has already attained to; or that he cannot be content with moderate power: but because he cannot assure the power and means to live well, which he hath present, without the acquisition of more.

It may seem, at first, that many people simply do not have this lust for power. But we must bear in mind that by *power* Hobbes means only the possession of the capacity to get what you want. In that sense of "power," we *would* probably all like to have more power than we do.

Given this picture of human life and human nature, Hobbes goes on to ask what life would be like in a stateless society, without a recognized authority; without someone able to maintain control, if necessary, by force. Hobbes calls the condition of people without government a **state of nature**. He argues that, given the circumstances of human life that he has described, we cannot hope for security in a state of nature. For we have no reason to think that someone who wants something we have will not take it, killing us, in the process, if it is necessary.

> Hereby it is manifest, that during the time when men live without a common Power to keep them all in awe, they are in that condition which is called War; and such a war, as is of every man, against every man. ... In such condition, there is no place for Industry; because the fruit thereof is uncertain: and consequently no Culture of the Earth; no Navigation, nor use of the commodities that may be imported by Sea; no commodious building; no Instruments of moving, and removing such things as require much force; no Knowledge of the face of the Earth; no account of Time; no Arts; no Letters; no Society; and, which is worst of all, continual fear, and danger of violent death; And the life of man, solitary, poor, nasty, brutish and short.

That is Hobbes's famous and rather bleak picture of what life would be like without government. But Hobbes believed that any reasonable person could recognize that if we followed certain principles, which he called (rather misleadingly, as we shall see) **Laws of Nature**, we should be able to escape these perils of the state of nature.

Among the "laws" are such principles as these, which Hobbes called the first four "laws of nature."

1. You should seek peace, wherever it is possible; but if you cannot achieve peace, you should defend yourself, by all means at your disposal.
2. You should give up the right to defend yourself, to the extent that it is necessary to achieve peace, provided other people accept the same limitations.
3. You should keep your promises.
4. You should not give other people who keep their promises reason to regret them.

It is not hard to see why Hobbes's calling these principles "laws of nature" was misleading. In his day, the laws of nature were thought of as moral rules, with divine authority, which everyone was obliged to obey even outside the constraints of the state. These laws were essentially conceived of as the moral laws that governed relations between people – and, in particular, between subjects and their monarchs – pre-existing and over-riding the laws of any state. They were known to us by reason, because God, who made us, had given us, in reason, the capacity to recognize His will.

Now just as Hobbes's use of the term "power" was rather special, so we must bear in mind that his use of the idea of a "law of nature" was distinctive. For his natural laws involve no moral ideas at all: they are, as he sometimes said, "maxims of prudence," rules that our reason reveals to us it would be in our own interests to follow. Indeed, Hobbes thought that in the state of nature there *are no* moral principles. Morality is made possible by the state.

The view that moral considerations cannot apply outside a state is one that Hobbes does not seem to defend; and it is certainly not one that most of us would agree with. It is a natural view that moral principles not only *do* but *should* operate among the Mbuti. They think certain actions are right and others are wrong: they criticize those who are unkind or irresponsible. And even if they did not, that would not mean that *we* could not criticize people in those circumstances for those vices.

Hobbes's defence of his laws of nature, then, is not that they are morally right, but simply that any reasonable person can see that we would be better off if everybody obeyed them. But he also believed that even once we do see this, we will not obey the laws of nature without the threat of sanctions.

All of us, for example, may seek to avoid obeying the laws of nature, where it suits us, provided we think we can get away with it. This is because what reason shows is not strictly that we will profit if we obey these rules, but rather that we have reasons for wanting everybody *else* to obey them. If we all agreed to obey these rules as long as everybody else did, I might try to get the benefits from your obeying the rules by *appearing* to obey them myself, while secretly deviating from them whenever I thought no one would find out. Pretending that I would go along with the rules might be enough to get everybody else to keep obeying them, as long as I wasn't caught. Provided I can get the benefits of your obeying a rule by simply appearing to obey it myself, I have no special reason to obey it in fact: I would have no reason at all, if I was as purely self-interested as Hobbes supposed all human beings to be.

Without effective policing, then, Hobbes doubted that human beings would ever obey the laws of nature; and thus, he thought, we would remain in a state of nature unless these (and other) laws could be enforced. It is for this reason that Hobbes held that it was essential to establish a state, with somebody exercising a monopoly of ultimate authority. We need a "common power" that will force us to keep the laws of nature if we are to achieve the benefits that reason shows us we can gain from keeping to them.

> The only way to erect such a Common Power . . . is, to confer all their power and strength upon one Man, or upon one Assembly of men, that may reduce their Wills, by plurality of voices, unto one Will.

By making such an agreement or *covenant* a group of people is "united in one Person ... called a COMMON-WEALTH."

> A *Common-wealth* is said to be *Instituted*, when a *Multitude* of men do Agree, and *Covenant, every one, with every one,* that to whatsoever *Man,* or *Assembly of Men,* shall be given by the major part, the *Right* to *Present* the Person of them all, ... every one, as well he that *Voted for it,* as he that *Voted against it,* shall *Authorize* all the Actions and Judgements, of that Man, or Assembly of men, in the same manner, as if they were his own, to the end, to live peaceably amongst themselves, and be protected against other men.

Hobbes went on to argue that reasonable people would agree to such a covenant only if it gave the sovereign enough power to do the job of securing the peace. And, he argued, to be able to do this job, the sovereign must have absolute power: the only exception he made was that we have the right to defend our own lives against the sovereign, because our lives are the major thing that the sovereign is supposed to protect.

Thus, to give someone the sovereign power, for Hobbes, is both to allow them to regulate society by any methods they deem appropriate, including the use of force against citizens, and to recognize their right to do so.

Once we give someone the sovereign power, we enter into **civil society**, society organized in the form of a state. Hobbes, who lived in England when it was an absolute monarchy, suggested that we ought to give this power to a *monarch*, a king or queen. We are better off, he argued, handing it over to a monarch, even though we then run the risk of the monarch's using the power thus acquired to rob, bully or kill us. But because the justification for the sovereign's power, which we each accept as a matter of self-interest, is that our lives would be at risk without it, we can reasonably rebel against a king or queen who so abuses the power that authority brings as to put our lives at risk. So long as we are better off under the sovereign than we would be in the state of nature, however, we have no basis for complaint.

Notice that on Hobbes's view, there is a very intimate connection between the factual and the evaluative conditions for authority. For it is only if sovereigns satisfy the factual condition, and are able to enforce rulings, that they can protect us from our fellow citizens, and thus meet the evaluative condition by protecting us from a life that is "nasty, brutish and short." This feature of Hobbes's theory is a very important one, for it shows that the connection between the factual and the evaluative conditions is not arbitrary. Hobbes's view does seem to set minimum conditions on what can be called a state. For a government to be legitimate it must both try to make the lives of citizens better than they would be in a state of nature, and have some success in the attempt. Someone who failed even to try to improve on the state of nature could not legitimately claim, according to Hobbes, to be a sovereign, with the right to govern.

Though this seems to be right, there are many problems with Hobbes's view. If he has correctly identified a minimum condition for being a government at all, he has not established that the only demand we can make of government is that it should improve on the state of nature. Let us consider some of the reasons why.

6.3 Problems for Hobbes

Because Hobbes does not derive the authority of the state from moral considerations, but from considerations that are meant to appeal to the rational self-interest of each of us, his view can be called **prudentialist**. We would be prudent, according to Hobbes, to confer on an absolute sovereign the power to regulate everybody's lives.

Hobbes makes a number of crucial steps in the long argument to his prudentialist conclusion. First, because the covenant is among the citizens, and not between the citizens and the sovereign (whether the sovereign is one person or an assembly), he holds that the sovereign has no obligations to the citizens. Second, he assumes that once you enter into the meeting, to decide whether you should set up such a covenant, you are obliged to accept the majority verdict, whether you voted for it or not. Third, he assumes that because we ought to keep our promises, once we have entered into such a covenant, we are bound by it, so that we should not break it under any circumstances, short of a direct assault by the sovereign on our lives. Fourth, he assumes that the sovereign can only protect us from the dangers of the state of nature by having **absolute** power; that is by being unrestrained by any constitutional checks and balances. Finally, as I have already said, he assumes that outside a state moral considerations do not apply.

I shall consider some objections to the first three assumptions in a moment, and I have already argued that the last assumption is unjustified. But many of us would surely want to follow up our objection to the last assumption by objecting very strongly to Hobbes's claim that the sovereign must have absolute power.

The existence of the Mbuti suggests that, at least in a society with a very simple level of material life, Hobbes's view of the dangers of the state of nature is somewhat exaggerated. The dangers of a tyrannous sovereign with no obligations to the citizenry look considerably less attractive than the dangers of Mbuti life. So long as the Mbuti got along without the protection of a sovereign, they would have had no reason to enter into a Hobbesian absolute state. It is surely reasonable to suggest that most people with a little familiarity with the history of humanity would not willingly enter into a covenant to create an absolute sovereign, with all the attendant risks of tyranny, if the alternative was the free, if simple, life of the Mbuti pygmies.

Nevertheless, it does seem clear that, on the whole, we profit enormously from the existence of settled government. But, of course, we have achieved a system – democracy – which substantially reduces the risk of the abuse of the sovereign power. It does not guarantee that majorities will not oppress minorities, but it makes it less likely that a minority, let alone a majority, will ever be oppressed. Even if we do not need an absolute sovereign to protect us from the perils that Hobbes imagined in a state of nature, we all have something to gain from the existence of a government, provided it is not too oppressive. So a more reasonable reaction than Hobbes's would be to argue for a covenant which gave the sovereign effective powers, but limited his or her rights to just those powers that were necessary for enabling us to escape the perils of the state of nature. Which rights the sovereign should have is a question to which we shall return.

But this is only the first problem with Hobbes's argument. For his whole view depends, as we have seen, upon supposing that a political arrangement has been set up by agreement. Once we have made this agreement, according to Hobbes, we should stick to it. But not everyone is likely to find this argument convincing, for four sorts of reasons.

First of all, while we *might have* agreed to a covenant in a state of nature, we certainly *didn't* freely enter into one. Most of us, who were not naturalized as citizens of our countries, were simply born into them. And even those who were naturalized were not offered a contract they could enter into freely; for there was no negotiation. The Immigration and Naturalization Service of the United States simply says, as the Congress required it to, "take it or leave it." And "it" includes the Constitution and all the laws of the United States. Since no one anywhere in the world is free nowadays to choose to live entirely outside any state, the fact that someone accepts citizenship of a country as their best option does not necessarily mean that they would prefer it to living in no state at all.

If Hobbes answered this objection by saying that the fact that we *would have* accepted the covenant is a reason to do what it requires, we can ask whether this is true of agreements in general. And the answer is plainly no. Otherwise, if I would have agreed to buy your car if you'd offered it to me for $100, then, by a similar argument, I would owe you $100 if you gave me your car, even if I hadn't agreed to buy it! So the first objection is that since we didn't enter freely into a covenant, it is hard to see why it should be binding on us.

The second sort of objection, however, is even more damaging. For, even if we *had* agreed to a covenant, there is no reason to suppose that reasonable people would have accepted the particular covenant that Hobbes suggests. We have already seen that there is reason to doubt that any of us would willingly have instituted an absolute sovereign, one, that is, who had no obligations to the citizens. We have thus good reason to question Hobbes's first assumption.

But the third objection is that there is a further reason for doubting that we would have accepted the terms of Hobbes's covenant. It is that, even if we had agreed to set up a meeting to agree to a covenant, we would be most unlikely to have agreed to the meeting being governed by the rules he suggests. Why, for example, should we have agreed that the meeting to make the covenant should be governed by a majority vote? If we were out to protect our own self-interests, for example, we might have insisted on a rule of unanimity; and, as we shall see, other philosophers have thought that unanimity is preferable to being governed by the views of a majority. That is a reason for rejecting his second assumption.

Finally, Hobbes's claim that we would be bound by the agreement we made, whatever happened, is unconvincing. For Hobbes's justification for the state appeals – because it is prudentialist – simply to our self-interest. If, once we had set up the covenant, we discovered that there was a way of getting around it that was in our self-interest, why would it not be prudent to use that way out? That is a basis for rejecting his third assumption; and we now have reason to doubt every one of the five Hobbesian assumptions we began with.

Nevertheless, there is at the heart of Hobbes's argument a recognition of an important truth: the truth that we usually gain, from the existence of settled government, advantages that it would be most imprudent to give up, once we have them; or to refuse, if, like the Mbuti, we do not. The existence of the state is, for most people in most societies, better than the alternative.

6.4 Game theory I: Two-person zero-sum games

It would be interesting and important if we could make the sort of argument Hobbes offered more precise, so that we could say just why it is that the advantages of civil society over the state of nature ought to appeal to anyone. It would be especially interesting if we could do this in a way that was not open to the sorts of objections I have made against Hobbes. To do this, we should first need to show why it was a reasonable strategy to enter into negotiations with other people in the state of nature, in order to gain certain important advantages. Then we would need to show what sort of agreements rational people would come to in those circumstances. As the American philosopher Robert Nozick has put it:

> A theory of a state of nature that begins with fundamental general descriptions of morally permissible and impermissible actions, and of deeply based reasons why some persons in any society would violate those moral constraints, and goes on to describe how a state would arise from that state of nature will serve our explanatory purposes, *even if no actual state ever arose in that way.*

Unlike Hobbes, we would not be assuming that there are no moral principles which apply outside the state; we would not be relying on the fiction that we really did make a covenant; we need not be committed in advance to the particular form of absolute sovereign that Hobbes advocates, or to majority voting in the design of the state; and we could have a more plausible view than Hobbes's about when the state ceases to be advantageous and rebellion is in order.

Many recent philosophers, Nozick among them, have tried to make the sort of argument Hobbes offered more precise by making use of a very powerful modern theory about how rational people should deal with problems of this kind. This mathematical theory has been put to use in many areas of the social sciences, including, most importantly, economics. It is called **game theory** because it was first applied to some simple games; but game theory can be a very serious matter.

Game theory advances our understanding of rational decision-making in the way that formal logic deepens our grasp of rational argument. That, in itself, gives it a philosophical interest over and above its importance for recent political theory. But game theory is not only of theoretical importance: nowadays it is used by business executives to make corporate decisions and by strategic planners working out nuclear defense policy. Still, it remains easiest to explain the central ideas of game theory in terms of some (rather simple-minded) games.

For the purposes of game theory, a **game** is any set-up in which there are people – called, naturally enough, **players** – who are choosing strategies for their dealings with each other, in a way that determines what each of them gets as a **payoff**. Thus, in chess, there are two players; a strategy for each player consists of a (very complicated) set of rules about how he or she will react to any sequence of moves by the other player; and the payoff is a win, a draw or a loss.

Now one way to represent a game that has two players, A and B, each with two strategies, is to draw a matrix like the one at the top of the next page. Here, the pairs of values in the matrix represent what the players get as payoff if they adopt the strategies at the left of the row (for A) or the top of the column (for B). Thus, if A does A_1 and B does B_2, the payoffs are r, for A, and s, for B, and so on. (Obviously, this game is a lot less complicated than chess!)

		Player B	
		B_1	B_2
Player A	A_1	p,q	r,s
	A_2	t,u	v,w

Consider, for the sake of an example, this simple game. We both, first, put a dollar on the table. Then you hide a marble behind your back, in either your right or your left hand. I now have to say either "Left" or "Right." If I guess correctly, I get both dollars; if I guess wrong, you get them both. The matrix for this game looks like this:

		YOU	
		right	left
ME	right	$1.00	-$1.00
	left	-$1.00	$1.00

This simple game has a very important feature: if I win something, you lose it, and if you lose something, I win it. The total amount of payoff available is constant. For this reason games like this are sometimes called "constant sum" games. But they are also much more often known as **zero-sum** games: anything one player wins from the game the other loses, so that the sum of one player's losses (a negative amount) and the other's gains (a positive amount) will be zero. A zero-sum game is a game in which the players are most directly in competition; every cent or dollar or point I lose is a cent or dollar or point you win, and vice versa. (Notice that a zero-sum game has to be one involving two players.) In zero-sum games, we only need to write one of the entries in the box – usually the amount won by the player with his or her name down the left-hand side of the matrix; since, if it is a zero-sum game, every figure for one player's winnings implies an equal amount lost by the other. So we could just have written for the marble-guessing game:

		YOU	
		right	left
ME	right	$1,-$1	-$1,$1
	left	-$1,$1	$1,-$1

Because this game is just a guessing game, there is really no question of choosing a strategy. Since I do not know where you will hide the marble, I might as well pick sides at random. (Though, of course, if we played often and I discovered a pattern in the way you hid the marble, I might adopt a strategy conforming to that pattern.) But there are games in which there is a distinct advantage in sticking to one of your available strategies.

Here is such a game. Each of us puts $1.50 on the table, so there is $3 available in prize money for the pay-offs. There are three marbles in a bag, two white and one blue. You write either "blue" or "white" secretly on a piece of paper. I am then allowed to remove *either* both of the white marbles *or* the blue one from the bag. If I remove the white marbles, you get the blue marble. But suppose I take the blue marble. Then, if you had written "white," *you* get both the white marbles; and if you had written "blue," *I* get all the marbles. The payoff each of us gets is a dollar back from the "pot" of $3 on the table for each marble we win. Since each marble ends up being won by somebody this is a zero-sum game: every marble you don't get, I do.

	YOU	
	"White"	"Blue"
ME Take both white marbles	2 marbles	2 marbles
Take the blue marble	1 marble	3 marbles

Now you might think that I ought to take the blue marble in the hope that you had written "blue." But we are considering the game-playing of rational people, and I should take your reasoning into account in deciding what to do. And from your point of view, it is clear what you should do. If you write "white," the best that can happen is that you will get two marbles, because I take the blue marble; and the worst that can happen is that you get one marble, because I took the two white ones. If you write "blue," on the other hand, the best that can happen is that you get one marble; and the worst that can happen is that you get none at all. Since the *best* that can happen from your point of view if you choose "white" is better than the best that can happen if you choose "blue", and the *worst* that can happen if you choose "white" is the same as the best that can happen if you choose "blue," it seems obvious that, if you are reasonable, you will write "white." Since that is so, I should take both the white marbles (assuming you are reasonable) and leave you with just the blue one. For if I took the blue marble, you would get both the white ones.

The strategies in which you write "white" and I take the white marbles are called **equilibrium** strategies, because if either of us unilaterally deviates from that strategy, we will be worse off than we would be if we had stuck to it. If you adopted your equilibrium strategy and wrote "white," but I deviated from my equilibrium strategy and took the blue ball, then, instead of getting two white marbles – and two of the three available dollars – I would get only the blue marble – and only one dollar. And, as we saw, if I chose my equilibrium strategy, and took the white balls, but you had deviated from equilibrium by writing "blue," then you would get no marbles (and no money) at all. At equilibrium each of us is doing as well as we can expect, assuming the other person is rational.

In two person, zero-sum games, if there is more than one pair of equilibrium strategies then what each player gets is the same in each of them. In fact, if an equilibrium exists in the sort of game we have been considering, it is easy to find. The American mathematician and game-theorist Morton Davis has explained very clearly some of the main points about equilibrium strategies.

We start by looking at the question from the point of view of one of the players, Michael; and we consider what follows from the assumption that Michael has to tell Marina in advance what strategy he has chosen. Let's suppose that Michael's strategies are on the left of the matrix, and correspond to rows, while Marina's are across the top and correspond to columns. Michael knows that, since Marina is rational, she will choose a strategy which minimizes his payoff. So he knows that Marina will choose the strategy corresponding to the *minimum* value of the row in the game matrix that Michael chooses. As Davis says, Michael should, therefore, "choose a strategy that yields [for him] the *maximum* of those *minimum* values; this value is called the **maximin**, and it is the very least that [Michael] can be sure of getting."

We can now consider what would happen if the situation was the other way round, and Marina was deciding what strategy to choose if she had to tell Michael *she* had chosen. Michael would choose for himself the row in the column Marina has picked that gave him the *maximum*; so her obvious choice is the column that minimizes this maximum. That outcome is called the **minimax**. When the minimax is the same as the maximin, the payoff is called an **equilibrium point** and we call the players' strategies an **equilibrium strategy pair**.

Where there is an equilibrium point to a two-person zero-sum game, there is a compelling reason for both players to opt for it: each player wants to maximize his or her gains and thus, since the game is zero-sum, to minimize the gains of the other player. Provided each player, A, knows this fact about the other player, B, A has a reason to expect B to look for a strategy that maximizes the minimum B can get, whatever strategy A chooses; and, of course, vice versa. If there is a pair of strategies where both players maximize the minimum they can get, then each of them will want to stick with that pair of strategies.

In fact a **maximin** strategy seems like a good idea in any two-person zero-sum game, whether it has an equilibrium or not. For in a zero-sum game you can assume your opponent is trying to minimize what you get and so maximize his or her own payoff. The maximin strategy minimizes the harm that your opponent can do you. As game theorists have often pointed out, the appeal of the maximin strategy in the two-person zero-sum game lies in the fact that it offers security. If your opponent is irrational or takes risks, you might be able to do better than the maximin strategy: but the only way to do better is to risk something worse than the maximin strategy guarantees.

These simple ideas are at the basis of the theory of games. In order to apply the theory to any interesting problems, however, things have to be complicated a little. There are four main kinds of additional complexity in the full theory of games.

First of all, in the games I have been considering, the players only consider what are called pure strategies: these are strategies in which nothing is left to chance. With so-called **mixed strategies**, on the other hand, players do not decide among the options of getting A, B, C and so on. Rather, each strategy corresponds to a (specified) *chance* of getting A plus a *chance* of getting B plus a *chance* of getting C, and so on; where, of course, all the chances add up to 1.

It might seem crazy to suggest that you would do better adopting a mixed strategy than adopting a pure one. "Surely," someone could say, "making a rational decision will always be better than leaving things to chance." But there are situations where the case for a mixed strategy is compelling.

Suppose, for example, that you are playing a modified version of the first marble-guessing game as part of an experiment in a computer science lab. When other people have played against the computer they have lost all the time, because it has correctly predicted which hand they will choose to put the marble in. You are not so easily caught out. You toss a coin and put the marble in your right hand if it turns up heads, and into your left if it turns up tails. Since the coin is a chance device, the super-computer cannot predict how it will turn out: it has to "guess" at random. So, unlike all the others, you win 50% of the time.

It turns out not only that there are good reasons for adopting mixed strategies on some occasions, but that introducing mixed strategies allows the development of a very elegant mathematical theory of two-person zero-sum games. In particular, once you allow mixed strategies, there is always a solution to two-person zero-sum games: a pair of strategies which maximize the minimum each player can expect to get by playing that strategy over and over again. So that is the first complication.

A second complication arises because not every situation can be seen as a game that has payoffs in dollars and cents; and if we are going to use the idea of a game to help us understand the process of coming to settle on a system of government, we shall want to have some measure of payoff that takes into account such things as security from attack, which are difficult, if not impossible, to measure in monetary terms. The way to do this is to use the notion of utility I mentioned in the last chapter. The entries in the payoff matrices are now not dollars but units of utility.

I mentioned in the last chapter that it is not very easy to make sense of the notion of inter-personal comparisons of utility, so that you might reasonably doubt that we can make sense of a zero-sum game in terms of utilities. After all, if we can't compare our utility values, how can we know that when I gain some utility you lose an *equivalent* amount?

This is a serious difficulty for an attempt to define the difference between zero-sum game and non-zero-sum games, where the payoffs in both are utilities. But, fortunately for us, it is a problem we can avoid. For, as I have said, even if we could make sense of the idea of your getting as payoff an amount of utility which is equivalent to the amount I have lost, the "game" of political life is not one which we would expect to be zero-sum. Furthermore, in the theory of two-person games, as it turns out, we can often avoid making comparisons between the amounts of utility the two players get from the various strategies; all we need to do, instead, is to consider whether each of them gets more from one strategy than another. And that is something you can do without inter-personal comparison of utilities. As we shall see later, however, some answers – and in particular, John Rawls's answer – to the question of the justification of political authority presuppose that inter-personal comparisons of utility are possible.

But two further kinds of complication, which are of importance in the application of game theory to political philosophy, are also necessary. These are

(a) that we should consider games which are not zero-sum; and
(b) that we should consider, in particular, games with more than two players, which are called *n*-person games.

It is obvious why (b) is important; all real societies consist of more than two people. But to see why (a) is important, we can consider a very well-known non-zero-sum two-person game.

6.5   Game theory II: The prisoners' dilemma

In a two-person non-zero-sum game, we must obviously mark each element of the matrix with two numbers, representing the utility of each outcome to each player. This is because the sum of their utilities is not constant, so that we cannot tell what one player's payoff is just by knowing the other's. Consider the following non-zero-sum two-person game, one that has been very widely discussed.

Two suspects, Carrie and Larry, are being questioned about their role in an armed robbery. The police think that they committed the crime together, so the prisoners are kept apart, unable to communicate with each other. The police already have the evidence to convict each of them of a less serious offense – say, resisting arrest – but, without a confession, they do not have the evidence to get convictions for the more serious offense. So they offer each of the suspects the same deal. The deal is this:

(a) If one suspect confesses, and the other does not, the one who confesses goes free, and the other gets fifteen years in jail for armed robbery;
(b) If they both confess, they both go to jail for five years;
(c) If they both remain silent, they will both go to jail for six months on the charge of resisting arrest.

Here is the matrix which represents Carrie and Larry's options:

	CARRIE Confess?	
	Yes	No
LARRY Confess? Yes	(5 years, 5 years)	(Freedom, 15 years)
LARRY Confess? No	(15 years, Freedom)	(6 months, 6 months)

If we look at the situation from Larry's point of view, we should conclude that the right strategy is to confess. If Carrie confesses, Larry can either get five years, by confessing, or 15 years, if he doesn't confess. So, if Carrie confesses, Larry is better off confessing, too. But suppose Carrie doesn't confess. Then, if Larry confesses, he will get off scot-free; whereas, if he doesn't he'll have to spend six months in jail. Either way, then, Larry is better off confessing. Since the situation is symmetrical, Carrie has exactly the same reasons for confessing also.

That is the game-theory solution to the **prisoners' dilemma**, and, given certain assumptions, it seems to be the right one. Acting rationally without communicating and with no reason to trust each other, they will both get five years. But most people who have thought about this case notice immediately an important fact about the situation: if Carrie and Larry had some reason to trust each other, they could both keep quiet and both get away with just six months. The "rational" solution to the problem gives them each five years; but this co-operative solution, which they would both prefer, gives them both a shorter sentence.

The dilemma for Larry is whether to trust Carrie in the hope they will both get the six-month sentence – while risking for himself a very long sentence, if she confesses; or whether to refuse to trust her and probably get the five-year sentence, gaining the advantage that he avoids the risk of that long sentence altogether.

For this dilemma to arise it is essential that the game is not a zero-sum game: in a zero-sum game, since I win what you lose and vice versa, each of us can only lose by helping the other.

If we reconsider the Hobbesian state of nature, we can apply the game theory analysis to see why the choice of a state is one way of avoiding some of the situations which make life without government "solitary, poor, nasty, brutish and short." Without the state, deciding whether to co-operate may be like the prisoners' dilemma.

Suppose, for example, in the state of nature, I am trying to grow bananas. There is only one other person around – call her "Eve" – and she, like me, loves bananas. So we both grow them. In the state of nature, as Hobbes conceives of it, we shall each make raids on the other's banana plantations. In the ensuing skirmishes, some bananas will be damaged, and, more importantly – since we are, as Hobbes supposes, roughly equal in strength – we will each sometimes get hurt. Suppose we get fed up with this situation and both agree to observe a "covenant": I won't steal your bananas if you won't steal mine, and vice versa. Each of us is now considering whether to keep this covenant. (For the sake of simplicity I'll consider only two strategies – keeping and breaking the "covenant" – so a strategy of "wait-and-see," of keeping the covenant until the other player breaks it, is ruled out.) Here is the matrix:

		Eve's options	
		Make a deal but don't keep it	Make a deal and keep it
My options	Make a deal but don't keep it	Each of us gets most of our own bananas, loses some to the other person and steals some of theirs in return; since some bananas get damaged in fighting, we get less than our own full crops and we also risk getting hurt in our banana raids.	I get all my bananas plus some of Eve's plus freedom from her attacks. She gets many of her own bananas but loses some in my raids and also risks being hurt when I attack.
	Make a deal and keep it	I get most of my bananas, but lose some in Eve's raids and also risk being hurt in her attacks. She gets all her own bananas plus some of mine along with freedom from my attacks.	We both get all our own bananas plus freedom from attack by the other.

If Hobbes is right, and we are both self-interested in the state of nature, we are now in a situation like the prisoner's dilemma. If Eve keeps her word, then I shall do better if I break my word: I'll not only get freedom from her attacks and all my bananas, but I'll get some of her bananas as well. If she doesn't keep her word, then I shall still do better if I break mine: we'll both continue to risk being hurt, but at least I'll get back some of the bananas Eve steals from me by stealing from her.

Since the situation is symmetrical, Eve has just as much reason not to keep *her* word, so both of us choose the strategy of making the covenant and then breaking it: *and that puts us immediately back where we were in the state of nature without the covenant!* Notice that this matrix has exactly the structure of the prisoners' dilemma: we will end up in the top left-hand box of the matrix, when we would both rather be in the bottom right.

CHAPTER 6

That was Hobbes's great insight, expressed in game-theoretic terms: he saw that, if we human beings were self-interested in the state of nature, we needed to change the rules of the game before we had an incentive to co-operate. To see that this is correct, we need only consider a matrix for the same situation once the Hobbesian sovereign is in control.

		Eve's options	
		Make a deal but don't keep it	Make a deal and keep it
My options	Make a deal but don't keep it	Each of us gets most of our own bananas, loses some to the other person and steals some of theirs in return; since some bananas get damaged in fighting, we get less than our own full crops and we also risk getting hurt in our banana raids. We also both get punished regularly for stealing	I get all my bananas plus some of Eve's plus freedom from her attacks. However I also get punished whenever I am caught stealing. She gets most of her bananas; but she loses some to me and also risks being hurt when I attack. However she is never punished.
	Make a deal and keep it	I get most of my bananas, but lose some in Eve's raids and also risk being hurt in her attacks. However, I am never punished. She gets all her bananas plus some of mine; but she also gets punished whenever she is caught stealing.	We both get all our own bananas plus freedom from attack by the other. Neither of us is ever punished.

Suppose that the sovereign punishes banana thieves by taking away *all* their bananas; and suppose that the sovereign usually detects thefts. Then, as you can easily work out, Eve and I are now both better off if we keep the covenant we have made with each other: for whatever the other person does, the risks of being punished outweigh the advantages. Game-theory allows us to see very clearly why Hobbes thought self-interested people could not escape the state of nature unless they had a sovereign to enforce their agreements with each other.

6.6 The limits of prudence

I suggested at the end of 6.3 that there was a problem for Hobbes that followed from the fact that his theory was what I called "prudentialist." The problem was that if, once we had set up the covenant, we discovered that there was a way of getting around it that was in our self-interest, nothing would stop us from using that way out. Even after setting up the state and installing the sovereign, we cannot suppose that the sovereign would be infallibly able to detect wrong-doing; sometimes, even once the state is in place, a purely self-interested person would have reasons to disobey the law. It would be no use for Hobbes to appeal, at this point, to a general moral obligation to keep promises. For, as we have seen, Hobbes's argument is explicitly not meant to depend on moral principles. If we were allowed to draw on moral principles in defending the institution of the state, we could say a good deal more in its defence than Hobbes actually does. The institution of a state and of enforceable regulations can allow us to achieve many good things, other than security. It can allow the maintenance of moral ideals – such as the ideal of helping those in suffering – which Hobbes refuses to consider. Hobbes's argument provides no basis for these ideas.

More than this, if the principle that we should keep our promises were the basis of our duty to obey, then we should have to face up to a fact that I pointed out in the last chapter; namely, that we normally suppose that the duty to obey promises can be overridden by other considerations. Far from leading to Hobbes's conclusion that we should obey the sovereign except when our lives are at risk, basing our duty as citizens on keeping promises as a moral principle would suggest that our duty was severely limited by other moral obligations.

But there is a deeper objection to Hobbes's appeal only to self-interest: Hobbes's argument completely fails to capture the sense of allegiance to their states that many people have. Many people think not only that they would give their lives for their countries, but that this would sometimes be the right thing to do. To make sense of this belief, we need to appeal to something more than self-interest. Unless you are guaranteed a place in heaven, it is never, surely, in your self-interest to die; at least, where the alternative is living a life that is not unbearably distressing.

So other political philosophers have suggested answers to the question of justification have offered answers to the question of justification that offer some prospect of explaining a moral identification with the state you belong to that lies beyond self-interest. And one way to do this is to give up an assumption of Hobbes's that I have already suggested we should reject: the assumption, namely, that there are no moral principles that apply prior to the formation of the state. The two most important recent works of political philosophy both try, in different ways, to start from moral principles in a state of nature and derive from them an answer to the question of the justification of political authority. The first such proposal is in the works of the American philosopher John Rawls, whose most famous book is called *A Theory of Justice.*

6.7 Rawls's theory of justice
Rawls claims that a society is just – and that the authority of the state is therefore justified – if two conditions obtain:

First Principle

Each person has an equal right to the most extensive system of equal basic liberties compatible with a similar system of liberty for all.

Second Principle

If there are inequalities in liberty or in income

(a) they work out to the advantage of the worst-off, and
(b) the positions which are better off are open to all qualified people.

Rawls defends this theory by arguing that his conception of justice would be chosen by people in a suitably constructed bargaining game over the other available options including the state of nature. The bargaining game is an *n*-person non-zero-sum game, involving rational players, who make decisions on the basis of self-interest. The players share a desire to find some basis for reasonable cooperation – so that they are not, for example, people who enjoy the thrill of fighting so much that they actually prefer the "war of all against all" in the state of nature. Further, Rawls, like Hobbes, requires that no one is powerful enough to guarantee that he or she can dominate the others, "when all is reckoned together." These requirements on the participants are broadly similar to the requirements that Hobbes insisted on.

But Rawls adds two more requirements, which move his theory away from prudentialism; away, that is, from the assumption that the justification of the state can appeal only to rational self-interest. These further requirements characterize what Rawls calls the **original position**, which is the situation of the people playing his bargaining game.

There are, broadly speaking, two ways in which you might bring moral considerations into play in using this route to get from the state of nature to the state. One would be to forbid any strategy in which a player acted immorally – and I shall return to this possibility again in considering the work of Robert Nozick. But another, perhaps more subtle, way would be to construct the bargaining game in such a way that people were forced to take certain moral principles into account. John Rawls's proposal involves extra constraints of both these kinds.

The first constraint, which Rawls calls the **veil of ignorance**, effectively forces self-interested bargainers to consider other people's interests. It is the requirement that the participants do not know what their own position – or anyone else's – will be in the society that results from the bargaining game, and know very little about their own talents and abilities either. Not only are players in the bargaining game ignorant of their own skills and capacities; they do not know, behind the veil of ignorance, what their interests, or their goals or their conception of the good life will be. Apart from these limitations on their knowledge of their own position, the players in the bargaining game are extremely well informed: "They understand political affairs and the principles of economic theory; they know the basis of social organization and the laws of human psychology." But all this is general knowledge: what they lack is specific information about themselves. Let us reduce this requirement to a formula and say that behind the veil of ignorance *everyone is ignorant of their goals and their relative positions.*

The reason for this requirement is that self-interested bargainers who knew too much about their own goals and positions would obviously seek to set up the rules so they could profit from them. If I knew that I was going to be one of the tallest or the laziest people in the society, I might try to get specially good treatment for the lazy or specially bad treatment for short people. If I knew that property was going to be especially important in my idea of the good life, I might build in very strong property-rights. The veil of ignorance thus tempers the consequences of the assumption that the bargainers are self-interested: it requires us in a sense to take into account the interests of others, because, for all we know, we might end up in their position. We could say, in fact, that the veil of ignorance forces the participants to adopt the universalizing perspective that Kant identified as the mark of morality.

This, then, is a way of getting a certain moral principle

EQUALITY: Everybody should be taken equally into account

built into the outcome of the bargaining game, by constraining the players' knowledge, while still allowing them enough information to make some sort of choice between theories of justice. But, as I said, Rawls also builds into the bargaining game a requirement that rules out any strategy that fails to conform to a certain moral principle; namely, the principle that *the participants should not be envious.* He does this not directly by ruling out strategies motivated by envy, but indirectly, by saying that the participants in the game are not subject to envy.

One reason Rawls makes this requirement is, of course, that we do not want envy, which is an emotion that most of us think is morally reprehensible, to be part of the basis for judging the political institutions of the state. If we are ruling out morally unacceptable emotions in the participants in the game, however, we would surely also not want bare self-interest, which is also morally reprehensible, to be the basis for judgment either. Rawls needs a special reason for ruling out envy. And, as the American philosopher Robert Paul Wolff has argued, there is a much more telling reason why Rawls has to require that his bargainers are not envious: and explaining what that reason is allows us to see some of the advantages and problems of Rawls's theory.

6.8   The difference principle and inequality surpluses

Part (a) of Rawls's second principle is usually called the **difference principle**. It is a principle that can only apply if a society organized into a state is not a constant-sum game. To see why, consider a society which *is* a constant-sum game. We start from a position of equality, since every deviation from equal distribution has to be justified by the difference principle. But if it is a constant-sum game, then any inequalities that gave one person or group more goods or liberties than another would be bound to be unacceptable, since Jane's gain would have to have come from John's loss. If we are starting from equality, giving something to Jane would immediately make at least one person worse off.

As Wolff points out, however, we know very well that societies are not like this, because in many of our social practices there is what Wolff calls an **inequality surplus**. He explains this idea in terms of a very clear case.

Consider a factory in which sixty people work to make shoes. There are six basic tasks involved in the business: tanning the leather, cutting it, stitching, gluing, packing, and selling. Suppose that the net receipts (before wages) each year are $600,000, which is distributed equally to the workers, who therefore get $10,000 a year each.

Let us also suppose that if the tanners and the sales staff were to work harder, sales and profits would rise markedly. The tanners limit the rate of the production of shoes, because their work is difficult and tiring; and the salesmen and women limit profits because they tend to work only hard enough to keep the inventory down below the level where it would fill up the store-room. If we paid the tanners and the sales staff not $10,000 but $15,000, productivity increases would lead to net receipts of $700,000. But, since the extra tanning and selling are hard work, the tanners and sales people will not do the extra work for less. Now

> after the fifty regular workers are paid their $10,000 each, and the [tanners and the sales staff] are paid $15,000 each, there will be a pot of $50,000 left over, which can be spread around among the fifty regular workers, raising their wages to $11,000 each. *That $50,000 is an inequality surplus* – it is the surplus income remaining after all the occupants of the roles of an unequally rewarded practice have been paid enough to draw them into the several roles.

Since $15,000 is the minimum wage necessary to get the sales people and tanners to increase their productivity, trying to give the others more than $11,000 in these circumstances will actually lead to a reduction in total productivity. It won't leave enough money to pay the tanners and the sales people what it takes to increase their productivity. In situations where there is an inequality surplus the worst-off can be better off than they would be without the inequality.

Now, as Wolff points out, we can see immediately why Rawls needs to have his assumption that the bargainers are not envious. If one of the stitchers – say, Joe – was envious, he might prefer the original less productive arrangement, even though he would get $1,000 less, because he was willing, in effect, to pay $1,000 to avoid being in a situation where someone was better off than he. In effect, for Joe, the envious stitcher, the entry in the pay-off matrix looks like this:

	NEW SCHEME	OLD SCHEME
ENVIOUS STITCHER	$11,000 plus the pain of seeing others get $15,000	$10,000 plus the pleasure of knowing nobody gets more than you

Provided the utility Joe attaches to the payoff in the old scheme is greater than in the new one, Rawls's difference principle would rule out the new scheme *if he did not have the requirement that the players were not envious.* Because of the non-envy requirement, however, Rawls need never consider an objection to inequality of this sort.

Now, many people believe that the existence of inequalities is a large part of what gives rise to the tremendous productivity of modern economies. Rawls is saying, in effect, that provided these inequalities are just what is necessary to create the incentives that produce extra goods, even the worst-off person can be seen to be profiting from them: and, if that is true, only envy – which is, after all, a disreputable feeling! – could account for even the worst-off objecting to those inequalities.

6.9 A critique of Rawls

Those are the constraints on the players in the original position: they are self-interested but not envious, and they operate behind the veil of ignorance. The game requires them to agree *unanimously* on a system of ground rules for the state; those rules being the principles of justice. We need now to consider the argument for the claim that the two principles would be unanimously chosen by self-interested, non-envious rational people behind the veil of ignorance in the original position.

Rawls's arguments for this claim are long and complex. They depend, in essence, on comparing his two principles with other principles of justice – like utilitarianism, which says that what is just is what maximizes utility – that have been offered. He then shows why the players in the original position would prefer his two principles both to these other options, and, of course, to the state of nature.

But the core of his argument is that maximin considerations require people behind the veil of ignorance, who are ignorant of their own position, to accept only principles that protect the worst-off; that way they will be maximizing the worst that can happen to them, once the veil of ignorance is lifted and they discover what their position is to be. That is why they will want to guarantee themselves equality with others, unless it is essential to protect the worst-off.

Many kinds of criticisms can be raised of Rawls's defence of his two principles. Some of them have to do with detailed aspects of his presentation; and these I shall not consider. But there are crucial objections that can be made to his arguments, objections that go right to the heart of his project.

I shall mention one preliminary criticism only to put it aside: given the difference principle, Rawls is committed to inter-personal comparisons of utilities. This is because we are to consider all the possible social institutions and see which one does best for the worst-off. But since different people will be worst-off in different institutions, Rawls must be able to compare the utilities of different people. I have already said that there is reason to doubt that this can be done; but, for the moment, let us suppose that it can.

Rawls's argument is

(a) that his principles would be chosen as the result of a certain *n*-person non-zero-sum bargaining game, and

(b) that, once we understand why that game is constructed as it is, we shall see that this offers grounds for thinking that his principles are indeed just.

There are, therefore, two major sorts of criticism we can make of his work. First, we can argue – against (a) – that he has not shown that his principles would be chosen by rational people in the game he describes; second, we can argue – against (b) – that they would not be justified, even if we could show that they would be chosen in that game.

I will start with an objection to (a). Rawls claims that his principles would be chosen in the bargaining game because the players will find that they are preferable to the various alternative theories of justice he considers, provided they apply the maximin criterion. But there is no reason to suppose, as Rawls requires, that all reasonable people will adopt maximin as their rule in this game.

Let me try to explain why. I said earlier, in 6.4, that there were reasons for choosing a maximin strategy in two-person zero-sum games. The basic reason was that in a zero-sum game you can assume that your opponent is "out to get you;" and, thus, that you should act in such a way as to make you least vulnerable to your opponent's choices. But in non-zero-sum games, especially those involving more than two people, it is not at all clear why we should use the maximin rule. There is no reason to suppose your fellow players are out to get you, since;

(a) they are not envious, and
(b) because the game (like all n-person games) is non-zero-sum, "getting" you won't necessarily do them any good anyway.

Now, I also argued earlier that the idea of a zero-sum game cannot be made to apply in cases where the payoffs are, as Rawls requires, in utilities. But the point remains that, in the sort of bargaining game we are considering, there is generally no reason to think that you will prefer outcomes in which I have less utility to outcomes in which I have more.

Thus, suppose that we cannot make inter-personal comparisons of utility, so that we cannot compare Fay's utilities with Ray's. We can represent this state of affairs by using different units for each of us: call Fay's utilities fs and Ray's rs. If we cannot make inter-personal comparisons of utility, we cannot say how many fs is worth one r. Fay and Ray might be involved in a situation where the payoffs are like this:

	Ray	
Fay	(10 fs 5 rs)	(20 fs 8 rs)

In this case, even though we cannot compare the utilities of the two players, we *can* see that Fay has no reason to think that Ray will prefer outcomes where she has less, to outcomes where she has more. To put it another way, if we had any way of measuring how many units of Fay's utility were worth one unit of Ray's, whatever the ratio of f to r, this would not be a zero-sum game. It is hard to see why, in circumstances where this sort of non-competitive outcome is possible, reasonable people should adopt the maximin rule. And if the people in the original position would not adopt the maximin rule, it is not at all obvious that they would prefer Rawls's principles to other ways of deciding whether a state is just; for example, utilitarianism. Self-interested people will accept rules, like Rawls's two principles, which protect the worst-off people, if they are applying maximin, because they want to make sure that if they turn out to be the worst-off, their lives will be as good as they can be. But if they are not applying maximin – but gambling, for example, that they will *not* be the worst off – they might very well opt for a system of social justice that is less concerned for the poorest. And unless Rawls can show that *any* reasonable person in the original position will adopt maximin principles, there is no reason to suppose that they will all agree on his two principles.

There is, indeed, a reason for thinking that reasonable people in the original position might well do a different sort of calculation; a reason why someone might indeed be willing to gamble on an outcome different from Rawls's. In the original position, you are provided with a very great deal of general knowledge about people, so that though you do not know how any paricular person will act – because you are ignorant of everybody's goals and relative positions – you can make statistical predictions about the sorts of ways in which people will behave.

Suppose, in particular, your general knowledge told you that very few people would be really badly off if your society was run, not according to Rawls's principles, but according to the utilitarian principle that we should maximize average utility. (To do this, we should have to continue to assume, with Rawls, that inter-personal comparisons of utility were possible.) And suppose it also told you that if you adopted Rawls's principles, the worst-off would be better off, *but everybody else would be worse off.* Why should a self-interested person, who knows this, seek to protect the interests of the worst-off, when he or she is very unlikely to be one of them? To adopt maximin in this case would be to assign a very great deal of weight to an extremely unlikely outcome.

To make this question vivid, suppose, in particular, that one of the rules being considered in the original position would set up a compulsory lottery that made a few people who had the bad luck to get the wrong ticket into slaves who had to do some nasty but necessary jobs. Suppose, too, that the economists told us that this would produce a massive increase in the goods available to everybody else; and nobody would volunteer to do these jobs for the sorts of pay that our society could afford. If there were enough people, the chances of any particular person getting caught by the lottery could be very small indeed and everyone might accept the lottery. (Rational people often take small risks for large benefits; nobody would think it irrational to take the small risk of dying in a car accident to drive to fetch a million-dollar lottery prize.) Since no moral considerations prohibit the players in the original position from adopting this rule – and remember, the only requirement on them is that they mustn't be envious – there would, apparently, be no reason in these circumstances for Rawls to reject this option.

The general point is this: maximin may save you from the worst that can happen, but – especially in conditions of scarcity – it may also reduce your chances for a really worthwhile life once the veil of ignorance is lifted.

6.10 The status of the two principles

A second kind of objection to Rawls's theory focuses, as I have said, on the question: Why would the fact that the two principles could be derived in this sort of way show that they were justified? We posed a similar problem to Hobbes's theory, when we asked why the fact that we would have accepted certain arrangements in the state of nature should bind us now. As we saw, there were two main reasons why Hobbes was unable to reply: "Because you ought to keep your word." One was that we *didn't* give our word. The other was that there was no reason to think a purely self-interested person would be impressed by the claim that promises are binding; and Hobbes rules out appeal to moral principles in the state of nature, anyway.

But, unlike Hobbes, Rawls is free to make appeal to moral ideas in defense of his principles; and, in fact, he offers two sorts of reason for thinking that the fact that the two principles would be chosen in the bargaining game is an argument in favor of them. One is a moral reason, which depends on a conception of a fair bargain:

> Since everyone's well-being depends upon a scheme of cooperation without which no one could have a satisfactory life, the division of advantages should be such as to draw forth the willing cooperation of everyone taking part in it, including those less well situated.

The less well situated will quite reasonably refuse to cooperate if they think the way in which resources are allocated in the society is unfair. So only a system where the costs are fairly distributed is morally appealing. But, as Robert Nozick has pointed out, if we examine the way the deal looks from the point of view of the better situated, we may wonder whether the two principles really do reflect a fair deal. Nozick imagines the less well situated (or, as he says, "endowed") making their pitch:

> "Look, better endowed: you gain by cooperating with us. If you want our cooperation you'll have to accept reasonable terms. We suggest these terms: We'll cooperate with you only if we get *as much as possible.* That is, the terms of our cooperation should give us that maximal share such that, if it was tried to give us more, we'd end up with less."

Now Nozick points out that if it is fair for the least well-off to argue like this, it would seem to be fair for the better endowed to do likewise. But that would lead to a radically different arrangement from the one suggested by Rawls. On this scheme, we should allow an increase in wages for the poorest only if it benefited the richest: and that sounds not like justice but like exploitation!

Indeed, the very words that the worse-endowed have to utter sound not so much like the offer of a fair-minded person as the threats of a blackmailer: "We can spoil the whole system," the worse-endowed are saying, "so, if we don't get everything we can, we'll bring down the whole house of cards." Rawls's argument here is unconvincing.

A second way to try to justify the principles – a way we considered in the case of Hobbes – is to argue that they are principles you would choose if you were having to decide what principles to accept in getting out of the state of nature. I said about Hobbes that this argument seemed simply unsound: I, at least, would not choose Hobbes's potentially tyrannical sovereign over the life of the Mbuti pygmies. But the reason why this sort of argument will not work for Rawls is rather different.

In the original position we are behind a veil of ignorance, which deprives us of knowledge of our own goals and our relative positions. In a certain sense, everything that makes me distinctive is thus eliminated. Rawls cannot say that *I* would have chosen the two principles in the original position, because the veil of ignorance wipes *me* out. The fact that someone like me in the original position would choose a certain set of principles for regulating society gives me no special reason to like those principles: for that person doesn't know enough about me to take my interests properly into account.

It is a good thing, therefore, that Rawls does not offer the argument that we would choose the two principles if we were getting out of the state of nature. The reason why he doesn't is that his official explanation of the role of the original position is very different from Hobbes's discussions of the meetings in the assembly that gathers in the state of nature to institute the commonwealth.

What Rawls says is roughly this: the role of these reflections is to provide a way of organizing our moral intuitions about political life. Our basic ideas about politics are disorganized and often inconsistent. We need, therefore, to find a way of systematizing them in order to deal with the inconsistencies and root them out. One way to do this is to find a story – like the story of the original position – that allows us to derive our central moral ideas about political life, and then to make our ideas consistent by eliminating those notions that cannot be derived from that theory. We should move in our thinking back and forth between particular intuitions and the general theory, trimming each to the other, until we reach what Rawls calls **reflective equilibrium**. At reflective equilibrium our intuitions and our theory will coincide.

The difficulty with this view is not with the idea of reflective equilibrium; it is rather with the particular sort of theory that Rawls wants to bring into equilibrium with our intuitions. For unless there is some reason to think that the general theory supports the particular claims that are derived from it, there is no reason to eliminate from our inconsistent set of intuitions just those that don't fit with the theory.

Suppose we have a theory, T_1, from which we can derive all our moral intuitions except intuition I. We can always construct a different theory, T_2, from which we could derive all our moral intuitions, including I, *except those which are inconsistent with I.* (To do this, we simply look at the class of possible worlds in which T_1 is satisfied – the class, W, of worlds that are morally good according to T_1 – and construct T_2 as a theory that is satisfied in all the members of W in which I is true.) We cannot say I is to be rejected because it cannot be derived from a theory: it can be derived from T_2. True T_2 may not deliver some of our other intuitions, the ones inconsistent with I; but since our intuitions are inconsistent we have to give some of them up anyway. Still, just as there is no reason to reject I because it *cannot* be derived from T_1, there is no reason to accept it just because it *can* be derived from T_2. To reject I, on the basis that it can't be derived from T_1, we should need to have a reason for preferring T_1 to T_2 in the first place.

We can apply this analysis to Rawls's argument. Consider Jerry, who is a utilitarian. He derives his ideas of justice from considering what will maximize human utility: call this view T_1. Rawls advocates the two principles, deriving them from his bargaining game: call this T_2. These theories both fit with our moral intuitions in many cases, as Rawls would admit. Consider, now, some intuition that is derivable from Rawls's theory T_2, but not from Jerry's theory T_1: the intuition, say, that it is right to limit the income of the richest person, in order to make the poorest off slightly better off, even if the result is to make everybody in between much worse off also. Now, as I have just argued, to accept this intuition on the basis of T_2, we should need to have a reason for preferring Rawls's theory. But, as we have just seen, we have no good reason in Rawls's case to suppose that the derivation of the two principles from his bargaining game offers any independent reason for supposing those principles to be right.

6.11 Are the two principles right?

I have been concentrating on Rawls's derivation of his two principles. But even if his derivation of them was unsuccessful, they might still be correct. Anyone who finds utilitarianism attractive, however, will doubt that Rawls's theory can be right. Rawls would require us to avoid increasing the utility of everybody except the very worst-off group in the society a great deal, if it would not increase the utility of the worst-off. This is inconsistent with a very deeply ingrained moral idea: the idea that, all things considered, it is better that people have more rather than less of what they want.

There is, however, a more fundamental respect in which Rawls's theory can be challenged. Rawls's full theory has a feature which I have not so far mentioned. It is that he has, over and above the two principles, a rule for the **priority of liberty**. This says, in essence, that certain fundamental rights – which, taken together, he calls *liberty* – cannot be limited for the sake of anything else. Liberty, Rawls says, can be restricted only for the sake of liberty. This can occur in two ways:

(a) a less extensive liberty must strengthen the total system of liberty shared by all;
(b) a less than equal liberty must be acceptable to those with the lesser liberty.

Thus, suppose – rather implausibly! – that everybody would be richer if freedom of speech was restricted to politicians. Rawls would say that, in those circumstances, we could not limit freedom of speech, *however much better off everybody would become.* Suppose, on the other hand, that if everybody was free to say what they knew about a country's defenses, then an enemy would be able to take over, and that would lead to the abolition of free speech altogether. Restricting freedom of speech would be allowed in this case because it was necessary to protect the system of liberty.

There is no doubt then that Rawls intends us to take certain rights – the ones that he calls "liberty" – very seriously. But, as Robert Nozick has argued, Rawls's way of thinking about these rights goes against the grain of some of our deepest moral ideas. The reason is that Rawls's principles are what Nozick calls **end-result principles**: for Rawls, a society with a certain system of liberty and a particular distribution of goods is just provided it fits a certain pattern, independently of how it came about. Now Nozick argues that most of us favor what he calls **historical principles** of justice. A historical principle is one that holds "that past circumstances or actions of people can create differential entitlements or differential deserts."

It is easy to give examples of historical principles. Thus, as Nozick points out, if there are people in prison for war crimes, we don't assess the justice of the punishment by looking only at what resources the criminals have, and comparing them with everybody else's share. We think it relevant to ask whether they did something to *deserve* a lesser share of the good things of life.

A familiar, and less serious, historical principle governs our thinking about the fairness of certain lotteries. Lotteries organized by state or national governments to raise funds change the distribution of goods in the society. Furthermore, they do so without regard for the desert of the winners, allocating money simply on the basis of a random process. But, provided the lottery is fairly conducted, most people hold that the resulting re-distribution of goods is as fair as the original distribution.

This sort of historical principle is often invoked in assessing the justice of certain legal institutions, as we shall see in the next chapter. But its importance here is that if some of the principles of justice are historical principles, then Rawls's two principles are certainly not the whole story. In particular, if some of our rights – say, our rights to property – derive from history – say, from the way we acquired the property – then Rawls's theory of justice would fail to capture this important fact. Robert Nozick's contribution to recent political philosophy has been to provide a vigorous defence of historical principles of justice.

6.12 Beginning with rights

Though Rawls insists on the priority of liberty, the major thrust of his book deals with questions about when allocations of money and goods are just. He is concerned mostly to argue about what is called **distributive justice**, which is the set of issues that have to do with what makes the distribution of resources – who has what goods – in a society right or wrong. Nozick's main concern, however, is with rights. The first sentence of his book *Anarchy, State and Utopia* runs:

> Individuals have rights, and there are things no person or group may do to
> them (without violating their rights).

Nozick's aim in the book is to consider the question of the justification of political authority from the starting point of this claim. Once we know what rights people have, we can ask whether a state could be set up without violating those rights. If it could not, then the justification for the state would require at least that we showed that it offered us something morally valuable to outweigh these rights violations. But even if it could, that would still not show that any actual state is justified, since it might have been set up in a way that violated people's rights.

Like Hobbes, Nozick begins with a state of nature: but unlike Hobbes, it is a state of nature in which people should and do respect certain moral ideas. In fact, Nozick's state of nature is patterned after the one conceived by the English philosopher John Locke in his *Second Treatise on Government*, which was first published in 1690. In this essay, Locke wrote that the state of nature was a state of perfect freedom and equality.

> But though this be a *state of liberty*, yet *it is not a state of licence* . . . The
> *state of nature* has a law of nature to govern it, which obliges every one:
> and reason, which is that law, teaches all mankind, who will but consult it,
> that being all *equal and independent*, no one ought to harm another in his
> life, health, liberty, or possessions . . . Every one, as he is *bound to
> preserve himself*, and not to quit his station wilfully, so by the like reason,
> when his own preservation comes not in competition, ought he, as much
> as he can, *to preserve the rest of mankind*, and may not, unless it be to do
> justice on an offender, take away, or impair the life, or what tends to the
> preservation of the life, the liberty, health, limb, or goods of another.

Nozick's list of rights also includes the right not to be attacked or killed when you are doing no harm and the right to keep your property and to do with it what you like, so long as you don't violate any one else's rights in the process.

Nozick agrees with Locke – and disagrees with Hobbes – that even without government these rights exist and that we have the right to enforce them in this way. But he and Locke also agree that there are many "inconveniences of the state of nature". Locke immediately argues that the "proper remedy" for these inconveniences is "*civil government*"; but Nozick sets out to ask the question whether there is anything less than the institution of a state that will do the job.

One reason that Nozick adopts this more conservative approach is that he takes **anarchism** – the claim that the state can never be justified – to be a serious option. Against an anarchist, especially one who agrees with Locke that we have many rights in the state of nature, it would be important to show how a state of a certain sort could arise without violating anyone's rights. Otherwise the anarchists really might be right in thinking that the state was morally unjustifiable.

Since you know how Hobbes and Rawls justified the state, you might expect Nozick to defend his theory by arguing, like them, that people would choose in the state of nature to hand over certain rights to the state, and come, by an agreement to "institute the common-wealth." But Nozick proceeds in a different way.

He begins by considering how rational and self-interested people in the Lockean state of nature could come to make deals with each other to form what he calls **protective associations**. These are groups of people who agree to help each other to deal with anyone outside the organization who poses a threat to anyone within it; and to settle conflicts between members of the association where necessary. The key point which distinguishes protective associations from organized banditry is that such associations seek to enforce those rights which people have in the state of nature and to enforce them according to the laws of nature: unlike a protection racket, a protective association has a basis in morality.

Using the idea of a protective association Nozick offers an explanation of the origins of the state in the state of nature. He seeks to show how

> without anyone having this in mind, the self-interested and rational actions of persons in a Lockean state of nature will lead to single protective agencies dominant over geographical territories . . .

The dominant protective association of a region will claim, according to Nozick, a monopoly of the sort of authority that I said at the beginning of this chapter characterizes the state. A dominant protective association of Nozick's kind he calls a **minimal state**. It is *minimal* because it is "limited to the narrow functions of protection against force, theft, fraud, enforcement of contracts and so on." This puts it in stark contrast with Rawls's ideal state, where the government spends a lot of its time on issues of distribution of income, in order to ensure that the difference principle is obeyed.

Now the reason why Nozick seeks to show that something very like a state can develop in this way is that he is convinced that a theory of justice must be based on historical principles. And the only way you can tell if a state is justified on historical principles is to see whether it was produced by a just process.

Plainly, if Nozick is correct in saying what our rights are in the state of nature, and correct in arguing that we could end up with a state without violating those rights, then he has made a convincing case against anarchism. He has not shown that any particular actual state is justified, but he has shown that the anarchist is wrong to claim that no state could be justified.

But Nozick also claims that the sort of state that would be derived in this way from the Lockean state of nature is the *only* sort of state that can be justified; and that is a much more doubtful claim. Even if we conceded that any other, non-minimal state involved the violation of rights, it would only follow that the state was unjustified *all things considered* if there were no compelling moral points in the state's favor. If a non-minimal state offered us things that were morally valuable and outweighed the violations of rights, then we might still think it right to develop and defend it. In saying that only a minimal state is justified, Nozick supposes that only a very restricted class of moral considerations can be brought to bear in deciding whether a state is just.

Just how minimal the minimal state is – and just how restricted are the moral considerations that Nozick brings to bear – becomes clear if we turn from Nozick's account of the minimal state to his theory of distributive justice.

6.13   The entitlement theory

Nozick's theory of distributive justice is very different from Rawls's. He calls his view of distributive justice an **entitlement theory** of justice. In outline it consists of four claims:

1. A person who acquires property in accordance with the principle of justice in acquisition is entitled to that holding.
2. A person who acquires property in accordance with the principle of justice in transfer, from someone else entitled to the holding, is entitled to the holding.
3. A person who acquires property in accordance with the principle of rectification of holdings is entitled to that property.
4. No one is entitled to property except by (repeated) applications of 1, 2, and 3.

The **principle of justice in acquisition** tells you what entitles you to come to possess something that does not already belong to anybody else; the **principle of justice in transfer** tells you what entitles you to possess something that used to be owned by somebody else; and the **principle of rectification of holdings** tells you how you can become entitled to something because someone else got it from you in violation of justice in acquisition or transfer. Nozick's treatment of these principles is rather sketchy, but he does say enough to suggest a plausible line of objection.

We can begin by asking what consequences Nozick draws from the fact that an action would violate somebody's rights. He suggests that we could interpret this as meaning not that avoiding these violations is a goal of our moral lives, but that it is what he calls a "side-constraint" on our actions. **Side-constraints** are boundaries that it is always morally wrong to cross. We may pursue all sorts of goals, both moral and personal, but, on this view, we may only do so in ways that avoid violating the rights of others.

If that is so, and given his entitlement theory, he is committed to some fairly surprising claims about what anyone, let alone a government, can do. Thus, for example, suppose you are entitled to the drugs in your medicine cabinet – you got them justly from someone who was entitled to them – and they are the only drugs in town that can save a child with a serious biochemical disorder. You are out of town. If respect for property rights constitutes a side-constraint on action, then it would be wrong for any one, including a judge, to order that the drugs be taken and used to save the child without your consent. The child has no right to the drug and nor has the judge. In a minimal state the child would have to be allowed to die in order not to offend against property rights. It won't do to say that the child has a right to life, which we would be ignoring if we respected your property rights, as Nozick himself points out.

> A right to life is not a right to whatever one needs to live; other people may have rights over these other things. At most, a right to life would be the right to strive for whatever one needs to live, provided that having it does not violate anyone else's rights

(along with, of course, the right not to be killed when you pose no threat to others.)

This objection to Nozick's view was raised by the American philosopher Judith Jarvis Thomson. It is a crucial objection because it undermines one of the most startling claims that Nozick makes in his book, which is that any taxation which is intended to even out inequalities in resources – any *purely re-distributive taxation* – is morally indefensible. For this conclusion depends on the assumption that it is always wrong to disregard property-rights for any purpose whatsoever. For Nozick, respect for property-rights is a side-constraint on the state's actions.

Thomson points out also that Nozick is not entirely consistent in his application of the idea of rights as side-constraints. Thus she observes that when he is discussing the rights of animals, Nozick leaves open the possibility that we can "save 10,000 animals from excruciating suffering by inflicting some slight discomfort" on an innocent person. But if innocent people have a right not to be discomforted against their will, and this right is a side-constraint on our actions, then we ought never to consider saving these animals (provided not saving them does not infringe on their rights). If rights are side-constraints then they cannot be violated to achieve otherwise desirable goals. This makes them, in effect, as Thomson says, infinitely stringent: that is, no moral consideration, however weighty (apart, perhaps, from another right) will justify over-riding a person's rights to their property.

> This wobbling in the degree of stringency of rights . . . makes it very unclear just how Nozick is to get from his starting point, which is that we have rights, to his thesis that a government which imposes taxes for the purpose of redistribution violates the rights of its citizens. . . . [For] surely it is plain as day that property rights are not infinitely stringent.

And if they are not infinitely stringent, Nozick has lost the basis of his claim that only the minimal state can be morally justified. For it is the infinite stringency of property rights that limits the ways in which the state can justify taxation to the minimal tasks that Nozick allows.

This is only the beginning of a discussion of Nozick's work, which includes some very interesting applications of game theory. But it does suggest that Nozick would need to offer more arguments before we should accept his claim that our fundamental rights include rights to use our property that cannot be over-ridden by any other moral purpose. That is, perhaps, a good thing: if Nozick were right, every state in the present world would be in serious violation of its citizens' rights, just because it uses tax revenue to pay for education!

6.14 Conclusion

In this chapter, I have looked at some questions about the over-arching institutions of the state. From the very earliest times, philosophers have asked such questions about the nature and the justification of the institutions of their own societies. We have seen that the question of the justification of political authority was raised naturally by the question: What is a state? Hobbes and Rawls and Nozick all agree that there are certain demands that we should make of a state if it is to be justified in its monopoly of coercive power. But Rawls's and Nozick's conditions for a just state are goals to aim at, not conditions that must be met if there is to be a state at all. I shall take up again in the next chapter the question whether any system that meets Hobbes's very minimal demands can be called a "state." Even if we reject his claim that the sovereign may do anything, provided the citizens are better off than they would be in the state of nature, we might still be able to accept his view that a system that meets this condition deserves to be called a "state."

In the next chapter I will look at an institution within the state, namely the legal system. With a grasp of the central issues of political philosophy, we can turn, now, to the philosophy of law.

7 Law

What is a law?

When should we obey the law?

When is punishment morally justified?

7.1 Introduction

Governments in many countries and at many times have made laws that are morally repugnant. Many governments, for example, have wanted their citizens to obey laws that were racist, discriminating between citizens simply on the basis of their supposed "racial" origins. Sometimes – regrettably, not often enough – citizens of these countries have been so outraged by these racist laws that they have sought to have them changed. And when legal means of changing the law have been exhausted, some have chosen to resist their governments by civil disobedience. That is, they have set out to resist these evil laws by deliberate acts of law-breaking. In civil disobedience law-breaking is usually undertaken in order to draw attention to the evil law, to express a citizen's repugnance to it, and to create political pressure to get it repealed. Sometimes, civil disobedience involves breaking the hated law itself: laws segregating public transport were broken by their opponents, both as an expression of their rejection of racial segregation, and in an attempt to force the states and municipalities to change their laws.

But there are some evil laws we cannot oppose by breaking those very laws. If, for example, you thought that a law requiring capital punishment for thefts above a certain value (which was common in Europe until quite recently) was evil, there was no obvious way you could break that law. You might have tried to stop the government executing convicts, but this would probably have been too difficult and too dangerous. Even where you *can* break the evil law itself, doing so may not be enough to force the government to change. So civil disobedience often involves breaking laws – for example, laws against blocking highways – that most citizens generally respect and regard as justified.

As we saw in the last chapter, philosophers have sought to justify the existence of the state by arguments that appeal to moral ideas: the ideas, for example, of keeping your word (in Hobbes) or of equality (in Rawls) or of rights (in Nozick). We did not come to a simple conclusion about when the state is justified. But – unless you elect to be an anarchist – you will accept, in the end, that sometimes a government meets the general conditions that entitle it to a monopoly of the justified use of force. So that *if* a government is justified in using force to coerce citizens into meeting their political obligations, then those citizens have a duty to obey the laws it promulgates . . . at least until they have a good countervailing reason not to do so.

It follows, then, that anyone who undertakes civil disobedience in a society whose government meets the conditions of justification for the exercise of coercive power ought to think carefully about whether their actions are justified. For in such a state every citizen gains benefits from the state's existence, and, as Rawls argued, fairness requires that the burdens of a system be shared as well as the benefits.

Now in many real cases, it is doubtful that the state meets even minimal conditions of justification. Indeed, a state many of whose laws are racially discriminatory is likely to lose its justification on any view that says, with Rawls and Nozick, that a state must give equal recognition to every citizen's basic political rights. So one answer to the question "When is civil disobedience justified?" is to say that civil disobedience is justified where a government has ceased to be justified, because it fails to meet the minimum conditions for legitimacy. Many people felt that the Nazi government in Germany did not meet those minimum conditions necessary to make its laws morally binding on its citizens. Civil disobedience is justified in such a state because the government lacks overall legitimacy: it has no moral call on the citizen's obedience.

We may still, of course, have moral reasons for doing what the regulations enforced in such a state require: the fact that your government lacks legitimacy is no reason to feel free to commit murder. We may also feel that it is prudent to obey a wicked government, because it carries out its threats. If, however, the government lacks legitimacy we have no moral duty to obey a law simply because it is the law.

But this is a rather extreme case. Not everybody who believes some particular law is wicked thinks that the whole state that made the law is so morally bankrupt as to have lost all justification. Those Americans who marched in the great Civil Rights marches of the sixties largely maintained their faith in the rightness of the American Constitution and the legitimacy of the American state. They believed that racially discriminatory laws were not only wrong but inconsistent with what was best in the American political system: many of them thought – rightly, as it turned out – that the government and the courts would eventually act to overturn segregationist laws, provided there was enough continuing political pressure.

The Civil Rights marchers would have disagreed, no doubt, about what it was that made civil disobedience in defiance of racist laws right. But some of them argued that some rules are so bad that they cannot be regarded as laws at all. A law, on such a view, is a regulation that is legitimately promulgated by a legitimate state. Civil disobedience can be justified, these people claimed, not only when the state lacks overall legitimacy – because it fails to meet certain minimum moral standards – but also where particular rules, proposed as laws, are illegitimate – because *they* fail to meet certain minimum moral standards. In these cases, they said, it can be proper to practice civil disobedience, in order to get the state to acknowledge that these particular rules do not count as laws.

The view that a rule has to meet certain moral conditions before it can be regarded as a law at all is the central tenet of what have called **Natural Law** theories. They are called Natural Law theories because they are associated with the view that valid laws in human societies are justified by their being based on something more fundamental than social customs or human agreements. For Natural Law theorists (or "Natural Lawyers") valid laws are natural in the sense that they are not man-made. Natural Law theorists have usually held, like St. Thomas Aquinas, the most influential European theologian and philosopher of the Middle Ages, that the contents of Natural Law, the moral boundaries within which legitimate laws must fall, can be discovered by reason. Laws, Aquinas said, must be *ordinances of reason*; that is, they must be rules that we can see, by using those capacities for reasoning that all normal human beings have by nature, to be right. Indeed, Aquinas defined a law as "nothing other than an ordinance of reason for the common good, made by whatever authority has the community in its care." For Aquinas the contents of Natural Law were the "Laws of Nature" that I discussed in connection with Hobbes.

Now many people who supported the Civil Rights marches, and were even in favor of civil disobedience in order to induce the Congress and the President to enforce the civil rights of Afro-Americans, would have rejected a Natural Law theory. They would have said that some segregationist laws were perfectly valid as laws and that the fact that they were unjust, because they were racist, was an argument for getting them changed, not a reason for denying that they were laws in the first place.

In arguing thus, these supporters of the Civil Rights movement were following in the steps of the philosophy of **legal positivism**. For a positivist, the task of **analytic jurisprudence**, which is the systematic study of laws and legal institutions, is to discover what the laws of a country are, independently of whether or not they meet moral standards. Generally, the positivists have argued that the laws of a state are those regulations issued by the government and enforced by its monopoly on coercion.

The nineteenth-century British legal philosopher John Austin, who was one of the leading figures in the development of legal positivism, defined laws simply as the "commands of the sovereign." Since Austin defined a command as an order accompanied by a threat, any rule that was promulgated by the legitimate government – the sovereign power in a state – and was enforced by the use of the state's monopoly on coercion was a law, however good or bad it was. As Austin said, in a famous passage of his book, *The Province of Jurisprudence Determined*:

> The existence of law is one thing; its merit or demerit another. Whether it be or be not is one enquiry; whether it be conformable to an assumed standard, is a different enquiry. A law, which actually exists, is a law, though we happen to dislike it . . .

It might seem that this dispute is simply a matter of definition: and a definition of a word is to be decided by asking how competent speakers of the language use it. But, as we shall see, there may be reasons for preferring one definition; reasons more complex than the fact that it reflects the way the word is ordinarily used.

7.2 Defining "law" I: Positivism and Natural Law
Nevertheless, we must still *start* by trying to find a definition that accurately reflects the way the word is used. So let us ask how we do in fact decide whether a rule is a law. Like

AQUINAS

St. Thomas Aquinas (c. 1224-1274) was born at Roccasecca in Italy and educated by the Benedictine monks of Monte Cassino, going on to university in Naples, before he entered the Dominican order – much against the wishes of his family – in 1244. He then studied philosophy and theology at Paris for some years before going to work with Albertus Magnus at Cologne in Germany. From Cologne he went back to teach at the University of Paris, before returning to study and write in Rome. In the decade beginning in 1259, Aquinas worked for his order and for the Papacy; and before the end of his life he had come full circle, teaching again at the University of Paris and at the University of Naples. Aquinas died at Fossanova in Italy on his way to a Church Council in Lyons, France, and was canonized by Pope John XXII in 1323. Like all Christian philosophers of his era, Aquinas was very deeply influenced by his study of Aristotle. Aquinas distinguished philosophy from theology by the fact that theology starts with judgments accepted on the basis of religious faith, which means that they are beliefs which are accepted only because the believer chooses to accept them. Philosophy, on the other hand, takes judgments from evidence and reason,

accepting only what they require. In his ethics Aquinas also placed a great deal of emphasis on the role of reason: to be good, he argued, is to regulate your actions and your feelings by your reason. Aquinas wrote many works apart from the massive *Summa Theologiae* – a compendium of philosophical and theological arguments on many topics – including commentaries on Aristotle and on the Bible; and he remains one of the leading authorities in Catholic theology.

---

many philosophical questions, this question seems very difficult in theory, even though we appear to know how to answer it in practical cases. We all think we can recognize the laws of our own society with no difficulty. Yet, presented with an imagined society, very different from ours, we may be unclear whether we want to call something a law or not. Consider, for example, the following case:

> The Oligarch family seized power in Doulia twenty years ago: they have consolidated their power over the unwilling but terrified populace with the help of the well-paid thugs who make up the "army" and the "police"; and they now enforce a system of rules whose sole aim is, they openly admit, to further their own interests.

It seems to me that we would not want to call these rules "laws," even if the threats the Oligarchs made were carried out by "courts." And, given the discussion of the previous chapter, we can say why.

The reason is that there are certainly *some* minimum moral standards that someone must meet if the rules they issue are to be regarded as laws. For there are some minimal standards that people must meet if they are to be regarded as forming a government at all. As we saw in our discussion of the idea of the state, the bare power to enforce your wishes, without any right to do so, does not make you a legitimate government; certainly, the bare power to enforce its wishes does not distinguish government from successful banditry.

But positivists can still say that, even conceding that moral questions are involved in deciding who *has* the authority to govern, once we have identified the government, any rules they promulgate, however morally repugnant, are still laws.

It is important that this is a concession. For it means that in deciding whether some rule is a law, we must rely on at least some moral claims: the claims, namely, that are needed in order to distinguish between power, which is a purely factual question, and authority, which is an evaluative one.

Of course, if we accept the positivist's concession, we do not have to go so far as the Natural Lawyers. For, once it is clear that a government does not lack overall legitimacy, we certainly call some of the rules it promulgates and enforces "laws," even if they are quite evil. Even those of us who think that the laws of slavery were morally appalling still recognize that they *were* laws: like Austin, we can say that "the existence of law is one thing; its merit or demerit another."

How, then, could the Oligarchs change their way of controlling Doulia in order to make themselves a legitimate government, so that their rules might become valid laws? If Hobbes was right, the minimum they need to do is to succeed in ensuring that their citizens are better off than they would be in a state of nature. But it seems pretty clear that this would not be enough. Even in the case as I originally described it the Oligarchs might truly claim that the citizens were better off than without any government at all. There is no reason to think that the interests of the Oligarchs conflict with guaranteeing some degree of good order: an ordered citizenry is easier to keep in control. All they require, perhaps, is that everybody should give a few days of unpaid service in the Doulian gold-mines each year. So their "police" might enforce rules against murder, just so as to ensure the supply of orderly labor.

Even if the Oligarchs met Hobbes's condition, then, they could still be in no position to claim that their orders were laws. But it is also true that we would probably not say that what the Oligarchs were running was a state: so that we can now see that Hobbes's minimum conditions for being a state are too undemanding.

So what else would they have to do? One answer to this question is provided by Aquinas, in the passage I cited earlier: he said, you will recall, that a law was "nothing other than an ordinance of reason for the common good, made by whatever authority has the community in its care." The key thing that is lacking in the case of the Oligarchs is any concern for the common good. Their rules are intended entirely for their own convenience. Even their enforcement of good order is intended only to make their own lives easier. They do not even pretend that their rules are made "for the common good."

Our definition of the state, then, must require not only that a legitimate government should have the power to enforce its rules but that its authority to do so should derive from the fact that at least some of its regulations aim at the common good.

We do not require, however, that the laws the Oligarchs make should actually *succeed* in promoting the common good. Perhaps the Oligarchs believe, wrongly, that the gods will bring misfortune on Doulia if they allow people to sing on Wednesdays. A rule against singing on Wednesdays will not promote the general good. All it will do is to deprive people of the pleasure of song one day a week. Perhaps the Oligarchs are so incompetent that almost every rule they make fails to contribute to the common good. Still, if they genuinely believed their rules were for the common good, we might call their rules "laws."

If we do not require that the Oligarchs' rules should succeed in promoting the common good, nor do we require that the *only* aim that they pursue with the power of the state should be the common good. There are many states with systems of law that are strongly biased in favor of one sectional interest; and some, though fewer, where this is acknowledged to be so. But provided at least a significant part of what the Oligarchs do is aimed at the common good, we can say that Doulia is a state and they are its legitimate government.

Of course, they are not a very good government. And Rawls and Nozick would both insist that we can make moral demands of them beyond simply doing the minimum to ensure legitimacy. But it seems that now they not only have the power to control the citizens of Doulia, but also meet enough conditions to be recognized as the political authority there.

We might suggest, then, with this understanding of "legitimacy," that

> Laws are rules, backed by the threat of force, promulgated by a legitimate government to regulate the behavior of people subject to its authority.

What this means is that all that is morally required to turn a system of rules into a legal system is that it should be enforced by people who both have the power to enforce them, and seek to exercise that power, at least sometimes, for the common good. But there are compelling reasons for thinking this is too simple an answer.

7.3 Defining "law" II: Legal systems and the variety of laws

Suppose that the Oligarchs, recognizing and regretting that they are not legitimate, want to take the first steps in the direction of legitimacy. They announce some rules that they claim are aimed at the common good: murder is proscribed and theft is banned; and they decide to replace forced labor with taxes. From time to time they announce more such rules. And they say what the penalties will be for breaking them. When people are found to be disobeying these rules and the Oligarchs hear of it, they have them locked up or beaten, usually exacting the penalties that they originally threatened.

But these rules are not systematically enforced, and there is no system for investigating when the rules have been broken; no way of objecting that a punishment is not the one that they announced; and no procedure for trying to persuade them that you did not commit the offense they are punishing you for. Furthermore, some of the rules are inconsistent with each other and the Oligarchs are inclined to punish someone who breaks one rule in order to keep another. Doulia might still be a state, but these rules would not be laws.

The reason is that laws have to be part of a *legal system*; and to be a system of laws a set of rules has to be both

(a) systematically organized, and
(b) systematically enforced.

The unsystematic character of the Doulian system shows that my first attempt at a definition of law needs to be modified to take into account the systematic character of law.

But my definition is inadequate for another reason. When we think of laws, we very generally think first of criminal laws. In the legal systems with which we are familiar, however, there are many other sorts of laws, some of which are not backed with threats at all. There are two very important kinds of such laws.

First of all, there are laws like the laws governing the writing of wills. These laws – which I shall call **constitutive laws** – allow people to do things – in this case, making a will; but they do not punish anyone who does not chose to take advantage of them. There is no penalty for not writing a will. Of course, if you do not write a will, the state will take it upon itself to allocate your property when you die. But this is not a punishment (and it is certainly not a threat of force against a dead person!) but simply an activity that is required because the property of a dead person must belong to somebody. Once you do write a will, and provided it is properly drafted, the state will recognize it; and if anybody tries to take away the property you have left to your children, they will be punished by the criminal laws against theft. But the regulations about the making of wills only govern people who chose to be governed by them.

Laws that govern wills allow citizens to enter into legally defined relationships – they *constitute* those relationships. In essence, they allow people to use the state to help regulate their relations with each other. Many areas of civil law, such as the laws of marriage and contract, are in this respect like the regulations that tell you how you must draft a will.

Notice that even though we do not *have* to make wills or contracts or marriages, if we *do*, we place legal obligations on ourselves and on others; and those obligations may be enforced by threats. Nevertheless the laws that tell you how to get married, or make a will or a contract, differ importantly from criminal laws, because they largely govern the behavior of people who have chosen to accept certain legal responsibilities – the executor of a will, the married couple, the parties to a contract – and are not binding on citizens who do not choose to accept them.

The second class of rules that are not backed by force either are the laws that determine how certain legal institutions should operate. There are many such laws. One class, for example, says which courts should deal with which sorts of problems: these are laws governing **jurisdiction**. If a state judge tries a case that should really be decided under federal law, he or she will not be punished. Rather, the judgement will simply be set aside by a higher court. The rules about how judges should try cases are certainly laws, but they are not all backed by threat of force. (Of course, some laws governing the behavior of judges – those against taking bribes, for example – *are* backed by the state's coercive power.) Let us call laws that regulate how courts should act, but that are not backed by threat of force, **institutional laws.**

The British philosopher H.L.A. Hart, one of the modern defenders of legal positivism, has developed a theory of the kinds of structure we require in a system of rules if they are to be properly regarded as laws; and that theory both recognizes the systematic character of the legal system and allows for the existence of constitutive and institutional laws.

7.4 Hart: The elements of a legal system

Hart begins by asking us to imagine a society very like Mbuti society. There are many rules that govern Mbuti life, rules that are recognized and largely obeyed by most Mbuti people. But there are no officially organized sanctions for breaches of these rules. People who disobey them regularly will be criticized and, perhaps, in the end, ostracized. But there are no judges, no policemen, no courts. These basic rules – rules that are necessary if people are to live together in a society at all – Hart calls **primary rules.** They say what a member of the society may or may not do. Typically, there will be primary rules against taking other people's property, against using unnecessary violence in disputes, and against breaking one's freely-made promises. Primary rules include more than the precepts of morality: for example, because morality does not determine exactly how property should be transferred between generations. But many of the primary rules will be moral rules: rules against murder and lying, for example. According to Hart, this minimum structure of primary rules captures the truth in Natural Law theories; any group of people that failed to recognize even these basic rules would hardly constitute a society at all.

Primary rules are not enforced by officials; as in the case of the Mbuti, there may be no state to enforce them. And, in a society with only primary rules, there is plainly no legal system.

Now the Doulians certainly have more than primary rules, because they do have some officials – what they call "policemen" and "policewomen," for example. But, as we have seen, they still do not have a legal system. Hart argues that what we need to add to the system of primary rules in order to create a legal system is not merely a set of sanctions enforced by officials – otherwise the Doulian system would be a system of law – but a number of other kinds of rules. These other rules he calls **secondary rules.**

Secondary rules, Hart says, "are in a sense parasitic upon" primary rules.

> For they provide that human beings may by doing or saying certain things introduce new rules of the primary type, extinguish or modify old ones, or in other ways determine their incidence or control their operations.

Hart sees secondary rules as introduced to meet a number of deficiencies in the system of purely primary rules that the Mbuti have; deficiencies that would need to be remedied if the Mbuti were to move from a society organized in small groups to the larger-scale of society in which almost all human beings now live.

The first deficiency that Hart identifies is that a system of primary rules is *uncertain*. What he means by this can be made clear enough in the Mbuti case. For a system of primary rules has two kinds of uncertainty. One kind of uncertainty arises when it is not clear, on the basis of the evidence available, which of two rules applies in a given case.

Suppose, for example, that the Mbuti held that a man's bow and arrows should be inherited by the son who is the best hunter. And suppose they also held that a person could give away (or sell) his own bow and arrows. Then when a man died, it would not always be clear who his bow and arrows should go to.

Now suppose that in some particular case everybody knew that the best hunter in a certain family was the eldest son. If one of his younger sons claimed that he had been given the bow and arrows before his father died, then this younger son could claim that the rule of inheritance need not be invoked. For, at the moment of death, the bow and arrows no longer belonged to the father. There would now be a dispute between the two sons about who owned the bow, and there would be no mechanism for deciding who should get it.

But systems of primary rules are open to another kind of uncertainty; a kind of uncertainty of an even more troubling kind. For in a system of primary rules, even if the facts are agreed, there is no way of deciding, in a disputed case, what rules actually apply.

For example, if the eldest son claimed that there was a rule that said that a father could not give his bow and arrows away on his death-bed – that it was wrong, by Mbuti custom, to do so – there would be no way of checking to see whether this was, in fact, a rule of their society. There would also be nobody who could decide definitively whether the eldest son was right and then enforce that decision.

The first kind of secondary rule, therefore, that Hart argues a legal system must have is what he calls a **rule of recognition**. A rule of recognition is a rule that tells us how the question whether a rule *is* a law in our society is to be decided. In the United States, for example, as in all modern societies, there is a highly complex set of rules of recognition. These rules of recognition say, very roughly, that a rule is a Federal law if it is

(a) a Constitutional provision, or
(b) a law created by the Constitutionally defined process of law-making, or
(c) a rule that was established by the courts in the common law tradition that grows out of the legal tradition that pre-existed the Constitution and that has not been explicitly cancelled or superseded by rules made under the Constitution.

Similar considerations determine whether a rule is a law in the several states. It also tells us which laws are to be applied in cases where there is conflict; in some matters, federal laws, and in others, state laws take precedence.

The rules of recognition of a society, even of a modern industrial society, do not need to be written; British judges do not rely on a written document telling them to apply laws made by the British Parliament and signed by the Queen. The role of the rules of recognition in the British system depends on the fact that judges have learned, in the course of their education and their practice as lawyers, how the legal system decides whether a rule is a valid rule of law.

But rules of recognition are not the only secondary rules that are needed to turn a collection of primary rules into a legal system. A second class of secondary rules is needed to remedy a second defect of the Mbuti system; namely, that there is no way for the Mbuti to *change* their rules explicitly. Rules of this kind – **rules of change**, Hart calls them – are embodied in the American Constitution in the sections setting out the powers of the President, the legislature and the judiciary. Once more the position is complex, and can only be very roughly described in a brief compass: but one rule of recognition says, roughly, that if a rule has

(a) been through the procedures necessary to be passed by the legislature, and
(b) been signed by the President (or returned to the legislature and passed by a majority sufficient to override a Presidential veto),

it will be recognized by the courts, provided it is not in conflict with the Constitution. If, in interpreting these laws, the courts declare that certain rules follow from the statutes explicitly passed by the Congress or from the Constitution itself, then

(c) those rules become incorporated in the law also.

Finally, Hart argues, there is one other deficiency in the system of primary rules exemplified in Mbuti society: it is highly inefficient. When there is a dispute about whether a rule applies, there is no settled procedure for determining the issue; and even if it is clear which rule applies, there is no one who is given the job of stopping offenders, or punishing them.

The addition of rules of recognition and rules of change would not, by themselves, remedy this deficiency. The reason is obvious enough. I have already talked of which rules courts recognize; and obviously, what is needed to gain the advantages of the other secondary rules is a set of rules that create something like courts. These rules should determine which individuals have the task of deciding, in which cases, which rules apply. This third sort of secondary rule Hart calls a **rule of adjudication**.

In most societies it will also be thought necessary to assign to somebody the task of enforcing the decisions in those cases, since there is an obvious advantage in having officials – like bailiffs, police officers and prison-guards – who make sure both that the decisions of the courts are carried out and that those who ignore the rules are punished.

But Hart says that these further officials are not essential to the existence of a legal system. In a small-scale society it might simply be that, once the courts had decided that someone was to be punished, anybody could punish them. What is required for a legal system is only that there be officials charged – by the rules of adjudication – with determining what the rules are, and a relatively clear set of principles – the rules of recognition and change – by which they make those decisions.

If you believe that the element of coercion by the government is central to the idea of law, then you will want to add to Hart's claims the thesis that the rules which the courts decide are applicable should be enforced by the government, through its agents. And so you might want to add a fourth kind of rule – **rules of enforcement**, say – that create a class of officials who have the responsibility of punishing offenders and enforcing the judgements of the courts. But you can still agree with Hart's basic definition of a legal system as "the union of primary and secondary rules."

In line with Hart's proposals, then, we can thus modify my original definition of laws:

> Laws are rules, backed by the threat of force, promulgated by a legitimate government to regulate the behavior of people subject to its authority, and which belong to a system containing both primary rules, and secondary rules of recognition, change, adjudication and enforcement.

Institutional laws, governing the way courts should operate, are secondary rules of adjudication; and constitutive laws, such as the laws governing the creation of wills, are, in effect, part of the system of rules of change. For such laws allow people to create rules – my property should go to my designated heirs – that will then be applied by the courts.

If the Doulians were to change their system in such a way as to create rules of recognition, change, adjudication and enforcement, and if these rules were actually operative in Doulia, then many people would surely say that Doulia had – at last! – achieved a legal system. Once there was such a system, generally directed to the common good, they would say, with Austin, that even a bad law that was not aimed at the common good was nevertheless a valid law of the Doulian legal system. But this would not mean that they had agreed entirely with the positivist tradition: for this second definition makes it a condition of being a legitimate government (and thus a condition of being a source of valid law) that you should have instituted a system of rules aimed at the common good.

This second definition is much closer to the Natural Law position than is Hart's, because it requires that the system of laws be enforced by a legitimate government; and this implies some moral constraints on the content of a legal system because a legitimate government must aim to promote the common good. But some philosophers have argued that this is not the only way in which moral ideals play a part in determining what sorts of rules and procedures can be recognized as part of legal systems. They have argued, following the Natural Law tradition, that there are certain moral constraints, internal to the idea of law, that mean that the rules and procedures of a legal system must answer to certain moral ideals. So I propose now to examine this claim in the case of one particular kind of procedure: namely, the institution of criminal punishment. If, as I have suggested, any legal system must have rules of enforcement, then any moral ideals that constrain punishment are part of the concept of law.

7.5 Punishment: The problem

Before we take up these questions, however, it will help to say a little more about why the nature and justification of punishment is so central a question in the philosophy of law. We can begin, once more, with an attempt at a rough definition of how the term is used. We call "punishment" the infliction of penalties on offenders, by people in authority over them, for offenses they have committed. This rough definition will cover both the punishment of children by parents and teachers, and the punishment of criminals by courts. In each case there is a class of people who are entitled to punish – those in charge of children, courts – and they inflict a penalty of some kind because of an offense the offender has committed. Now inflicting a penalty involves doing something to someone that they have a right not to have done to them for no reason. We may not spank children just for the fun of it; we may not lock people up or take their money (as a "fine") without offering an explanation of why the normal moral rule against doing so does not apply in this case.

So what makes criminal punishment cry out for justification is the fact that it involves inflicting on people either some suffering or the deprivation of some liberty (or – in the extreme case – of life), and that each of these is, in itself, something we should normally avoid. When Jeremy Bentham, one of the founding utilitarians and a great nineteenth-century British philosopher and social reformer, said that all punishment in itself was evil, that was what he meant.

He did *not* mean that all punishment was wrong. Indeed, as we shall see in a moment, Bentham developed in great detail one of the main philosophical accounts of how the infliction of punishment could be justified. But one of the major reasons why we ought to be concerned about the morality of punishment is that it *does* involve using the coercive apparatus of the state to treat people in ways that would be quite wrong *without* justification.

7.6 Justifying punishment: Deterrence

Bentham thought that the reason why punishment, though evil in itself, was justified, was fairly clear.

> General prevention ought to be the chief aim of punishment and is its real justification. If we could consider an offense which has been committed as an isolated fact, the like of which would never recur, punishment would be useless. It would only be adding one evil to another. But when we consider that an unpunished crime leaves the path of crime open, not only to the same delinquent but also to all those who may have the same motives for entering upon it, we perceive that the punishment inflicted on the individual becomes a source of security to all.

The position that Bentham puts here is called the **deterrence** theory of punishment. It says that punishment is justified to the extent that it succeeds in discouraging or *deterring* crime.

Bentham was a utilitarian. It follows that he thought that the punishment should only be of the minimum severity necessary to avoid the harm done by crime. If the severity of the punishment produced more disutility in the offender than the disutility of the offenses it was meant to deter, then it could not be justified. Making life-time imprisonment with hard labor the punishment for all crimes would, no doubt, reduce the disutility caused by criminals very substantially: but, according to Bentham, it would have too high a cost.

First of all (and granting, for the sake of argument, that it is possible to compare the utilities of different people), the total disutility caused by people stealing small sums of money is nothing like as great as the disutility that would be caused by punishing many people so severely.

Second, any criminal justice system will make some mistakes. We saw in Chapter 2 that there were good reasons for accepting fallibilism – the view that any of our beliefs about the world might be incorrect. If that is so, then, however careful we are in our criminal trials, sometimes we will punish innocent people. The disutility caused to these innocent people must be taken into account along with the disutility suffered by criminals.

There is something very appealing, I think, in the idea that punishment is justified by its deterrent effect. However much we may disapprove of criminals, or dislike them, and however strong the desire we sometimes feel for revenge, it would surely be a good thing if the harm done to convicted offenders – and especially to innocent people wrongly convicted – was justified by its contributing to the common good. Certainly, many people would think that if it could be shown that the threat of punishment made no difference – that people would commit no more crimes even if there were no more punishments – there was something wrong with a system that inflicted so much harm to no positive effect.

7.7 Retributivism: Kant's objections

Yet there are at least two major kinds of objection to Bentham's view: and one of them begins by denying exactly this last claim. This first objection was put very forcefully by Immanuel Kant.

> Even if a Civil Society resolved to dissolve itself – as might be supposed in the case of a People inhabiting an island resolved to separate and scatter themselves through the world – the last Murderer lying in prison ought to be executed before that resolution was carried out. This ought to be done in order that every one may realize the just desert of his deeds. . .

What Kant is saying here is that, quite irrespective of the supposed deterrent effects of punishment, offenders ought to be punished because they *deserve* to be punished. Unlike Bentham, Kant thinks that punishment is justified not by its consequences, but by the fact (and to the degree) that the offender has offended. Any view that says we may only punish people for their offenses is called **retributivism**; for such people see punishment as retribution for crime. Kant's position is stronger than this; though he is a retributivist because he thinks we may only punish the guilty, he also holds that we *must* punish them.

As I have already said, many people would object to this conclusion. They would do so, in part, on the grounds that it reflected only a primitive desire for revenge on the offender. "Surely," they would say, "two wrongs don't make a right?" The world is a worse place because Kant's murderer has deprived a person of life; but if our revulsion against murder derives from a belief in the value of human life, how can taking another life improve the situation, except by making other killings less likely?

If we wish to see the force of Kant's view, however, we should consider the second major objection to Bentham's theory. Bentham says that punishment is justified if, on balance, it produces more utility than the disutility it creates. But if that is the only reason why punishment is justified, then why limit ourselves to trying to punish the guilty? Suppose it turned out that we could deter crime by flogging people at random, or by punishing people we knew to be innocent while claiming, dishonestly, that they were guilty. If the disutility produced in this way were outweighed by the utility produced by the reduction in the crime-rate, Bentham's utilitarian principles would lead us to do these things. And, surely, that would be wrong.

Let us follow a suggestion made by the philosopher Ted Honderich and call the practice of doing harm to innocent people in order to increase overall utility **victimization**. Kant's first objection to victimization would be that, however much good it did, victimization would be wrong because the victim didn't deserve the punishment.

But he would go on to say that to treat people in this way is to fail to respect their autonomy. To flog victims is to treat them as means to the end of reducing crime; it is to take no account of the fact of their innocence, or of the fact that the crimes we are hoping to prevent are not their fault.

7.8   Combining deterrence and retribution

Some philosophers recently have suggested a sort of halfway position between Bentham and Kant. Respect for the distinction between guilt and innocence means that we must not inflict penalties on the innocent. But even if someone is guilty, we may only punish them if the penalty is inflicted by a system that succeeds in deterring crime. It might be argued that if people were not deterred by punishments, then no good would be achieved by punishing them; and so, we ought not to do it. So the middle way is to say that punishment may be carried out for its deterrent effects, but only when it is applied to the guilty.

This middle way between Bentham and Kant is initially attractive. But Bentham's way of justifying punishment by reference to overall utility also suggests another reason why it might be justified, even if deterrence were ineffective. Once a person has committed a crime, we might decide to lock them up, not because this would deter anyone else, but because it would stop them doing it again. Once more, the disutility to offenders would be justified by the utility to potential victims of their potential future offenses.

Even this rationale is open, however, to the same sort of Kantian objection. If we lock criminals up because they are a danger to the public and call this "punishment," why should we not lock up people who are a danger to the public *before* they have committed any crime? As psychological theory gets better it may become possible to predict who will commit crimes. We could try to treat such people; but if the treatment failed, what objection could Bentham have to locking them up?

It is plain that Kant would have an objection to this sort of policy too. For a person who is *going to* commit a crime has not yet done anything to deserve punishment. It is one thing to punish someone for planning a crime or for conspiring to commit crimes with others; another to penalize a person who is going to commit a crime, even if they have not yet formed an intention to do so. To inflict a penalty on such a person would, once more, be to treat them as a means to the public good, ignoring the question of whether they were guilty of any offense.

We could modify the middle way, then, to say that we may punish offenders in any way that contributes to the public good – by protecting the innocent or in some other way – and not just in ways that produce deterrence. We would thus keep the core of retributivism – only the guilty may be punished – while taking into account the deterrence theorist's basic idea that we should only do this if some good comes from it.

But this concession will not satisfy the retributivist. For the retributivist insists that punishment is retribution *for* an offense: not only can we punish only offenders but we can only punish them for their offenses. And that means that, in some sense, the penalty inflicted must reflect the nature of the crime.

There are at least two ways in which it can be thought that the punishment must "fit" the crime. I shall consider one less obvious way later. But the obvious way in which punishments may fit crimes is that there may be some proportion between punishment and offense.

Thus, suppose that Virginia has parked her car illegally and that a police-car chasing an assassin has hit her car and thus allowed the assassin to escape. Suppose the assassin has killed a much-loved public figure. Then many of us might gain a great deal of relief if Virginia were severely punished, even though what she had done – parking illegally – was not a serious offense. Even if it would produce a great deal of utility for many people if an offender were severely punished (because, say, it satisfied a desire for revenge), it would be wrong, the retributivist says, to punish her more than she deserves.

Most people, I think, would accept these retributivist claims about punishment. However much good it may do for the rest of us, the degree of suffering we may impose on an offender must be limited by the seriousness of the wrong they have done. More than this, a harm inflicted on a person who is innocent, or that is out of all proportion to their offense, should not be called a punishment at all. There are certain moral constraints internal to the concept of punishment – constraints captured in the idea of *desert* – just as the Natural Lawyers claimed there were certain moral constraints internal to the concept of law. Even if it is a good thing that punishment deters – even if there are reasons for increasing the efficiency of its deterrent effects, for example by publicizing trials and sentences – these are only goals that we can use the criminal justice system to pursue if we first respect the rule that the penalties must be deserved.

The difference between retributivists and deterrence theorists is another example of a dispute between the two types of moral principle that Nozick called end-result and historical principles. Retributivists, unlike Bentham and deterrence theorists, require that we look beyond the end-result of our system of punishment, beyond the allocation of utility that it produces; they require us to respect the historical principle that punishment should be given only to those who have done something to deserve it.

7.9 Deterrence theory again

Deterrence theorists are not without resources to respond to the retributivists' objections. They have argued, for example, that the requirement that we should only punish the guilty comes from the fact that there would be so much disutility associated with the fear we would all feel if we knew that our society practiced random victimization. The retributivist can counter that this effect could be avoided by keeping the practice secret. (Needless to say, we couldn't keep it secret from the innocent people we victimized or the guilty people who escaped punishment.) Even if we did keep it secret from most people, so that most people escaped the disutility of fearing arbitrary victimization, victimization would still be wrong. But the deterrence theorist can reply that even if it were possible to keep this secret from most people, having a secret system risks very serious abuses. If we had a system that allowed victimization to masquerade as punishment, then officials of the system could use the law to exercise their private grudges: if we want to maintain a democracy, official secrecy is simply very dangerous.

Just as deterrence theorists can try to explain in this way why only the guilty should be punished, so they can explain why we believe there should be some proportion between crime and punishment. The reason, of course, is that deterrence theory is based on the recognition that "punishment in itself is evil." It follows, as I have already pointed out, that a deterrence theorist will not allow the penalties for crimes to exceed the minimum necessary to avoid the harm of offenses.

But each of these replies depends on the deterrence theorist being right about very complex social facts: How much fear would really be created by a system of publicized victimization? Would that really be worse than the offenses it might deter? Is the harm done by those offenses we think should be punished seriously always greater than the harm done by those offenses that we regard as trifling?

There are many factual conditions that would have to hold if the deterrence theorist's views are to fit with what we normally believe to be right. Let us call these conditions the **presuppositions of deterrence**. Then one important factual question to consider is whether the presuppositions of deterrence are true.

The answer to this question is almost certainly no. But even if the deterrence theorist's factual claims were true, they would still not establish that the deterrence theorist was right. For, as we have repeatedly seen, most of us believe that the retributivist's constraints on punishments should be respected even if the presuppositions of deterrence were false. Our moral views are views about what would be right not just in this world but in other possible worlds where the facts are different.

What this means is that it is no defense of the utilitarian view of punishment to show that, given the way the world actually is, it will lead us to do just what retributivists require. For in thinking about the justice of punishment we are trying to understand not only which punishments are right but *why* they are right. And to decide that, it is necessary to consider what we would do if the facts were different.

I mentioned earlier two ways in which a punishment might fit a crime, but I gave only one of them. We can see, finally, how different the basic conceptions of punishment held by deterrence theorists and retributivists are if we consider this second way in which punishments and crimes might fit each other.

Suppose offenders were obliged to compensate the victims of their offenses. Not every crime has a victim – who is the victim of my speeding on the highway? – and not every harm can be compensated – you can't give someone back a lost limb. But, some retributivists have said, where possible it is a virtue in a legal system if offenders make reparation to their victims. Being obliged to make reparation to your victims is an especially fitting punishment where it is a practical possibility.

The retributivist will see compensation as internal to the system of punishment, as flowing from the very meaning of the idea. But Bentham, who would agree that the compensation of victims was desirable, would say that it was a separate question how they should be compensated. Maybe it would be more efficient if the government took on the task of compensating victims, using taxes or, perhaps, fines and the proceeds of prisoner's labor to pay for it. If that was true, Bentham would see no advantage in making the offender compensate the victim directly. The deep differences between the views of those who see moral ideas as internal to the very idea of law and punishment – the Natural Lawyers – and those positivists who do not, have very different consequences for social policy.

7.10   Why do definitions matter?

I said, at the end of section 7.1, that there might be reasons for preferring a definition of a complex term like "law" other than that it is simply the one that competent speakers of the language seem to use. Many terms have a certain "open texture" to them, which means that ordinary usage does not determine precisely how they should be applied in every case. One task of a philosophical definition is to try and explain not just how we use a term but why there are good reasons to use it that way. Such an explanation allows us to fill in the gaps where ordinary usage leaves this open texture. The dispute between Natural Law and legal positivism reflects two such competing explanations of why we have a concept of law; and these two different explanations have different consequences for how we should fill in the open texture of our everyday use of the words "law" and "punishment."

CHAPTER 7

Thus, the Natural Lawyer's objection to the positivist view is *not* that the positivists have misdescribed the way people ordinarily use the word "law," but that their view has serious moral and political dangers. Unless we insist that law must have a certain moral content, we may find ourselves accepting as legal – and, therefore, in some sense, binding – horribly immoral laws, like the racist laws of Nazi Germany.

The positivists reply that what the law is is indeed a question of fact and not of value. Far from obliging us to respect bad laws, their view forces us, once we have decided the factual question of what the law is, to face the separate normative question of whether we should obey it. We can best keep our eyes open to the possibility that laws should *not* be obeyed by keeping clear the distinction between the two questions:

(a) What rules are operating in this society?
(b) Is it a good thing that this particular rule is operating?

Indeed, positivists have argued that it is the Natural Lawyers who risk giving bad laws a respect they do not deserve. Building too much of morality into your definition of law can confuse people into thinking that they ought to obey even bad laws, because it leads them to *identify* law and morality.

One problem with the Natural Law view, then, is that it may lead people to think that every law is morally binding. But equally worrying for the positivists is the possibility that a conflation of law and morals can lead people to think that every moral rule should be legally binding.

Thus, for example, someone might be led to defend censorship laws that said that people may not look at pornography (irrespective of whether it leads them to do harm to anyone else), even if their enforcement involved a substantial interference in the private lives of citizens. Keeping law and morals apart allows us to entertain the possibility that some of our moral ideas should not be imposed on others: that some moral rules should not be legally enforced because to enforce them is to fail to respect the citizen's autonomy.

Yet this hardly seems to be a fair objection to the position of the Natural Lawyer. People who see the criminal law as Bentham did, regarding it simply as a device for maximizing utility, have no special reason to respect autonomy; all that they require is that we maximize utility. It is the Natural Lawyers who argue that a system that fails to respect the citizen's autonomy is not a system of law, and that victimization is not a form of punishment. They argue this precisely because they hold that respect for certain moral ideals, among them autonomy, is internal to the concept of law. And in claiming this, they are not simply expressing a disagreement with positivism about the word "law" (or "punishment"), but appealing to a different view about the proper function of government.

At the end of Chapter 5 I argued that autonomy was an important value; and, as we have seen, respect for autonomy is important in distinguishing between the justified use of punishment and bare coercion. Building the idea of desert into the very definition of punishment reflects a commitment to the value of autonomy. For respect for the distinction between those who do and those who do not deserve punishment flows from a recognition that we should treat each other as responsible agents.

But autonomy is an important issue not only in the enforcement but in the creation of law. If we respect people's autonomy, we may wish to enforce only those criminal laws that are necessary to protect citizens from each other. Suppose there was no evidence that pornography led people to do harm to others. If we thought that the desire for pornography was, nevertheless, immoral, making someone avoid pornography would still not make them a better person; what would make them better would be to persuade them that looking at it was wrong. Even if you think that looking at pornography is intrinsically wrong, therefore, you might still agree that simply *forcing* someone not to look at it with the threat of punishment, even though they want to and do not see that it is wrong, is an abuse of the powers of the state.

The view that the heart of a system of law is respect for the citizen's autonomy has powerful consequences. If we respect the autonomy even of the offender, we must insist that criminal trials and punishments should be able to show the offender why he or she is being punished, and to offer him or her a justification for the severity of the punishment. If this is to be possible, the courts must be able to argue that the offense was an offense against a rule that can be justified because it is aimed at the common good; that the punishment is consistent with our moral view of the offense; and that the court has taken into account the offender's reasons for doing what he or she did. A system of courts that did not meet these conditions would not deserve the respect of offenders, because it could not seek to show them why they were being punished.

These are difficult and important questions. And it is important also to see that these sorts of questions can be central to the reasons why people adopt one or other position in the debate between Natural Law and positivism. In thinking about the merits of the various views I have discussed, I hope you will keep in mind the fact that they are not just arguments about the meanings of words. At the heart of the dispute are some of the most important questions about how we should conduct our lives together.

7.11   Conclusion

In this chapter we have seen how the dispute between Natural Law and positivism has widespread consequences for our understanding not just of the nature of law itself, but also of the institution of criminal punishment and of the nature of the state. Positivists believe law is a descriptive notion and they leave the question of evaluation to be settled after the legal system has been identified. Natural Lawyers, on the other hand, see law as an essentially moral idea and so demand of a system of rules that it satisfy certain moral constraints if it is to be called a legal system at all.

This belief flows through into their view of punishment: that, too, they hold is a moral idea and victimization is no more punishment than a system of rules aimed at the private satisfaction of the Oligarchs is a system of law. Retributivism's objection to victimization stems from the Natural Lawyer's recognition that there are constraints – constraints that deterrence theorists fail to recognize – on the proper use of the coercive power of the state. Reflecting on these issues also leads to the view that Hobbes's positivist view of the state is wrong; and that Aquinas was, surely, right when he said that to be a government you must have not only power but also the purpose of aiming at the common good.

We have also seen that the dispute between positivism and Natural Law is not simply an argument about words: underlying the disagreement about what "law" means are deep differences about politics and morality. The idea of autonomy that is central to the Natural Lawyer's conception of courts and trials is the same notion as the one that played so central role in Kant's conception of morality. And respect for autonomy in legal philosophy leads to the rejection of consequentialism, a rejection that I argued was at the heart of Kant's ethics. This interconnectedness of issues is inevitable. In thinking about the law, as a specific set of institutions within the state, our views are bound to be connected with more general questions about the state – with political philosophy – and, in the end, with the most fundamental questions of morality.

8 Philosophy

How does formal philosophy differ from folk-philosophy?

Or from religion and science?

Can there be equally adequate but incompatible ways of conceptualizing the world?

8.1 Introduction

In many a village around the world, in cultures traditional and industrialized, people gather in the evenings to talk. In pubs and bars, under trees in the open air in the tropics, and around fires in the far North and South of our globe, people exchange tales; tell jokes; discuss issues of the day; argue about matters important and trivial. Listening to such conversations in cultures other than your own, you learn much about the concepts and theories people use to understand their experience, and you learn what values they hold most dear.

It would be natural enough, as we built a picture of those values, theories, and concepts in another culture, to describe what we were doing as coming to understand the philosophy of that culture. In one sense, the philosophy of a person or a group is just the sum of the beliefs they hold about the central questions of human life; about mind and matter, knowledge and truth, good and bad, right and wrong; about human nature and the universe we inhabit.

At their most general, as I say, these beliefs are naturally called "philosophy" and there is nothing wrong in using the word this way. There are many continuities between conversation about these universal questions – what we might call **folk-philosophy** – and the kind of discussion that has filled the chapters of this book.

All human cultures, simple or complex, large or small, industrial or pre-industrial, have many of the concepts we have discussed – or, at least, concepts much like them. Issues about what is good and right, what we know and mean, what it is to have a mind and to think, can arise for people living in the simplest of societies. Indeed, at least some of the problems of the philosophy of mind, of epistemology, and of ethics surely do arise naturally for any curious member of our species. We might suppose, as a result, that people have reflected on these questions everywhere and always. If any thought about these questions counts as philosophy, then philosophy is likely to be found in every human society, past and present – wherever there are people struggling to live – and make sense of – their lives.

But it is important, too, that there are discontinuities between folk-philosophy and the discussions of this book. Philosophy, as it is practiced and taught in modern Western universities, is a distinctive institution that has evolved along with Western societies. I mentioned towards the start of Chapter 4 that science – unlike minds and knowledge and language – has not existed in every human culture. The problems of the philosophy of science occur only in cultures that have the institution of science; and just so, political philosophy and the philosophy of law raise questions that only matter if you live – as not all human beings have lived – in a society organized as a state.

The differences between folk-philosophy and the discussions of this book are not, however, simply differences in subject matter. Along with the new problems of the philosophy of science and law, social change has also produced new ways of tackling the old problems. One way to focus on what we have learned about the character of modern Western philosophy, the kind of philosophy that I have tried to introduce in this book, is to contrast it both with the folk-philosophy of other cultures and with other styles of thought in our own culture. In doing this it will help to have a name for the style of philosophical thought that I have been engaged in. I suggest that we call it **formal philosophy**, to contrast it with the informal style of folk-philosophy.

In the next few sections I am going to contrast formal philosophy with the traditional thought of pre-literate cultures, with Western religious thought, and with science. Each of these contrasts will allow us not only to learn more about philosophy, but also to ask some important philosophical questions.

8.2 Traditional thought

If you have ever read any anthropology, you are bound, I think, to be struck by the astonishing range of ways in which human beings have tried to understand our world. The Mbuti, for example, whom I have mentioned often already, think of the forest around them as a person – what we might call a god – and they think that the forest will take care of them. If they have a run of bad luck in their hunting, they suppose not that the forest is trying to harm them, but that it has lost interest in them; that it has, as they say, "gone to sleep." When this happens they try to waken the forest by singing for it, and they believe that if their songs please the forest, their luck will turn.

Not only do most Westerners find such beliefs surprising, they are likely to think that they are unreasonable. Why should a forest care about anything, let alone human singing? And even if it did, how could it determine the success of a hunt for honey or for game?

This sense that Mbuti beliefs are unreasonable is likely to grow when you are told that the Mbuti know very well that other people who live nearby, people with whom they have complex social relationships, believe quite different things. Their neighbors, in the villages on the edge of the Ituri rain-forest where they live, believe that most bad luck is due to witchcraft – the malevolent action of special people whom they regard as witches.

In these circumstances, it is surely very curious that the Mbuti do not worry about whether they are right.

Both the fact that the Mbuti know that other people believe different things, and the fact that this does not seem to concern them, mark their way of thinking off from that of Western cultures. Most Westerners would worry if they discovered that people in the next town got on very well without believing in electricity. We think our general beliefs can be justified; and if others challenge our beliefs, we are inclined to seek evidence and reasons for our position and to challenge their reasons and their evidence in response. The anthropologist and philosopher Robin Horton has used the term **adversarial** to describe this feature of Western cultures. We tend to treat our intellectual disputes like our legal disputes, trading evidence and argument in a vigorous exchange, like adversaries on a field of intellectual battle. Horton uses the term adversarial to contrast this Western approach to argument with what the Nigerian Nobel Laureate, Wole Soyinka, calls the **accommodative** style of many traditional cultures. Traditional people are often willing to accept and accommodate the different views of other groups.

Indeed, the Mbuti, like many traditional peoples, tend not to give the justification of their general beliefs much thought at all. If we asked them why they believed in the god-forest, they would probably tell us, as many people in many cultures have told many anthropologists, that they believe it because it is what their ancestors taught them. Indeed many traditional cultures have proverbs which say, in effect, "everything we know was taught us by our ancestors."

Justifying beliefs by saying they have the authority of tradition is one of the practices that demarcates traditional cultures from formal philosophy. Even where I have cited distinguished philosophical authorities from the past – the "ancestors" of Western philosophy, like Plato and Descartes – I have considered their arguments and tried to understand and criticize them. The fact that Plato or Descartes or Kant said something is not, by itself, a reason to believe it.

We should be careful, however, not to exaggerate the differences in the way Mbuti people and Westerners *ordinarily* justify their beliefs. Most of what you and I believe, we too believe because our parents or teachers told it to us. Some of the differences between the Mbuti and formal philosophy reflect differences not so much between traditional and Western people, as between formal and informal thought.

Nevertheless, Westerners (and Western-trained people generally) are more likely to ask even their parents and teachers not just *what* they believe but *why* they believe it. And when Westerners ask why we should believe something, what they want is not just an authority, but some evidence or argument. This is especially true in formal philosophy. Throughout this book I have tried to offer and examine reasons for believing the claims I have made; and the philosophers I have discussed have done the same.

I have also tried to proceed *systematically.* I have tried, that is, to connect arguments made on one subject – fallibilism, for example – with other apparently remote questions – the inevitability that our courts will sometimes punish the innocent, the underdetermination of empirical theory. And this shows up another contrast with traditional thought. Though anthropologists often try to make a system out of the thought of traditional peoples, they do not usually get much help from the people whose thought they study.

Sir Edward Evans-Pritchard, one of the founders of modern cultural anthropology, attempted, in his book *Witchcraft, Oracles and Magic Among the Azande*, to explain the theory of witchcraft implicit in the practice of the Azande people of southern Sudan. But when he discovered inconsistencies in their claims – it turned out that if you followed the Zande beliefs about the inheritance of witchcraft through, everybody was a witch! – they didn't seem to be very concerned about it.

The urge to give arguments and evidence for what you believe, and to make your beliefs consistent with each other so that they form a system, is one of the marks of formal philosophy. We can say that formal philosophy aims to be systematic. But though this urge to theorize is important to philosophy, it is also central, as we saw, to science; and it is not hard to see that it is central to the whole range of modern intellectual life. In short, the systematic character of philosophy is not special to the subject. It is an outgrowth of the systematic nature of our current modes of thought.

The reason why the Azande did not theorize systematically about witchcraft in the way that Evans-Pritchard did is that *they did not want to*. Their lives made sense to them in terms of the theories they had, and, so far as they could see, there was plenty of evidence for their beliefs. The evidence that witchcraft exists was as obvious to them as the evidence that electricity exists no doubt seems to you. People who were ill got better after the application of spiritual medicines; people died regularly after their enemies had appealed to powerful spirits. Of course, not every one who is treated with spiritual medicine gets better; but then the lights don't always go on when you turn on a switch! The reason why the Zande did not think much about the evidence for their theories, in other words, is that they had no reason to suspect that they might be wrong.

Now I imagine that you have been supposing that it is quite obvious that the Azande not only *might* be wrong, but that they *are*. You probably also think that your belief that they are wrong is one that you can justify with evidence and reason, and that Azande people who respected rational argumentation and sensible principles of evidence would eventually come to agree with you.

If I had started not with Zande beliefs about witchcraft but with their moral beliefs, by contrast, I suspect you would suppose that the same would not apply. I suspect, in other words, that you probably believe there is some truth in moral relativism but none in relativism about such factual questions as whether there are any witches. Yet just as moral relativists hold that what is good depends on who you are (or where or in what culture or when you live), so some people have recently argued that what is true about factual questions depends on who you are (or in what culture or when you live).

Relativism about factual matters is usually called **cognitive relativism**; and if you are not a cognitive relativist, then it is an important philosophical question whether you can defend your position. Relativism is important because its truth would set limits on the role of evidence and reason; and evidence and reason are central to formal philosophy.

So it is important, too, that it turns out to be harder than you might think to defend the non-relativity of factual beliefs; and if we imagine what it would be like to argue with a convinced Azande, we shall see why.

8.3   Arguing with the Azande

Azande beliefs about witchcraft were rich and complex; but it does not take more than a brief summary to get to the heart of the difficulty I want to address. So, let me try to give you an idea of their main beliefs in a brisk summary.

The Azande believed that *mangu* – which is the word that Evans-Pritchard translated as "witchcraft" – was a substance in the bodies of witches. *Mangu* produced a spiritual power that could cause ill-health or other misfortune to its victims, even without the conscious intention of the witch. *Mangu's* physical manifestation was supposed to be a black substance – perhaps in the gall-bladder – which was inherited from males to males and females to females.

Witches were supposed to do their evil in two major ways. Sometimes the "soul" of a witch travelled through the air – visible in the daytime only to other witches but at night visible to all as a flame – and devoured the "soul of the flesh" of the victim. On other occasions, witches projected "witchcraft things" into their victims, causing pain in the relevant place; but this substance could be removed by the professional healers and seers whom Evans-Pritchard called "witch-doctors".

These witch-doctors were experts in the use of various kinds of Zande magic; but most ordinary Zande people knew many spells and rituals that were intended to help them control their world by, for example, bringing rain, curing disease, ensuring success in hunting or in farming, or guaranteeing the fertility of men and women.

Witchcraft, for the Azande, was involved in the explanation of all those unfortunate happenings that do people harm. But the Azande did not deny the role of other kinds of influence. They understood the interaction of witchcraft and other causes of harm through an analogy with hunting. When they went elephant hunting, they called the man who plunged in the second spear *umbaga*; and he and the man who plunged in the first spear were held to be jointly responsible for the elephant's death. The Azande compared witchcraft to *umbaga*. When, for example, a man was killed by a spear in war, they said that witchcraft was the second spear: for sometimes a spear thrust does not kill its victim and the "second spear" is needed to explain why, in *this* case, the man died.

If you asked the Azande what evidence they had for the existence of witchcraft, they would point, first, to many of the misfortunes of human life, and ask how else they could be explained. But they would also tell you that they had a number of ways of discovering more precisely how witchcraft operated: and these various ways of finding out about witchcraft they called *soroka*, which Evans-Pritchard translated as "oracles."

The Zande used many kinds of oracles: ways of finding out what was going on in the world of spirits, in general, and witchcraft, in particular. They regarded dreams about witchcraft as oracles, for example. But the highest in the hierarchy of oracles, in terms of reliability, was their "poison oracle"; and they used it regularly in their attempts to discover who had bewitched them.

The oracle involved administering a special poison to young chicks; and then questions were put to it and whether the chicken died determined the answer. In a typical case, an Azande man – and, in Zandeland, it always was an adult male – would administer the poison to a chicken and ask the oracle whether So-and-so had bewitched them. If the fowl died, the accusation was confirmed: but the question had now to be put the other way round, so that, on the second test, it was the fowl's *survival* that confirmed that there had been witchcraft. Thus, on the first test, the oracle's operator might say: "Have I been bewitched, oracle? If so, kill the chicken." And on the second test, he would say "Have I been bewitched? If so, save the chicken."

Even given this little sketch of some Zande beliefs, you might think that you had enough to begin to persuade a reasonable Zande person that they were wrong. After all, surely, on many occasions, the oracle would give contradictory answers. Suppose someone put the two questions I just suggested to an oracle and the chicken died both times? Wouldn't that show the oracle was unreliable?

Unfortunately, things are not so simple. Like many traditional people, the Azande believed that there were many taboos that should be observed in every important area of their lives; and the oracle was no exception. If the operator had broken a taboo – for example, by eating certain prohibited foods – the oracle was supposed to lose its power. So, if an oracle proved unreliable, they could say that one of the operators had broken a taboo. But they also believed that powerful witchcraft could undermine the working of the oracle; that would be another possible explanation for the failure. In short, when an oracle failed the Azande had plenty of resources within their theories to explain it.

Evans-Pritchard noticed this feature of Zande thought; and he said that the reason why they didn't notice that their oracles were unreliable was that they were able to make these explanatory moves, which he called *secondary elaborations.* And Evans-Pritchard observed that "the perception of error in one mystical notion in a particular situation merely proves the correctness of another and equally mystical notion." The problem is that it is not so clear that, in making these secondary elaborations, the Zande were being unreasonable.

For, as Evans-Pritchard noticed, the system of witchcraft, oracles and other kinds of magic formed a coherent system of mutually supporting beliefs.

> Death is proof of witchcraft. . . . The results which magic is supposed to produce actually happen after the rites are performed . . . Hunting-magic is made and animals are speared. . . . Magic is only made to produce events which are likely to happen in any case – e.g. rain is produced in the rainy season and held up in the dry season . . . [Magic] is seldom asked to produce a result by itself but is associated with empirical action that does in fact produce it – e.g. a prince gives food to attract followers and does not rely on magic alone.

And he also gave many more examples of the ways in which they can explain failures when they occur.

Consider, now, for the sake of comparison, what you would say if you did a simple experiment in chemistry which came out differently on two successive occasions. You would say, quite reasonably, that you had probably not done the experiment quite the same way both times. Perhaps one of your test-tubes wasn't quite clean; perhaps you hadn't measured the reagents quite carefully enough; and so on. In other words, it would take systematic observation, experimentation (where possible) and thought.

Now why shouldn't an Azande say to you that your explanation here is just as much a case of defending one mystical notion – the idea of chemical reactions – in terms of another – the idea that there is an invisible quantity of some reagent in the test-tube? Your theory, too, constitutes a set of "mutually supporting beliefs"; and that, far from being an argument against it, seems to be a point in its favor. Nevertheless, unless you already have some faith that the world is made of atoms and molecules which react according to definite rules, there is no obvious reason why a few experiments should persuade you of this general theory. And, similarly, there is no reason why the failure of even a good number of experiments should make you give it up.

At this point you may recall something I said in the chapter on science. I said there that our theories are **underdetermined** by the evidence for them. This meant that the contents of our empirical beliefs are not fully determined by the evidence we have for them. I argued also that much of the language we use for describing the world is theory-laden: the ways we commit ourselves to the existence of objects and properties beyond our sensory evidence is partly determined by the theories we happen to have. What Evans-Pritchard noticed was, in effect, a consequence of the fact that Zande observation was theory-laden also. They interpreted what they heard and saw in terms of their belief in witchcraft. But if theory-ladenness is a feature their theories share with our scientific beliefs, that fact is not, by itself, an argument against them.

In practice, then, we should have to do more than point to a few cases where the oracle seemed to give inconsistent results if we were to persuade a reasonable Azande person that their theory was wrong. What more would it take?

The answer, surely, is that it would take the collection of a lot of data on oracles; examining carefully the question whether anyone had broken a taboo; looking to see if we could find grounds to support the claim that witchcraft was interfering in those cases where the oracle failed and no one had broken a taboo; checking to see that the reason one chicken died and the other did not was not that different quantities of poison had been administered; and so on.

Notice that we could do all this, while still using the language of the Azande to describe what we were doing. We would not need to assume our own theories were correct. We could *use* our theories in order to see if we could construct cases where the oracle would fail; but we would still leave it up to the actual experiments to decide whether we were right. Because we share with the Azande some of the concepts we use for describing the world – *chicken, person, death* – we could agree that, in some cases, the results had come out in ways that didn't fit Zande theory; in others, that it had come out in ways that didn't fit ours.

In the long run, after much experimentation of this kind, some Azande might come to give up their theory. But there is no guarantee that this would happen. For, just as it is always possible for *us* to explain away experimental results by supposing that something – though we are not sure what – went wrong, so this move is open to the Azande, also.

Nothing I have suggested presupposes that it has to be *us* that raise doubts about Azande beliefs. Because the problem of consistency with the evidence can be put without presupposing that Zande theory is false, it would have been open to them to carry out these experiments. So, perhaps, if the Azande were wrong, they could have found it out for themselves.

I shall return in section 8.5 to the question of whether we should expect the Azande to come, after experiment and systematic thought, to agree with us; and not simply to assume a development of their own witchcraft theory. But it is worth spending a little time first to consider why it is unlikely that the Azande would have done either of these things on their own. For even if the Azande of Evans-Pritchard's day had started to worry about their beliefs, they would have been severely limited in their ability to theorize about them and to carry out these sorts of experiments – not because they were not clever enough, but because they lacked at least one essential tool. For the Azande did not have writing. And, as we shall see, much of what we take to be typical of formal philosophy derives in large measure from the fact that formal philosophy, unlike folk-philosophy, is written.

8.4   The significance of literacy

It is very striking that the founders of Western philosophy – Socrates and Plato – stand at the beginning of the development of Western writing. There is something emblematic in the fact that Plato, the first philosopher whose writings are still important to us, wrote dialogues which reported in *writing* the *oral* discussions of Socrates. Plato made Socrates important to us by writing down his thought. The fact that formal philosophy is written is tremendously important, and it pays to think about why this is.

Imagine yourself in a culture without writing and ask yourself what difference it would make to your thought. Consider, for example, how you would think about some of the questions we have discussed in this book. Could you remember every step in any of the arguments I gave for the claim that knowledge is not justified true belief, if you were not able to read and re-read the examples, to think about them and then read them again? Could you check, without written words to look at, that what you had decided about the nature of the mind was consistent with what you thought about knowledge?

Writing makes possible a kind of consistency that pre-literate culture cannot demand. Write down a sentence and it is there, in principle, for ever; and that means that if you write down another sentence inconsistent with it, you can be caught out. It is this fact that is at the root of the possibility of the sort of extended philosophical argument that I have made again and again in this book. Philosophical argument, as I said in the introduction, is rooted in a philosophical tradition. But this is possible only because we can re-read – and thus re-think – the arguments of our philosophical forebears.

It is this fact that is at the root of the possibility of our adversarial style. How often have we seen Perry Mason ask the stenographer to read back from the record? In the traditional culture the answer can only be: "What record?" In the absence of writing, it is not possible to compare our ancestors' theories in their actual words with ours. Given the limitations of quantity imposed by oral transmission, we do not even have a detailed knowledge of what those theories were. We know more of Plato's thought two millennia ago about epistemology than we know about the views of the entire population of the Azande a century ago about anything.

The Azande would have had great difficulty in testing their system of beliefs in the way I have suggested because they had no way of recording their experiments and their theorizing about the world. That is the main reason why systematic theorizing of the kind that we have been engaged in would have been difficult for the Azande.

But literacy does not matter only for our ability to examine arguments over and over again and to record the results of experiment and experience. It has important consequences also for the *style* of the language that we use. Those of us who read and write learn very quickly how different in style written communication is from oral. Indeed, we learn it so early and so well that we need to be reminded of some of the really important differences.

Consider, for example, the generality and abstractness of many of the arguments I have offered and how much these features depend upon writing. A simple example will help make this dependence clear.

Suppose you found a scrap of paper, which contained the following words:

On Sundays here, we often do what Joe is doing over there. But it is not normal to do it on *this* day. I asked the priest whether it was permissible to do it today and he just did this.

A reasonable assumption would be that someone had transcribed what someone was saying. And why? Because all these words – "I," "here," "there," "this," "today," and even "Joe" and "the priest" – are what logicians call **indexicals**. You need the context in which the sentence is uttered to know what they are referring to: you need to know who the speaker or writer was to know what "I" refers to; you need to know where that speaker was to know where "here" refers to; and so on.

When we write we have to fill in much of what context provides when we speak. We must do this not only so that we avoid the uncertainty of indexicals, but also because we cannot assume that our readers will share our knowledge of our situation; and because, if they do not, they cannot ask us. We can now see why trying to avoid these possibilities for misunderstanding is bound to move you towards abstract and general questions, and away from questions that are concrete and particular. The need for generality becomes clear if we consider the difference between the judgments of a traditional Zande oracle, and those of experts in a written tradition. A traditional thinker can get away with saying that if three oracles have answered that the carver, Kisanga, has stolen a chicken, then he has. But in a written tradition, all sorts of problems can arise.

After all, everybody knows of cases where the oracles have been wrong three times because they were interfered with by witchcraft. On a particular occasion, where the possibility of witchcraft has not been raised, it will seem silly to raise this objection. But if we are trying to write an account of the oracle, we shall have to take other cases into account. The literate theorist has to formulate principles not just for the particular case, but more generally. Rather than saying

Three oracles have spoken: it is so

he or she will have to say something like this:

Three oracles constitute good *prima facie* evidence that something is so; but they may have been interfered with by witchcraft. This is to be revealed by such and such means. If they have been interfered with by witchcraft, it is necessary first to purify the oracle . . .

Literate theorists, in other words, will have to list those qualifying clauses that we recognize as the mark of written scholarship.

Literacy forces you to consider general claims, because it requires you to make claims that are relevant beyond the particular conversation you are having. And it is easy to see that literacy also encourages abstraction in your language. Consider a traditional proverb that has been orally transmitted. Take this proverb from the Akan region of Ghana:

If all seeds that fall were to grow, then no one could follow the path under the trees.

When someone says this they are usually expressing the view that if everyone were prosperous, no one would work. But the proverb is about seeds, trees, and paths through the forest. The message is abstract, but the wording is concrete. The concreteness makes the proverb memorable – and in oral tradition nothing is carried but what is carried on in memory. But it also means that to understand the message – as I am sure only Akan-speaking people did before I explained it – you have to share with the speaker a knowledge of his or her background assumptions.

The proverb works because, in traditional societies, you talk largely with people you know; all the assumptions that are needed to interpret a proverb are shared. And it is because they are shared that the language of oral exchange (including, of course, the conversation of literate people) can be indexical, metaphorical and context-dependent.

Once you are writing, therefore, the demands imposed by trying to cater to an unknown reader move you towards both greater generality and greater abstraction. Because readers may not share the cultural assumptions of writers, written language becomes less metaphorical in contexts where communication of information is important. This is another reason we are less able to get away with the inconsistencies of our informal thought.

For if we speak metaphorically, then what we say can be taken and reinterpreted in a new context; the same proverb, precisely because its message is not fixed, can be used again and again. And if we can use it again and again with different messages, we may fail to notice that the messages are inconsistent with each other. After all, the proverb is being used in *this* situation, and why should we think *now* of those other occasions of its use?

Evans-Pritchard wrote:

> [Although] Azande often observed that a medicine is unsuccessful, they do not generalize their observations. Therefore the failure of a single medicine does not teach them that all medicines of this type are foolish. Far less does it teach them that all magic is useless. . . .
>
> Contradictions between their beliefs are not noticed by the Azande because beliefs are not all present at the same time but function in different situations. . . .
>
> Each man and each kinship group acts alone without cognizance of the actions of others. People do not pool their ritual experiences.

But we can now see that, without literacy, it would be very hard indeed to generalize in this way; or to bring beliefs from different situations together to check their consistency; or to share the full range of Zande ritual experience.

Neither the impulse towards universality and abstraction and away from metaphorical language, nor the recognition of inconsistencies of the traditional world view, leads automatically to formal philosophy. But without literacy it is hard to see how formal philosophy could have got started: it is not a sufficient condition for formal philosophy, but it certainly seems to be necessary. And, as we have seen, it is literacy that explains some of the features of formal philosophy.

8.5 Cognitive relativism

The problem of cognitive relativism would not be solved even once the Azande had writing and all that it entails. Indeed, it would become more acute. For suppose they had come to develop a view that was abstract, general and systematic in exactly the ways that formal philosophy is. We could still ask whether they would have any reason to end up agreeing with *us.* The Chinese did, after all, develop writing before any contact with the West, and their theories were abstract, general, systematic, and quite different from ours.

Suppose, then, that history had been different and the Azande *had* invented writing for themselves. Suppose, too, that they had started the process of systematic critical theorizing on their own. And suppose they had come to develop a theory, based still on belief in *mangu,* but modified, as a result of their accumulated experimental experience, to deal with the cases where the old theory seemed to have failed. We began our consideration of the Azande in order to address the question of whether cognitive relativism was true. So we must now ask ourselves whether, even if the Azande had developed in this way, we have good reason to believe that we could still persuade them that they were wrong.

CHAPTER 8

Some philosophers (and many anthropologists) have argued recently that we have no reason to believe that we could. In other words, they have defended versions of cognitive relativism. And their reasons for defending this view have to do with very general considerations about the nature of our theories of the world.

Begin with the fact that the concepts we use to organize our sensory and perceptual experience are themselves theory-laden. Terms like "gene," as we saw in Chapter 4, get their meaning from their place in a complex network of beliefs – a theory. Recent cognitive relativists have started with this fact, and gone on to argue that because our terms gain their meaning from such networks of beliefs, we can only ask whether a claim is true relative to some such network. These networks of beliefs that define our concepts are usually called **conceptual frameworks** or **conceptual schemes**.

If you agree that our concepts gain their meaning from such conceptual schemes, you might argue as follows. The Azande have one conceptual scheme, we have another. As they develop their ideas, to eradicate some of the inconsistencies between their theories and their observations, their theories will become better by the standards set within their conceptual scheme. The same is true of us. But if meaning, and thus truth, only applies with respect to a conceptual scheme, there is no point in saying that their theories are false by *our* standards.

Some of their theories may be false by *their* standards, and they might discover this by experimentation. But they are no more under an obligation to test their theories by our standards than we are obliged to test our theories by theirs. Since this is so, we have no reason to believe that they must come to accept our theories in the long run; just as they have no reason to expect that we shall end up believing theirs.

There may, at first glance, seem to be little to worry about in the possibility of cognitive relativism. But I think a little reflection suggests that we should not be complacent about this possibility. Suppose the cognitive relativists are correct. Then reasonable people, on the basis of reasonable interpretations of their experience, can come to have different and apparently incompatible theories of the world, and there may be no evidence or argument that can show which of them is right. What is true relative to one scheme may be false relative to another.

Before we go on to discuss this view, it is important to notice that I have moved between a weaker and a stronger version of cognitive relativism in the last few paragraphs. **Strong relativism** holds that what is *true* is relative to a conceptual scheme and that what is true for one may be false for another; **weak relativism**, that what it is *reasonable to believe* is relative to a conceptual scheme, and that what it is reasonable to believe in one conceptual scheme it may not be reasonable to believe in another. Weak relativism follows logically from strong relativism but not vice versa.

I think that there is a simple and powerful argument against strong relativism that draws on Frege's insights about meaning. If the argument is right, then, since strong relativism is not a logical consequence of weak relativism, weak cognitive relativism might still be correct. But I want to begin by putting strong relativism behind us.

8.6 The argument against strong relativism

It is essential to the form of relativism that I have been discussing that different theories which are true with respect to different conceptual schemes can nevertheless be incompatible with one another. Nobody worries about the possibility that what is true relative to the conceptual scheme of genetic theory might be different from what is true relative to the conceptual scheme of meteorology. Genetics and meteorology are about different subject matters. They are not incompatible with each other, they are merely mutually irrelevant. The argument against strong relativism begins with the recognition that the troubling kind of cognitive relativism – like the troubling kind of moral relativism – has to do with views that make incompatible claims about the *same* subjects.

One way of seeing what is involved here is to recognize that if two theories are incompatible, then they make competing claims about the universe. But there is only one universe – and all of us inhabit it. It follows that at most one of us is right. Strong cognitive relativists seem to want to deny this. They seem to think that two people in the same universe could both rightly make opposing claims about the truth. This view is apparently absurd: can we offer an argument that makes it clear why?

Consider two conceptual schemes, ENGLISH and AZANDE, associated with two languages, say English and Zande. The strong relativist says that there could be a sentence, $S_{ENGLISH}$, which was true relative to ENGLISH and whose translation, S_{AZANDE}, into Zande, was false relative to AZANDE. Now, as we saw in the chapter on language, Frege argued that the meaning of a sentence in effect determined what the universe would have to be like if it were true. Suppose this is right. Since a sentence of Zande is a translation of an English sentence if and only if they mean the same, there are two ways in which a strong relativist could now apply Frege's theory.

On one of them, we would say that, in order for S_{AZANDE} to be a translation of $S_{ENGLISH}$, it would have to be a sentence that would be true relative to AZANDE in the same circumstances that $S_{ENGLISH}$ would be true relative to ENGLISH. But that would make strong relativism impossible. For there could be no sentence which was both

(a) true relative to AZANDE – and thus a translation of $S_{ENGLISH}$, which is true relative to ENGLISH; and
(b) false relative to AZANDE – and thus evidence of strong cognitive relativism.

There could be no such sentence, that is, unless Zande contains sentences which are both true and false at once!

The other way to apply Frege's theory would be to say that, in order for S_{AZANDE} to be a translation of $S_{ENGLISH}$, it would have to be a sentence that would be true relative to AZANDE in the same circumstances that $S_{ENGLISH}$ would be true relative to AZANDE. But until we know how to translate $S_{ENGLISH}$ into Azande, how are we supposed to be able to tell whether it is true or false with respect to the Zande conceptual scheme? If Frege's theory of meaning is right, the Azande could only decide what $S_{ENGLISH}$ meant if they knew what it would be for it to be true for them. But there seems to be no way that we can explain this to them. In particular, because strong relativists believe truth is *always* relative to a conceptual scheme, they cannot, at this point, try to explain what it would be for S_{ENGLISH} to be not true-relative-to-ENGLISH or true-relative-to-AZANDE, but, simply, *true*. For if truth is not always relative to a conceptual scheme, then strong relativism is just false.

The general point is this. For two sentences, S and S', to be incompatible, it must be possible for us to recognize that S says what S' denies. But the only way of translating a sentence, S, in one language into a sentence, S', in another, so as to be in a position to confirm this incompatibility, is to suppose – as a minimum – that S and S' would be true in the same circumstances. It follows that strong relativism – the claim that we have reason to suppose that there are different conceptual schemes in one of which some sentence, S, is true and in another relative to which its translation, S', is false – is incoherent. For there could be no evidence that this was so.

8.7 The argument for weak relativism

But if there is an argument against strong relativism, the argument against weak relativism is harder to make. We could come to learn that the Azande had a concept of the soul, or *mbisimo*, of a person, which operated in certain ways, and that they took the behavior of conscious people to be evidence for the existence of that *mbisimo*. There seems to be, at least prima facie, no difficulty in understanding this claim. Nor does it seem difficult to understand that in their way of thinking – their conceptual scheme – what we took to be evidence that someone wanted meat was evidence that their *mbisimo* wanted meat. These seem to be different claims, and we might eventually feel that we understood what each of them meant. After learning English (and ENGLISH, with it) we could learn Azande (and AZANDE) in the way Zande children learn the language – not by translation, but directly. But we might still be able to think of no way of marshalling evidence that discriminated between these two ways of thinking about human mentality and behavior.

We might also agree that you could only use one of these conceptual schemes at a time, but that nothing in the evidence forced you to use one or the other. As Evans-Pritchard found, it is possible to get used to using extremely alien forms of thought.

I want now to argue that this sort of weak cognitive relativism is possible. I shall argue, more precisely, that it is possible, as Kant thought, that the way we think about the world – our conceptual scheme – helps to determine what it is reasonable for us to believe. I shall also argue that this is not too surprising.

To see why weak relativism is less puzzling than it might at first appear, all we need to do is to begin with a simple case. In the language spoken in Germany in the Middle Ages there was no word that translated our word "brown." The only word Middle German speakers had that covered brown things covered purple things also. They called things that were brown-or-purple *braun*. These people could certainly tell brown and purple things apart by looking at them. But if you had asked them to put marbles together into natural groupings, they would have put all the brown and purple marbles – all the *braun* ones – together.

This difference is connected systematically with other differences between Middle German and modern English, for it follows that they did not have a word that accurately translated "color," for example. They had the word *Farbe* instead. If *Farbe* translated "color," then every truth about color would correspond to a truth about *Farbe*. But they did not think that brown and purple marbles were of two *Farben*: they thought they were of one *Farbe*.

Still, it is not too hard to see how we would translate this language. *Braun* translates as "brown or purple"; *Farbe* refers to colors, excluding brown and purple, but including brown-or-purple.

There would be a difference between operating these two conceptual schemes. Middle German speakers might have remembered the *Farbe* of many things but not – or not so easily – their color. *We* would continue to remember colors. Each of us could work out what the other would remember and take to be important about the looks of things, but different things would continue to strike each of us as important. Now there might be reasons for preferring one scheme to another: perhaps all the brown mushrooms in our country are edible and all the purple ones poisonous. Sensitivity to color would help here, and *Farbe*-sensitivity might be lethal. But the problem would not be that one scheme said that something was true that the other said was false. These would be different ways of looking at the world; and evidence would lead them to say that brown things were *braun* and us to say that they were "brown." And it would not be a matter of evidence which way of looking at the world was right.

This simple case leads naturally into the more complex case of Zande belief in the *mbisimo*. Remember what I said in Chapter 1 about a functionalist theory of the mental. If there can be a functionalist theory of the mind, why could there not be a functionalist theory of the *mbisimo*? Indeed, if you remember what I said about functionalism in Chapter 1, you can argue that there *must* be such a theory. I said that, at the most general level, a functionalist theory explains the internal states of a system by fixing how they interact with input, and with other internal states, to produce output. But the only things we know about directly are the inputs and outputs. That is all the evidence there is. There seem, therefore, to be the same reasons for thinking that there must be a functionalist theory of the *mbisimo* as there are for believing there must be a functionalist theory of the mind.

If the Zande theory of the *mbisimo* and our theory of the mind made exactly the same predictions about what inputs would lead to what outputs, no amount of evidence would distinguish them. You might argue that this just showed that *mbisimo* meant the same as *mind*. But I think this would be wrong. For the internal states that the two theories proposed could operate in different ways. To put it in the terms of Chapter 1, the Ramsey-sentences of the two theories could have different structures, even if their consequences for input and output were the same.

The two theories might then differ, in the ways that Middle German and English differ. Classifications of states of the *mbisimo* that struck the Azande as natural might correspond to no natural classifications of ours. Perhaps, over time, the Azande would find that our theory suited them better; perhaps we could take a cue from theirs. Most likely, however, as our understanding of the world developed, both of us would change our theories. And there would be nothing to guarantee that we would end up with the same theory, at least so long as we continued to speak different languages.

If I am right, evidence and reason cannot, by themselves, lead us to one truth. There may be different ways of conceptualizing the one reality. To say this is to say more than that our knowledge of the world is fallible. We do, indeed, know that our own theories are not perfect. Many of the things that happen in our world we cannot explain; many others actually are inconsistent with our best current theories. But we also usually suppose that with time and effort we could make our theories better; explaining what could not be explained before, and modifying the theories to avoid their false consequences. Even those who believe that, because fallibilism is true, we are always at risk of being wrong think that it is possible to use evidence to get reasonable evidence that one theory – say, our everyday theory of belief and desire – is less adequate to the facts than another – say, neuro-physiological theories of the mind.

But if I am right, this is not so. Relative to one conceptual scheme, it might be natural to say "Jane believes that it's raining"; relative to another, it might be better to say "Jane is in neural-state X"; or even "Jane's *mbisimo* is in state Y." And it might be impossible for one person to make all of these equally their natural way of reacting to the evidence, so that, in that sense, these conceptual schemes were incompatible. The choice between the three "realities" would not be settled by evidence, but by asking: "Which conceptual scheme is it easier to live with?" There is no reason to suppose that two people in the same culture, let alone in different ones, would be bound to agree on the answer to this question.

This does not mean that reasons and evidence are not essential tools of thought in *every* conceptual scheme; it means only that our concepts are, in a sense, partly constitutive of the reality about which we offer evidence and reasons.

8.8 Philosophy and religion

The distinguishing marks of formal philosophy that I have so far identified are marks of intellectual inquiry in a literate culture. Like all such intellectual inquiry, it involves systematic, abstract, general theorizing, with a concern to think critically and consistently; sometimes in the company of thinkers long dead. These features reflect the fact that formal philosophy involves not just a way of thinking, but also a way of writing. The systematic character of philosophy shows up quite clearly as we think philosophically about philosophy's own character: **meta-philosophy** – systematic critical reflection on the nature of philosophy – is itself part of the philosophical enterprise.

I have argued that evidence and reasons are central to this systematic enterprise, even if they are not sufficient to pick one conceptual scheme as the only correct one. Even as the Azande became literate, they might have developed a style of thought with the marks of literate intellectual life, while still having a conceptual scheme different from ours.

But the development of literacy would almost certainly have one other important consequence for them, which it has had for the Western intellectual tradition. It would lead to an intellectual division of labor. Just as, in industrialized societies, there has been an increasing specialization of material production – think how many different skills go into the design, the making, the distribution and the sale of a car – so there are many different skills, trainings and institutions involved in the production and transmission of ideas. Even within, say, physics, there are not only many subdivisions of subject-matter – astronomy, particle physics, condensed matter theory – there are also many jobs within each of the fields – laboratory technicians, theorists, experimentalists, teachers, text-book authors, and so on. The division of labor in the West is so highly developed that, as the American philosopher of science Hilary Putnam has pointed out, we even leave the task of understanding some parts of our language to experts: it is because words like "electron" have precise meanings for physicists that I, who have no very good grasp of their meaning, can use them, and the same goes for the word "contract" and lawyers. These words, as my tool, only do their business for me because their meanings are sharpened by others.

One of the ways in which our high degree of intellectual division of labor shows up is in comparison, once more, with the intellectual life of the Azande. They did not have this substantial proliferation of kinds of theoretical knowledge. Though they did have what Evans-Pritchard called "witch-doctors," any adult male could conduct an oracle or perform magic or hunt, because most people shared the same concepts and beliefs. Any senior person in Zande society would be a source of information about their beliefs about gods, spirits, witchcraft, oracles and magic.

In the Western tradition, by contrast, many of our central intellectual projects are carried out by specialists. Questions about God – which, if there is a God, are as important as any questions could be for us – *are* studied in our culture by a variety of different sorts of experts. Though the philosophy of religion, for example, addresses theological questions, it shares that task with theology and with other kinds of Western religious thought. Similarly, theories of the ultimate constitution of nature are central to any folk-philosophy; and, once more, though metaphysics and the philosophy of science address these questions, they share them with the natural sciences.

But, unlike Zande religion, Western religions – Christianity and Judaism – are deeply bound up with writing; and, without writing, physics would be impossible. If literacy and its consequences mark formal philosophy off from traditional thought, how can we distinguish Western philosophy from Western religion and Western science?

It is easy enough to point to one thing that distinguishes formal philosophy from Western religion as a whole. Religion involves not only theories about how the world is and should be, but also specific rituals – the Jewish *seder*, the Catholic Mass, the Protestant Lord's Supper – and practices such as prayer. These are all practices a philosopher could engage in; but in doing so, he or she would not be acting as a philosopher but as a believer.

But there is, of course, a reason why it is so natural to think of philosophy and religion together; a reason that is connected with what I said at the beginning of this chapter. All religions – even those, like Buddhism, that believe neither in God nor in systematic theory – are associated with a view of human life, of our place in the world, and of how we ought to live. And such a connected set of views is often called a "philosophy of life." The philosophy of life of a modern woman or man is, in effect, the folk-philosophy of a literate culture.

The questions formal philosophers ask are relevant to these issues: studying formal philosophy can change your philosophy of life. For a literate intellectual, it is natural to think systematically about these questions. But if one is also religious, that systematic thought will involve not only the sorts of philosophical question I have raised in this book, but questions of theology also. It is important, therefore, to distinguish philosophy from theology, the critical intellectual activity that is a part – but only a part – of modern religion; as, indeed, it was only a part of the religion of the European Middle Ages.

One crucial difference between philosophy and most theology is that, in philosophy, we do not usually presuppose the truth of any particular religious claims. When philosophers address questions central to Christianity – the existence of God, or the morality of abortion – they do so in the light of their religious beliefs, but with a concern to defend even those claims that can be taken, within a religious tradition, for granted. But theologians, too, offer evidence and reasons for many of the claims they make about God. They are often concerned not only with setting out religious doctrines, but with systematizing them and relating them, through the use of reason, to our beliefs about the natural world. When this happens it is hard to tell where theology ends and the philosophy of religion begins.

Though there are, then, some ways of distinguishing most theology from most philosophy of religion, they have not so much to do with subject matter as with issues that have, in the end, to do with the way in which philosophy and theology have been institutionalized as professions. Philosophy of religion addresses religion with the training of philosophers: that means, in part, that it uses the same tools of logic and semantics, the same concepts of epistemology and ethics, that philosophers use outside the philosophy of religion. Christian theology, on the other hand, is closely bound both to traditions of interpreting a central text, the Bible, and to the experience of the Christian church in history. Jewish religious writing is similarly tied to the *Torah* and to other texts; and rooted, similarly, in its history. But because the central questions of theology are crucially relevant to the central questions of human life, it should not be a surprise that philosophers and theologians often come to ask the same questions. Someone who cares – as, surely, we should – about whether religious claims are true may want to follow both these routes to a deeper understanding of religion.

8.9 Philosophy and science

The distinction between philosophy and science is sometimes held to be, by comparison, a simple matter. Though Isaac Newton called his *Principia*, the first great text of modern theoretical physics, a work of natural philosophy, many philosophers since would have said that it was not a work of what I have called formal philosophy. The reason they would have given is that Newton's work was about (admittedly, very abstract) **empirical** questions – questions to which the evidence of sensation and perception is relevant. Formal philosophy, on the other hand, deals with questions which are **conceptual** – having to do not with how the world happens to be, but with how we conceive of it.

But this way of making the distinction between philosophy and science seems to me to be too simple. Much theoretical physics is very difficult to connect in any straightforward way with empirical evidence and much philosophy of mind depends on facts about how our human minds happen to be constituted. It will not do, either, to say that the use of empirical evidence in science involves experiments, while in philosophy it does not. For thought experiments play an important role in both science and philosophy; and many branches of the sciences – cosmology, for example – have to proceed with very few, if any, experiments, just because experiments would be so hard to arrange. (Imagine trying to organize the explosion of a star!)

Nevertheless, there is a difference – which, like the difference between philosophy and theology, is by no means absolute – between philosophy and physics: and it has to do with the fact that the kind of empirical evidence that is relevant to the sciences must usually be collected a good deal more systematically than the evidence that is sometimes relevant in philosophy.

Even this difference is a matter of degree, however. In the philosophy of language – in semantics, for example – we need to collect systematic evidence about how our languages are actually used if our theories of meaning are to be useful; and, as we saw in Chapter 2, the discovery of cases like the ones that Gettier thought up can play a crucial role in epistemology. But there is a pattern in the history of Western intellectual life, in which problems that are central at one time to philosophy become the basis of new, more specialized sciences. Thus, modern linguistics grows out of philosophical reflection on language, just as economics and sociology grew out of philosophical reflection on society, and physics grew out of Greek, Roman and Medieval philosophical reflection on the nature of matter and motion. As these special subjects develop, some of the problems which used to concern philosophers move out of the focus of philosophical attention. But the more conceptual problems remain.

This pattern is reflected in the fact that where philosophy and the specialized sciences address the same problem, the more empirical questions are usually studied by the scientists and the less empirical ones by the philosophers. That is the sense in which philosophy really is a primarily conceptual matter.

The division of labor between science and philosophy has been productive. While philosophical work has often generated new sciences, new philosophical problems are also generated by the development of science. Some of the most interesting philosophical work of our day, for example, involves examining the conceptual problems raised by relativity and quantum theory. To do this work – or, at least, to do it well – it is necessary to understand theoretical physics. But it also requires the tools and training of the philosopher.

8.10 The special character of philosophy

What can we say we have learned about the distinctive style of philosophical work? The first lesson, as I have just argued, is that philosophy, even when it is answering apparently particular questions – What is the difference between M and my mother? – approaches them in the light of broadly conceptual, abstract considerations, even though it would be foolish to do philosophy without one eye on the empirical world. That is why philosophical reasoning is so often *a priori*: for truths about conceptual matters can be discovered by reason alone. Nevertheless, as I have insisted, there is no sharp line between philosophical questions and those of other specialized areas of thought, such as theology or the sciences.

Another lesson, confirmed many times in this book, is that there is no area of philosophy that is independent of all the others. The subject is not a collection of separate problems that can be addressed independently. Issues in epistemology and the philosophy of language reappear in discussions of mind, morals, politics, law, science and, in this chapter, of religion. Questions in morals – When may we take somebody's property against their will? – depend on issues in the philosophy of mind – Are inter-personal comparisons of utility possible?; and are further dependent on metaphysical questions – What is consciousness?

What is at the root of the philosophical style is a desire to give a *general* and *systematic* account of our thought and experience, one that is developed critically, in the light of evidence and argument. You will remember that John Rawls used the notion of **reflective equilibrium** to describe the goal of philosophical thought. We start with an intuitive understanding of a problem, seeing it "through a glass, darkly"; and, from these intuitions we build a little theory. The theory sharpens and guides our intuitions, and we return to theorizing. As we move back and forth from intuition to theory, we approach, we hope, a reflective equilibrium where theory and intuition coincide.

If the history of philosophy is anything to go by, one person's reflective equilibrium is another person's state of puzzlement. Cartesianism seemed to many seventeenth-century thinkers a reasonable way of understanding the mind and its place in the world. To modern behaviorists, on the other hand, and to functionalists, it seems to raise too many philosophical difficulties. Perhaps the history of the subject is better represented by the picture suggested by the great German philosopher, Georg Wilhelm Friedrich Hegel.

Hegel thought that the life of reason proceeded by a continuing sequence of ideas. First, someone would develop a systematic theory – which Hegel called a **thesis**. It would then be denied by those who supported the **anti-thesis**; and, finally, a new view would develop which took what was best of each to produce a new **synthesis**. That is what we saw in the movement from Cartesianism to behaviorism to functionalism in the philosophy of mind; or from realism to emotivism to prescriptivism in moral philosophy. But this is not the end of the process. On a Hegelian view, a synthesis can itself become the thesis for some new anti-thesis.

Hegel also thought, however, that this process was tending toward a final goal, in which philosophy approached ever closer to the absolute truth. But if, as I have argued, both fallibilism and weak relativism are true, we need not accept this part of his view. As our understanding of the world changes, as we find new ways to live our lives, there will be new problems to address, new questions to ask, new syntheses to be created. Because fallibilism is (probably!) true, we will never be sure that our theories are right. And because weak relativism is true, it really will be a task of creation – the invention of concepts – as well as a voyage of discovery. As a result, philosophy, along with other intellectual specializations, can change both its tools and its problems.

In this chapter I have looked at the character of philosophy and suggested some contrasts between it and traditional thought, religion and the sciences. But the problems we have discussed in this book are explored with *all* the resources of literate culture. Thus, literature, too, examines moral and political ideas: and the novel explores the nature of human experience in society, and, sometimes – as in some science fiction – our understanding of the natural world. To claim that philosophy is important and enjoyable is not to say that we should not learn from and enjoy these other styles of thought, these other kinds of writing.

The questions I have asked in this book are some of those that are important to philosophy now. I have addressed them with some of the intellectual tools that philosophers now find useful. If you share our vision of a general and systematic understanding of the central problems of human life, they are questions you will want to ask also. I hope I have persuaded you that you *do* share that vision. And if you do, you will be irresistibly drawn to the questions of philosophy. In that sense they are, indeed, necessary questions.

Sources and acknowledgments

The sources for the material cited are given here, with the sections in which the citations occur. I have modernized spelling and sometimes modified translations. For classical works I have given chapter and section headings from the original, where appropriate, so that you may use any edition. Where I have given copyright details, I should like to thank the authors and the copyright holders for permission to reproduce material.

Chapter 1: Mind

1.2 The long quotation from the fourth part of the *Discourse* is loosely based on the translation of *A Discourse on Method, Meditations and Principles*, the Everyman edition, by John Veitch (Dutton, New York; Dent, London, 1912), p. 27. Compare F. E. Sutcliffe's translation *Discourse on Method and the Meditations* (Penguin, New York & Harmondsworth, Middlesex, 1968), p. 54.

1.3 References to Ludwig Wittgenstein's *Philosophical Investigations* translated by G.E.M. Anscombe (Macmillan, New York; Blackwell, Oxford, 1953), © Macmillan Publishing Company, U.S.A., © Basil Blackwell, U.K., are usually made to the numbered sections. The quotation is section 258.

1.7 The "simple theory of pain" is from Ned Block's "Introduction: What is functionalism?" in *Readings in Philosophy of Psychology*, Ned Block ed. (Harvard University Press, Cambridge, Massachusetts, 1980), Volume I, p. 174.

Chapter 2: Knowledge

2.2 The passage from Plato's *Theaetetus* is slightly modified from John McDowell's excellent translation (Clarendon Press, New York & Oxford, 1973), p. 94.

2.3 Irving Thalberg's "In Defense of Justified True Belief" (referred to here) is in the *Journal of Philosophy*, Volume 66 (1969).

2.3 In this chapter I have used the translation of Descartes' *Meditations* by G.E.M. Anscombe and P. Geach from *Descartes: Philosophical Writings*, translated by P. Geach (Bobbs-Merrill, New York, 1971), excerpted in *Reason at Work: Introductory Readings in Philosophy*, S.M. Cahn, P. Kitcher & G. Sher eds. (Harcourt Brace Jovanovich, San Diego, California, 1984). The long passages are from the First Meditation (p. 286 of *Reason at Work*) and the Second Meditation (p. 287 of *Reason at Work*).

2.4 & 2.5 The quotations from Locke's *Essay Concerning Human Understanding*, the Everyman edition, John Yolton ed. (Dutton, New York; Dent, London, 1961) are: Book 2, Chapter 1, Section 2, Volume I, p. 77; Book 2, Chapter 1, Sections 3 and 4, Volume I, pp. 77-8; Book 4, Chapter 11, Section 6, Volume II, p. 230; Book 4, Chapter 11, Section 7, Volume II, p. 230; Book 4, Chapter 11, Section 10, Volume II, p. 233. Most of the passages I have quoted are also in *Reason at Work*.

2.7 Gettier's "Is Justified True Belief Knowledge?" appeared originally in the journal *Analysis* 23.6 (1963). The example, including the quotation, is in *Reason at Work*, pp. 282-3.

2.7 Alvin I. Goldman's paper "Discrimination and Perceptual Knowledge," which appeared originally in the *Journal of Philosophy* 73.20 (1976), © the *Journal of Philosophy*, is reprinted in G. Pappas and M. Swain eds., *Knowledge and Justification* (Cornell University Press, Ithaca & London, 1978). The quotation is in *Knowledge and Justification*, p. 122.

Chapter 3: Language and Logic

3.2 The three quotations from Thomas Hobbes's *The Elements of Philosophy: Concerning Body* are from Chapter 2, Sections 1 and 3, reprinted in *Hobbes Selections*, F.J.E. Woodbridge ed. (Scribner's, New York, 1958), pp. 13-15.

3.3 Nim Chimpsky is described in *Nim: A Chimpanzee who learned Sign Language*, Herbert S. Terrace (Knopf, New York, 1979).

3.3 The quotation is from section 293 of Wittgenstein's *Philosophical Investigations.*

3.4 I have used Max Black's translation of Gottlob Frege's "On Sense and Reference" in *Translations from the Philosophical Writings of Gottlob Frege*, Peter Geach and Max Black eds. (Blackwell, Oxford, Second Edition, 1970). I am grateful to the translator for permission. The quotation is on p. 62.

3.6 The Frege quotation is from "On Sense and Reference", p. 67.

Chapter 4: Science

4.7 The quotation from Grover Maxwell is from "The Ontological Status of Theoretical Entities" in H. Feigl and G. Maxwell eds., *Minnesota Studies in the Philosophy of Science* III (University of Minnesota Press, Minneapolis, 1962), p. 7.

4.8 The quotation from Hume is from Section 4, Part II of *An Enquiry Concerning Human Understanding*, Eric Steinberg ed. (Hackett Publishing Co., Indianapolis, 1984), p. 24.

Chapter 5: Morality

5.2 The quotation from Hume is from Book III, Part 1, Section 1 of *A Treatise of Human Nature*, L.A. Selby-Bigge ed., revised P.H. Nidditch (Clarendon Press, New York & Oxford, 1978), pp. 469-70.

5.4 The quotation is from Alasdair MacIntyre's *A Short History of Ethics* (Macmillan Publishing Co., New York, 1966; Routledge & Kegan Paul, London, 1967), © Macmillan, pp. 252-3.

5.6 The quotations from Kant are from pp. 88-90 of *The Groundwork of the Metaphysic of Morals*, translated and analyzed by H.J. Paton (Harper Torchbooks, New York, 1964). The British edition is *The Moral Law* (Hutchinson, London, 1948).

5.7 The quotation from R.M. Hare is from *Moral Thinking* (Clarendon Press, New York & Oxford, 1981), p. 90.

5.10 The quotations from R.M. Hare are from sections 2.3 and 2.4 of *Moral Thinking.*

5.10 The quotations from Jonathan Glover's *Causing Death and Saving Lives* (Penguin, New York & Harmondsworth, Middlesex, 1977), © Jonathan Glover, are from pp. 73 and 79.

Chapter 6: Politics

6.1 My account of the Mbuti is based on Colin Turnbull's *Wayward Servants: The Two Worlds of the African Pygmies* (Greenwood Press, Westport, Connecticut, Reprint Edition, 1976) and *The Forest People* (Simon & Schuster, New York, 1968).

6.2 The quotations from Thomas Hobbes are all from Part I, Chapters 11 (pp. 160-8), 13 (pp. 183-8), and 15 (pp. 201-17), of *Leviathan*, C.B. Macpherson ed. (Penguin, New York & Harmondsworth, Middlesex, 1985). Chapters 13 and 15 – but not Chapter 11 – are also in Woodbridge's *Hobbes Selections*, cited above.

6.4 The quotation is from Robert Nozick's *Anarchy, State and Utopia* (Basic Books, New York, 1974; Basil Blackwell, Oxford, 1974), © Basic Books Inc., USA, © Basil Blackwell, UK, p. 7.

6.4 My exposition is based on Morton Davis's *Game Theory: A Non-technical Introduction* (Basic Books, New York, Revised Edition, 1983). The quotation is from p. 13.

6.7 The quotation is from John Rawls's *A Theory of Justice* (Belknap Press of Harvard University Press, Cambridge, Massachusetts; Clarendon Press, Oxford, 1971), p. 137.

6.8 The quotation from Robert Paul Wolff is from *Understanding Rawls* (Princeton University Press, Princeton, New Jersey, 1977), © Princeton University Press, pp. 31-2.

6.9 is much influenced by Wolff's *Understanding Rawls*; I am grateful, too, for his help in revising this section.

6.10 The quotation from John Rawls's *A Theory of Justice* is from p. 15.

6.10 The quotation is from Robert Nozick's *Anarchy, State and Utopia*, p. 195.

6.11 The quotation from John Rawls's *A Theory of Justice* is from p. 302.

6.11 The short quotation defining historical principles is from Robert Nozick's *Anarchy, State and Utopia*, p. 155.

6.12 The quotations from Robert Nozick's *Anarchy, State and Utopia* are from pp. ix, 118, and ix again.

6.12 C.B. Macpherson has a good edition of John Locke's *Second Treatise of Government* (Hackett Publishing Co., Indianapolis, Indiana, 1980). The

SOURCES AND ACKNOWLEDGMENTS

quotations are from Chapter 2, Section 6; p. 9 of Macpherson's edition.

6.13 Lawrence Davis formulates the outline I give of Nozick's theory in "Nozick's Entitlement Theory", which appeared in the *Journal of Philosophy* 73.21 (1976) and is reprinted in *Reading Nozick*, Jeffrey Paul ed. (Totowa, New Jersey, Rowman & Littlefield, 1981), p. 345.

6.13 The quotation from Robert Nozick's *Anarchy, State and Utopia* is from the footnote on p. 179.

6.13 I rely heavily on Judith Jarvis Thomson's "Some Ruminations on Rights," which appeared originally in *The University of Arizona Law Review* 19 (1977), reprinted in *Reading Nozick*. The quotations are from pp. 137-8 of *Reading Nozick*.

Chapter 7: Law

7.1 The quotation is from St. Thomas Aquinas's *Summa Theologiae* 1a 2ae 90.4; cited in R.A. Duff, *Trials and Punishments* (Cambridge University Press, New York & Cambridge, 1986), p. 74.

7.1 The quotation from John Austin is from *The Province of Jurisprudence Determined and The Uses of the Study of Jurisprudence*, H.L.A. Hart ed. (The Humanities Press, New York, 1965; Weidenfeld & Nicolson, London, 1954), p. 184.

7.2 The quotation is from p. 81 of R.A. Duff, *Trials and Punishments*, which has much influenced this chapter.

7.4 Chapters 5 and 6 of Herbert Hart's *The Concept of Law* (Clarendon Press, New York & Oxford, 1961), are relevant to section 7.4. The quotations are from pp. 70-9.

7.6 The quotation from Bentham is cited from Ted Honderich's *Punishment: The Supposed Justifications* (Penguin, New York & Harmondsworth, Middlesex, 1984), pp. 51-2.

7.7 The quotation from Kant is cited from Honderich's book, p. 22.

Chapter 8: Philosophy

8.3 & 8.4 The quotations from Sir Edward Evans-Pritchard's *Witchcraft, Oracles and Magic Among the Azande* are from Eva Gillies's abridged edition (Oxford University Press, New York & Oxford, 1976), © Oxford University Press, pp. 201-3.

Glossary

Some of the keenest debates in the history of philosophy are about how to understand certain concepts. Thus, to define a philosophical term is usually to take sides in a long-standing philosophical dispute. In this glossary I have tried to be as brief as is consistent with being helpful, and to provide readers with a reminder of the meaning of a term and a reference in parentheses to the section where its meaning is first introduced. (At that point in the text the word itself occurs in **bold** type.) The best way to learn how philosophical terms are to be understood is to see them used in philosophical argument; so these are reminders of meanings, not strict definitions.

a posteriori Used of propositions that can be known only on the basis of evidence drawn from experience – in contrast to *a priori*. (3.8)

a priori Used of propositions that can be known by reasoning, without evidence drawn from experience – in contrast to *a posteriori*. (3.8)

absolute sovereign A ruler who is not constitutionally limited in the exercise of power. (6.3)

absolutism In ethics, the view that certain acts are right (or wrong) irrespective of the consequences – in contrast to **consequentialism**. (5.9)

accidental generalizations True generalizations which do not follow from laws of nature. (4.10)

accommodative Used to describe traditional cultures that are highly *accommodating* of views that conflict with their own – in contrast to **adversarial**. (8.2)

action-guiding Moral beliefs are action-guiding because they commit us to action, independently of our preferences or desires. (5.3)

actual world In **possible-world semantics** the actual world is the **possible world** we are in. (3.7)

adversarial Used to describe Western culture, because intellectual differences often lead to

vigorous argument – in contrast to **accommodative**. (8.2)

ampliative inference Inductive inferences are ampliative because the conclusion contains more information than the premises. Deductive inferences are not ampliative. (4.8)

analytic jurisprudence The systematic study of laws and legal institutions. (7.1)

analytic An analytic sentence is true solely virtue of the meanings of the terms it contains: e.g. *A male child is a son*. A **declarative sentence** – such as *Joe has a son* – that is not analytic is **synthetic**. (3.8)

anarchism The view that no exercise of political authority is justified. (6.2)

antecedent See conditional. (3.9)

antecedent conditions See deductive-nomological model of explanation. (4.6)

anti-thesis See thesis. (8.10)

argument. In logic, an argument is a sequence of **declarative sentences**, which leads us to a final sentence, which is the **conclusion**. The other sentences, the **premises**, are supposed to support the conclusion. (3.9)

artificial language See natural language. (3.9)

assertion A **speech-act** in which a sentence is uttered with the intention of communicating that its **truth conditions** hold. (3.10)

attitudes An **action-guiding** mental state. If it disposes the agent towards something it is a **pro-attitude** to it; if against, a **con-attitude**. (5.3)

behaviorism The view that to have a mind is to be disposed to behave in certain specific ways in response to sensory and perceptual input. (1.2)

Cartesian The adjective from Descartes; hence **Cartesianism** refers to Descartes philosophical views. (1.3)

categorical imperative Kant's term for an imperative that is not **hypothetical**. Kant believed that moral *oughts* were categorical imperatives. (5.3)

causal theories of knowledge Causal theories interpret the **justification condition** as requiring that those true beliefs that count as knowledge must be appropriately caused. (2.7)

civil society Society organized in the form of a state. (6.2)

cognitive relativism Relativism about factual matters. A strong version holds that what is *true* is relative to a **conceptual scheme**; a weak version, that what it is *reasonable to believe* is relative to a **conceptual scheme**. (8.2)

cognitivism In ethics, the view that we can have moral knowledge; **non-cognitivism** is the view that we cannot. (5.3)

componentiality thesis *If two words or phrases have the same meaning, then we should be able to replace one of them with the other in any sentence*, S, *without changing the meaning of* S. The componentiality thesis is a very powerful tool for testing **semantic theories**. (3.4)

con-attitude See **attitude**. (5.3)

conceptual framework or scheme The networks of beliefs that define our concepts – as the **Ramsey-sentence** of common-sense psychology characterizes such notions as *belief*. (8.5)

conclusion See **argument**. (3.9)

conditional A sentence of the form "If *S*, then *T*" is a conditional; "*S*" is the **antecedent** and "*T*" is the **consequent**. (3.9)

confirmation theory The study of the processes by which scientific generalizations can be confirmed or supported by evidence, especially when it focuses on the **form** of the evidence-sentences and the generalizations. (4.10)

conjecture In Popper's philosophy of science, the development of theories is seen as the making of imaginative conjectures that are held onto only until experimental **refutation**. This is in contrast to **inductivist** views, which hold that theories and generalizations are *discovered* by observation and experimentation. See **falsificationism**. (4.9)

conjunction A sentence containing an *and*; in "*S* and *T*," "*S*" and "*T*" are called *conjuncts*. Also used to refer to the word *and*, as well as to the process of making a sentence with *and*. (3.9)

connective Words (or groups of words, such as *either . . . or . . .*) that can be used to form a sentence out of two (or more) other sentences. Conjunction and disjunction are both connectives, as is the **conditional**. (3.9)

consequent See **conditional**. (3.9)

consequentialism The view that an act should be assessed purely by its consequences – in contrast to **absolutism**. (5.9)

consistent A set of beliefs, theories or sentences is consistent if it is logically possible that they should all be true at once. (2.3)

Context of discovery Questions about how to set about deepening our scientific understanding – for example, How should we design experiments? – belong to the context of discovery. Questions that have to do with how we organize the data we collect from experiment and observation so we can decide whether it supports our theories belong to the **context of justification**. (4.2)

context of justification See **context of discovery**. (4.2)

contingent In possible-world semantics, true in only some **possible worlds** – hence, the opposite of **necessary**. (3.8)

contrary-to-fact conditional See **counterfactual**. (4.10)

copula In traditional logic the subject *S*, and the predicate *P*, were said to be connected by the copula *is* or *is not* to produce a sentence that said "*S* is *P*" or "*S* is not *P*." (5.2)

co-referentiality Two expressions are co-referential if and only if they have the same **reference**. (3.4)

correspondence rules See **received view of theories**. (4.5)

counterfactual A sentence that says what would have happened if something that didn't happen *had* happened; e.g. *If I'd been at the party, I would have seen Ruth.* (4.10)

declarative sentence Sentences that describe states of affairs, and can therefore be true (if the state of affairs is as they say it is) or false (if it is not). (2.6)

deductive closure principle *Take any two sentences, A and B: if you know that A and know that B, and if from A and B, together, C follows logically, then, if you believe that C, you know that C.* Compare with the **principle of deduction for justification**. (2.3)

deductive-nomological (or DN) model of explanation On Hempel's DN model of explanation, the *explanandum* is explained by deriving it from the laws of a theory and **antecedent conditions**, which characterize the situation in which the *explanandum* occurred. The laws and the **antecedent conditions** constitute the *explanans*. See section 4.6 for details. (4.5)

defeasible Evidence for *S* which is **consistent** with the falsity of *S* is defeasible; evidence which is *not* is **indefeasible**. (2.3)

demarcation problem The problem of saying what it is that distinguishes science from other kinds of intellectual activity. (4.1)

determinism The claim that every event has a cause. (4.10)

deterrence The deterrence theory of punishment says that punishment is justified to the extent that it succeeds in *deterring* crime. (7.6)

diachronic An approach that looks at the historical development of science is a diachronic approach – contrasts with a **synchronic** approach that looks at questions about science at a particular time. (4.2)

difference principle Rawls's view that inequalities in liberty or in income are justified only if they work out to the advantage of the worst-off. (6.8)

disjunction A sentence containing an *or*; in "*S* or *T*," "*S*" and "*T*" are called *disjuncts*. Also used to refer to the word *or*, as well as to the process of making a sentence with *or*. (3.9)

distributive justice A society is distributively just if its allocation of goods and resources is just. (6.12)

dualism The view that minds and bodies are two quite distinct sorts of thing – contrasts with **monism**. (1.2)

emotivism The view that moral sentences express not beliefs but feelings, preferences, or desires. (5.3)

empiricism Empiricists believe that most or all of our beliefs are justified by sensory and perceptual experience (including experience of our own mental states). The evidence experience provides is *empirical* evidence. (2.4)

end-result principles An end-result principle assesses the justice of an outcome independently of how it came about; **historical principles**, by contrast, assess the justice of an outcome at least in part by whether it came about justly. Rawls's principles of justice are end-result principles, Nozick's are **historical**. (6.11)

entrenched predicates A predicate is entrenched if it has frequently and successfully been used in **induction**. (4.8)

enumerative induction The process of arguing from many instances of *A*s that are *B*s to the conclusion that all *A*s are *B*s. It is the most basic kind of **inductive** argument. An *A* that is a *B* is an *instance* of the law "All *A*s are *B*s." (4.8)

epistemic logic Study of the **logical properties** of sentences containing the word *know*. (3.9)

epistemology Philosophical reflection on the nature of knowledge. (2.1)

equilibrium strategies In a game with two players, a pair of strategies such that each player will be worse off if he or she deviates unilaterally from his or her strategy in that pair. (6.4)

ethics Philosophical reflection on morality. (5.1)

existential quantifier See **quantifier**. (3.5)

explanandum Latin for *what is to be explained*. See **deductive-nomological (or DN) model of explanation**. (4.6)

explanans Latin for *what does the explaining*. See **deductive-nomological (or DN) model of explanation**. (4.6)

extension The extension of a predicate is its **reference** – that is, the class of things to which it refers – or, alternatively, the class of objects that **satisfy** it. The word extension is also used, more generally, to mean the **reference** of any expression: thus, the extension of a sentence would be a **truth value**, that of a name would be an individual, and so on. (3.5)

extensional context An **open sentence** that produces a sentence with the same truth value whenever we substitute an expression with the same reference for the blank is called an extensional context – contrasts with **intensional context**. (3.6)

fallibilism Fallibilists believe that any of our beliefs about the world could be wrong. (2.5)

falsificationism Popper's view that science proceeds by **conjecture** and **refutation**. So-called because of the importance he attaches to the way experiments can *falsify* theories. Popper's answer to the **demarcation problem** is that scientific theories are those that are subjected to rigorous and systematic tests, and it is thus crucial for him that theories be *falsifiable*; that is, capable of being refuted by observation or experiment. (4.9)

fanatics Defined by R.M. Hare as people willing to **universalize** maxims that allow them to do things to other people that they would not like done to themselves. (5.7)

first-order moral questions Questions about what is right and wrong, good and bad. Compare **meta-ethics**. (5.1)

folk-philosophy The sum of the beliefs a culture holds about the central questions of human life. The term is used to contrast this informal sense of philosophy with the kind of **formal philosophy** we have been doing in this book. (8.1)

form Two sentences share their form to the extent that they can be composed from the same **open sentence**. Logicians usually focus on certain specific aspects of form – for example, whether or not a sentence is a **conjunction**. (If it is, it is because it can be formed from the **open sentence** " – *and* –.") In particular, they study the way in which the form of the **premises** of an **argument** determines whether or not it is **valid**. (3.9)

formal philosophy See folk-philosophy. (8.1)

formal truth Also **logical truth**. Most often used to refer to a sentence that has a form which guarantees that it will be true independently of the particular **predicates** and names it contains: e.g. *Peter either is or isn't home*. More generally, any sentence of a **form** that guarantees that it is true. (3.9)

formally valid Logicians say that an **argument** is formally valid when a sentence with the **form** of the **conclusion** must be true if sentences of the form of the **premises** are true. If an argument is formally valid, we say that it has a **valid form**. (3.9)

foundational beliefs. The class of beliefs from which all knowledge is derived, according to **foundationalist epistemologies**. For foundationalist **empiricists**, this class is a class of beliefs derived from experience; for foundationalist **rationalists**, it is the class of truths known by reason. (2.5)

foundationalist epistemology According to all foundationalist epistemologies, (a) we need to find some class of beliefs, of which we have secure knowledge; and (b) once we find this class, we can then honor some of our other beliefs with the special status of knowledge by showing that they are properly supported by the members of this class of **foundational beliefs**. (2.4)

functional role The functional role of a state is the way it functions in mediating between input and output in interaction with other internal states. (1.4)

functionalism In **philosophical psychology**, the view that to have a mind is to have internal states that generate behavior in interaction with each other and with sensory and perceptual input. (1.4)

game theory A mathematical theory which has been put to use in many areas of the social sciences, including, most importantly, economics. For the purposes of game theory, a **game** is any set-up in which there are people – called, naturally enough, *players* – who are choosing strategies for their dealings with each other, in a way that determines what each of them gets as a **payoff**. (6.4)

Golden Rule "Do unto others as you would have them do unto you." (5.7) ·

hedonism The view that what is good is what makes people happy. (5.4)

historical principles See end-result principles. (6.11)

hypothetical imperative Kant's term for an imperative that presupposes something about the preferences of the person to whom it applies. (5.3)

idealism Idealism holds, in opposition to **realism**, that the existence of things depends in some way on their relationship to our minds. Both **verificationism** and **instrumentalism** are forms of idealism. (4.6)

indefeasible See defeasible. (2.3)

indexical If you have to know who is speaking, or when or where, in order to fix the reference of a term, then it is indexical: examples are *I, here, now*. (8.4)

induction The term is used, narrowly, to refer to **enumerative induction** and, more widely, to any reliable form of **ampliative inference**. Hume pointed out that there was a **problem of induction**, namely to explain how such ampliative inferences could be justified. Goodman's **new riddle of induction** – which involves his invented predicate *grue* – shows that there is a serious difficulty about trying to specify which inductive inferences are justified. (4.8)

inductivism The position that science does and should develop by **enumerative induction**. (4.8)

inequality surplus If a social system allows unequal distributions of goods, and produces, as a result, more goods than it would without that inequality; and if these extra goods are more than is needed to pay in the form of incentives to maintain the extra productivity; then that excess of goods is an inequality surplus. (6.8)

infinite regress An infinite regress argument shows (a) that a proposed solution to a problem only creates another one, and (b) that every time we use this proposed solution to deal with the new problem there will automatically be yet another problem to solve. (1.3)

institutional laws Laws that regulate how courts should act but are not backed by threat of force. (7.3)

instrumentalism The view that theories are merely *instruments* that allow us to predict **phenomena** and that the claims they make about unobservable matters are not literally true. (4.6)

intension This term is used in two senses. In the first, more particular, sense, an intension is simply the **sense** or meaning of a predicate. More generally, we say that the intension of a word, phrase or sentence is what is determined when we fix its reference in every possible world. This latter usage came about because it was believed that the **sense** of an expression could be fixed by saying what its **reference** (or **extension**) was in every possible world. But in 3.7 I argued that this was a mistake. (3.5)

intensional context An **open sentence** that does not always produce a sentence with the same **truth value** whenever we substitute an expression with the same reference for the blank – contrasts with **extensional context**. (3.6)

interactionism In philosophical psychology, the view that mental events can cause physical events, and *vice versa*. (1.2)

interpersonal comparison of utility. Comparing the **utilities** of two people in such a way as to make sense of such claims as that Sarah wants coffee twice as much as James does. Many economists and philosophers have argued that this is not possible. (5.9)

intuitionism In ethics, the view that we have a *faculty* – called **moral intuition** – that allows us to perceive moral qualities, just as we have the faculty of vision that allows us to see colors. (5.4)

jurisdiction Laws governing jurisdiction say which courts should deal with which cases. (7.3)

justification condition In epistemology, the condition that a true belief qualifies as knowledge only if it is *justified*. **Empiricists** and **rationalists** differ over what sort of justification is required. (2.2)

language-game A term invented by Wittgenstein to refer to any systematic rule-governed behavior involving the use of words. (1.3)

laws of nature Usually, moral rules, (often with divine authority), which everyone is obliged to obey even outside the constraints of the state. But, in Hobbes, maxims of prudence that would commend themselves to reasonable people in the **state of nature**. (6.2)

legal positivism The view that the concept of law is purely descriptive and that the task of **analytic jurisprudence** is to describe the law as it is. (7.1)

logic The study of **arguments**. (3.9)

logical constant Words whose meanings are fully determined by their **logical properties** are called logical constants. (3.9)

logical positivism A school of philosophy associated with a group of philosophers in Vienna in the 1920s, known as the *Vienna Circle*. This group included Wittgenstein and influenced Popper. Moritz Schlick, one of its leading members, referred to it as *consistent empiricism*. Their most influential doctrine was the **verification principle**, and much of their work was in logic, **philosophical semantics** and philosophy of science. (2.6)

logical properties The properties of words and phrases that affect the validity of arguments in which they occur. Thus, it is a logical property of *and* that when it joins two sentences to form their conjunction, we can deduce either **conjunct** from the sentence thereby formed. (3.9)

logical truth See formal truth. (3.9)

maxim of an action If you consider what your general reason is for some action then you are seeking the maxim of the action. (5.6)

maximin strategy A strategy of *maximizing* the *minimum* **payoff** that you can get in a game. Maximin strategies look like the safest bet in two-person **zero-sum games**; here, maximizing your own minimum is equivalent to minimizing your opponent's maximum **payoff** – the so-called **minimax strategy**. (6.4)

meaning-variance hypothesis The view that the meanings of terms used in reporting observations change when scientific theories change. (4.7)

meta-ethics Reflection on the nature, structure, and status of **first-order moral questions**. (5.1)

meta-philosophy Systematic critical reflection on the nature of philosophy. (8.8)

metaphysics A word coined early in the history of philosophy to refer to the works of Aristotle's that dealt with questions "beyond" or more general than his *Physics*. I have not tried to define this word in the text – it is one of the most widely and least carefully used words in the subject. Among the questions that have most often been seen as belonging to metaphysics are questions about *existence, freedom, necessity, causation,* and *reality*. The **logical positivists** sought to abolish all metaphysical questions on the grounds that they were based on misunderstandings of words and could be settled by analyzing verbal meanings. Most philosophers nowadays would deny that all metaphysical questions can be solved by analyzing meanings.

methodology The study of scientific method, including such questions as the proper design of experiments. (4.2)

mind-body problem The problem of explaining the relations of a mind and its body. (1.2)

minimal state The dominant **protective association** of a region constitutes, in Nozick's view, a minimal state, "limited to the narrow functions of protection against force, theft, fraud, enforcement of contracts and so on." (6.12)

minimax strategy See maximin strategy. (6.4)

mixed sentence See **received view of theories**. (4.5)

mixed strategy A mixed strategy corresponds to a (specified) *chance* of **payoff** A plus a *chance* of **payoff** B plus a *chance* of **payoff** C, and so on; where all the chances add up to 1. (6.4)

modal logic Study of the **logical properties** of sentences containing the words **necessary** and **possible**. Much progress in recent modal logic has been the result of the development of **possible-world semantics**. (3.9)

modus ponens The **valid** form of argument from "If *S*, then *T*" and "*S*" to "*T*." (3.9)

monism In **philosophical psychology**, the view that minds and bodies are both things of the same kind – contrasts with **dualism**. More generally, the view that there is only one kind of thing in the universe. (1.2)

moral content question What do moral judgments mean? (5.2)

moral epistemology The study of the justification of moral judgments. (5.2)

moral intuition See **intuitionism**. (5.4)

moral realism The view that moral beliefs are about an independent moral reality. (5.3)

moral relativism The view that what is good or right depends on who you are (or in what culture or when you live). (5.5)

myth of the given Wilfred Sellars' name for the idea that there must be some experiences that give us knowledge independently of any theory at all. (4.7)

Natural language Languages like English, French, and Spanish that were developed by human communities for communication, as opposed to the **artificial languages** used in computer programs, in mathematics, and in logic. (3.9)

natural Law In the philosophy of law, Natural Law theorists hold that valid laws in human societies are based on standards that are not man-made, and that these standards set limits on what can properly be called a *law*. Natural Law theories usually hold that the contents of Natural Law can be discovered by reason – these theories contrast with **legal positivism**. (7.1)

natural property See **non-natural property**. (5.4)

naturalism A term with many meanings. I have used it to identify a world-view that sees human beings and their philosophical problems as part of the wider world of nature and not as privileged observers of the natural world. (2.8)

naturalistic fallacy Usually, the error of deriving an *ought* from an *is*; though G.E. Moore originally defined it as the fallacy of identifying a **natural** with a **non-natural** property. (5.4)

necessary In **possible-world semantics**, true in every **possible world**. A sentence is necessary if its **negation** is not possible. (3.8)

necessary truth A sentence or belief that is true and could not have been false. (2.3)

necessity of identity The fact that true identity statements between names are all necessarily true. (3.8)

negation The negation of a sentence *S* is a sentence which is true if and only if *S* is false. Forming the negation of a sentence is also called negation. (3.9)

negative rights I have a negative right to do *A* if I am morally free to do *A*, and other people have an obligation not to hinder me if I choose to do it. I have a **positive right** to do *A*, if I am morally free to do *A*, and other people have an obligation to help me if I choose to do it. (5.11)

new riddle of induction See **induction**. (4.8)

nomically possible worlds A way the world might have been without violating the laws of nature. If **determinism** is true, then once the universe started there was only one nomically possible world. (4.10)

non-cognitivism See **cognitivism**. (5.3)

non-natural property G.E. Moore said that *goodness* was a non-natural property, in that unlike, say, yellowness, it could not be studied by natural scientists. Many people have taken Moore's distinction between **natural** and non-natural properties to be another way of making the distinction between facts and values. (5.4)

observation language See **received view of theories**. (4.5)

open sentence A sequence of words produced by removing some words or phrases from a sentence and replacing them with blanks. (3.5)

ordered pair A pair of things taken in a particular order; so that the ordered pair of *John and Mary* is different from the ordered pair of *Mary and John*. (3.5)

original position In Rawls, the situation of the players in the bargaining game that is supposed to produce the theory of justice. In the original position people are behind a **veil of ignorance** – so that they are ignorant of their goals and their relative positions – and they are not **envious**; otherwise they are self-interested and rational. (6.7)

ostensive definition In an ostensive definition we show what a term means by pointing to something it refers to. (1.3)

other-minds problem The problem of justifying

our belief that other people have minds. (1.2)

payoff See **game theory**. (6.4)

PDJ See **principle of deduction for justification**. (2.3)

phenomenology Systematic reflection on the nature of our conscious mental life. (1.1)

phenomenon Anything that can be observed with the senses. (4.4)

philosophical psychology Philosophical reflection on the mind. In contrast to experimental psychology, which investigates the mind's *a posteriori* character, philosophical psychology tends to be *a priori*. (1.1)

philosophical semantics Philosophical reflection on the nature of linguistic meaning. (3.4)

positive rights See **negative rights**.

possible world A way the whole universe might have been. (3.7)

possible-world semantics The study of problems of **reference** and meaning by associating words, phrases or sentences with their references in every **possible world** – that is, with their **intensions**. (3.7)

predicate An expression formed from a sentence containing no **quantifiers** by removing names or other expressions referring to individual people and things. Thus – *is tall* and – *is tall, dark and handsome* are both predicates. This syntactic account corresponds to a more traditional semantic account that says that they are expressions that, when attached to a name, produce a sentence that says something about the person or thing *named*, which is the **subject**. (3.5)

predicate logic The study of the interaction of the logical properties of **negation**, the **connectives** – **conjunction, disjunction** and the **conditional** – and the **quantifiers** *all* and *some*. (3.9)

premise See **argument**. (3.9)

prescriptive A claim about what we *should* say, or think, or do. (4.2)

prescriptivism R.M. Hare's view that moral language consists of **universalized** prescriptions. (5.8)

primacy of the sentence Frege's view that the meaning of a word or phrase is simply its contribution to the meanings of sentences in which it can occur; and thus that, in a sense, words uttered on their own do not mean anything (unless, like "Go!" the single word *is* a sentence). (3.4)

primary rules Hart calls the basic rules that are

necessary if people are to live together in a society at all **primary rules**. These contrast with the **secondary rules** of adjudication, change, enforcement and recognition that are needed to turn a system of primary rules into a legal system. (7.4)

principle of deduction for justification *If you take any two sentences,* A *and* B, *then, if you are justified in believing both* A *and* B, *and if from* A *and* B *together,* C *follows logically, then, if you believe* C, *you are justified in believing* C. Compare with the **deductive closure principle**. (2.3)

principle of the uniformity of nature The claim that the future will resemble the past, because the universe is *uniform*. Goodman's **new riddle of induction** raises doubts about whether this is such a clear idea. (4.8)

priority of liberty Rawls's claim that certain fundamental rights – which, taken together, he calls *liberty* – cannot be limited for the sake of anything else. (6.11)

prisoners' dilemma A problem in game theory. Suspects are told that if one confesses and the other does not, the one who confesses goes free, and the other gets fifteen years; that if they both confess, they will both go to jail for five years; and that if they both remain silent, they will both go to jail for six months. What should they do? (6.5)

private language argument Wittgenstein's argument against the Cartesian view that mental states are essentially private; discussed in section 1.3. (1.2)

pro-attitude See **attitude**. (5.3)

problem of induction See **induction**. (4.8)

projectible predicate One you can rely on when you project it inductively into the future. (4.8)

proposition The content shared by two sentences that *mean the same*; or, sometimes, by two sentences that *have the same truth conditions*. We often say that a sentence *expresses a proposition*, which means that it has a certain content. (3.4)

propositional attitudes Also called **sentential attitudes**. Expressions like "I doubt that –," and "I know that –," and so on, refer to the propositional or **sentential attitudes**; because what fills the blank is a sentence, which expresses a proposition. (3.6)

propositional logic Also called **sentential logic**. The study of the logical properties of **negation** and the **connectives** – **conjunction, disjunction** and the **conditional** – using **propositional variables**. (3.9)

propositional variable Also called **sentential**

variable. These are used, especially in **propositional logic**, to stand in for sentences. Thus, in "*S* or *T*," the symbols *S* and *T* are both **sentential variables**. (3.9)

protective associations In Nozick's political philosophy, groups of people, operating according to the laws of nature, who agree to help each other to deal with anyone outside the organization who poses a threat to anyone within it; and to settle conflicts between members of the association where necessary. (6.12)

psycho-physical parallelism The view that there are corresponding physical and mental realms that run in parallel, without any causal interaction. (1.2)

quantifiers Words like *some* and *all*. We sometimes write "For all *X*, such that . . ." for the **universal** quantifier that forms sentences saying that everything **satisfies** a certain **predicate**; and "There exists an X, such that . . ." for the **existential** quantifier that forms sentences saying at least one thing **satisfies** a certain **predicate**. The logical properties of these two quantifiers are studied in **predicate logic**. (3.5)

Ramsey-sentence The sentence produced by: (a) forming the **conjunction** of the sentences of a scientific theory; (b) removing all **theoretical terms**; and (c) replacing each of them with a variable and an associated existential **quantifier**. This procedure was invented by Frank Ramsey. (1.8)

rationalism The position that the major or only source of knowledge is reason – contrasts with **empiricism**. (2.3)

realism See **idealism** or **moral realism**.

received view of theories On the received view, a theory is stated in a language that contains, along with the logical terms, a vocabulary of observational terms, and of theoretical terms. The **observation language** consists of sentences containing only observational and logical terms. The **theoretical language** contains only theoretical terms and logical terms. There are also **mixed sentences**, containing both theoretical and observational terms. The theory itself contains two parts. One, the **theoretical postulates**, is stated entirely in the theoretical language, and describes the relations between the entities and properties that the theory postulates. These theoretical postulates connect with observation by way of **mixed sentences** called **correspondence rules**, which connect the entities postulated by the theory with things we are able to observe. These rules explain how theoretical sentences *correspond* to observational ones. (4.5)

reductio ad absurdum *Reductio*, for short. The form of argument in which we show that a

position is unacceptable because it has absurd consequences. (2.3)

reference What a word, phrase or sentence refers to: for a name, an individual; for a **predicate**, its **extension**; for a **declarative sentence**, its **truth value**. (3.4)

reflective equilibrium Rawls suggests that we should move in our ethical thinking back and forth between particular intuitions and general theory – trimming each to the other – until we reach what he calls reflective equilibrium, where our intuitions and our theory coincide. (6.10)

refutation See **conjecture**. (4.9)

relativism See **moral relativism** or **cognitive relativism**.

retributivism The view that punishment is justified not by its deterrent (or other) consequences, but by the fact (and to the extent) that the offender has offended. (7.7)

rules of adjudication Rules that charge certain officials – for example, *judges* – with the task of determining what the laws are. (7.4)

rules of change Rules governing the way laws may be changed. (7.4)

rules of enforcement Rules creating a class of officials who have the responsibility of punishing offenders and enforcing the judgements of the courts. (7.4)

rules of recognition Rules that say how the question whether a rule *is* a law in our society is to be decided. (7.4)

satisfaction Something, *O*, *satisfies* a predicate, *P*, if and only if we can form a true sentence from the predicate and *O*'s name. Thus, I satisfy the **predicate** – *is a philosopher*. (3.5)

secondary rules. See **primary rules**. (7.4)

semantic theory A theory that says what words, phrases, and sentences mean. In **philosophical semantics** we are interested in theories that say in a general way what the meanings of expressions are, not in giving the meanings of every expression in a language. This latter task is the job of the branch of linguistics called *semantics*. Nevertheless, both because it is hard to explore meaning in general without specific examples, and because what certain terms mean is itself a philosophical question, philosophers often make contributions to the semantics of particular words: for example, the **logical constants**. (3.4)

sense Frege's word for the *mode of presentation* associated with an expression. To know the mode of presentation of "the morning star," for example, you have to know that it refers to the heavenly body that often appears at a certain point on the horizon in the morning. It is not enough to know that it refers to Venus. For a name, then, a *sense* is something like a way of identifying the referent. For a sentence, it is a *thought* or the **proposition** it expresses. (3.4)

sentence-forming operator on sentences An expression, like *not* in English, that produces a sentence when added (in the appropriate way) to another sentence. (3.9)

sentential attitudes See propositional attitudes. (3.6)

sentential logic See propositional logic. (3.9)

sentential variable See propositional variable. (3.9)

side-constraints Boundaries that it is always morally wrong to cross. On Nozick's view, rights act as side-constraints. (6.13)

skepticism The view that we can know nothing about a kind of thing is skepticism about things of that kind. (2.3)

sound An **argument** is sound if it is valid and its **premises** are true. (3.9)

speech-act The act performed when a meaningful sentence is uttered. Apart from **assertions**, these include *orders* and *promises*. (3.10)

state of nature The condition of people outside – or prior to the existence of – the state. (6.2)

subject See predicate. (3.5)

supervenience If a class of properties *P* is supervenient on a class of properties *Q*, then no two things that have all the same *Q*-properties can differ in their *P*-properties. Chemical properties are supervenient on physical ones; moral properties, on non-moral ones. (5.8)

synchronic See diachronic. (4.2)

syntax To specify the syntax of a sentence is to say what words it is composed of and in what order. Thus, the syntax of a sentence is, in effect, its *form*. (3.9)

synthesis See thesis. (8.10)

synthetic See analytic. (3.8)

tautology A sentence which is logically or, more generally, analytically true. (4.8)

theoretical language See received view of theories. (4.5)

theoretical postulate See received view of theories. (4.5)

theory of meaning Philosophical proposals about the general form of **semantic theories** belong to the theory of meaning. (3.4)

theory reduction The process of showing that an old theory can be derived from a new one as a special case. (4.6)

theory-ladenness A statement is theory-laden if its meaning depends on some theory. Observation is theory-laden, because whenever we make a judgment on the basis of our sensory experience, the judgment commits us to the existence of objects, events or properties that go beyond that evidence. The fact that evidence always leads us to make claims beyond the evidence is called the **underdetermination of empirical theory**, because it means that the contents of our empirical beliefs are not fully *determined* by our evidence. (4.7)

thesis Hegel thought that the life of reason proceeded by a continuing sequence of ideas. First, someone would develop a systematic theory – which Hegel called a thesis. This was then denied by those who supported the **anti-thesis**; and, finally, a new view would develop which took what was best of each to produce a **synthesis**. (8.10)

truth condition The state of the world that determines whether a sentence is true or false. If you know what it would be for a sentence to be true, we say that you know its truth conditions. (3.4)

truth value Frege said: "By the truth value of a sentence I understand the circumstance that it is true or false." (3.4)

unanalyzable property G.E. Moore held that *goodness* was an unanalyzable property because you could not explain what "good" meant in terms of any other concepts. (5.4)

underdetermination of empirical theory See theory-ladenness. (4.7)

universal quantifier See quantifier. (3.5)

universalizability principle Kant's claim that: *You ought to act only on maxims which you can at the same time will should become universal laws of nature.* (5.5)

utilitarianism The form of **consequentialism** that says we should chose the action that maximizes (human) **utility**. (5.9)

utility Originally, a measure of happiness; now, in economics, a measure of the relative strengths of one's desires. (5.9)

valid An **argument** is valid when the **conclusion** must be true if the **premises** are true. If an argument is valid, we say that the conclusion *follows from* – or is a (deductive) **consequence** of – the premises. (3.9)

valid form See formally valid. (3.9)

veil of ignorance See original position. (6.7)

verifiable A sentence is verifiable if and only if there could be evidence that would provide grounds either for believing or for disbelieving it. (2.6)

verification principle The principle that every declarative sentence must be verifiable. (2.6)

verificationism The view, associated with the logical positivists, that if no amount of evidence can decide an issue, there is no real issue. Verificationism is a form of **idealism**. (2.6)

victimization The practice of doing harm to innocent people in order to increase overall utility. (7.7)

zero-sum game A two-person **game** in which anything one player wins, the other loses. (6.4)

Further reading

It is always a good idea to check in the *Encyclopedia of Philosophy*, Paul Edwards ed. (Macmillan & The Free Press, New York; Collier Macmillan, London, 1967) if you want to get either further information or advice about further reading. *A Dictionary of Philosophy*, Anthony Flew ed. (Macmillan, London, 1983) is also excellent. There are many good introductions to various fields of philosophy in the *Foundations of Philosophy* series (Prentice-Hall, Englewood Cliffs, New Jersey); and most of the individual philosophers of the period before the twentieth century that I have discussed are well introduced in the *Past Masters* series (Oxford University Press, New York & Oxford). I have mentioned some books in each series that I think are especially helpful. Where possible, I have given both British and American publication information. More advanced material is marked with an asterisk.

Chapter 1: Mind

* **Ned Block ed.**, *Readings in Philosophy of Psychology* (Harvard University Press, Cambridge, Massachusetts, 1980). Reproduces some of the best recent work in the philosophy of mind in two volumes.

* **Daniel Dennett**, *Brainstorms* (Bradford Books, Montgomery, Vermont; Harvester, Hassocks, Sussex, 1978). Provides some difficult but exciting reading about modern functionalism.

Descartes, *Meditations*. A great philosophical classic written in non-technical language. You should certainly read it. There are many published translations including F. E. Sutcliffe's *Discourse on Method and the Meditations* (Penguin, New York & Harmondsworth, Middlesex, 1968).

Jerry Fodor, "The Mind-Body Problem" in *Scientific American* 244.1, (1981), pp. 114-123. Great place to start reading about the relationship between dualism, behaviorism, and functionalism.

Paul M. Churchland, *Matter and Consciousness* (A Bradford Book from MIT Press, Cambridge, Massachusetts & London, 1984). A great introduction to the problems of the philosophy of mind as affected by the development of cognitive science. Highly recommended.

Thomas Nagel, "What is it like to be a bat?" in Ned Block ed., *Readings in Philosophy of Psychology*, Volume I, pp. 159-168. Relevant to the dispute about whether a phenomenological account of mental states is necessary.

* **Ludwig Wittgenstein**, *Philosophical Investigations* (Macmillan, New York; Basil Blackwell, Oxford, 1953). The major work of one of the most influential modern philosophers. Difficult but rewarding reading, relevant to philosophy of language and philosophy of mind.

Chapter 2: Knowledge

Alfred Ayer, *The Problem of Knowledge* (Penguin, New York & Harmondsworth, Middlesex, 1957). An introduction to epistemology by the philosopher who introduced positivism to the English-speaking world.

S.M. Cahn, P. Kitcher & G. Sher eds., *Reason at Work* (Harcourt Brace Jovanovich, San Diego, California, 1984). Contains or excerpts many important, classical epistemological texts, including Plato's *Theaetetus*, Descartes' *Meditations*, Gettier's famous paper, and Locke's *Essay Concerning Human Understanding*.

Jonathan Dancy, *Introduction to Contemporary Epistemology* (Basil Blackwell, New York & Oxford, 1985). Good modern survey of epistemology.

* G. Pappas & M. Swain eds., *Knowledge and Justification* (Cornell University Press, Ithaca, 1978). Good collection of recent work with a very useful introduction, which provides a good starting point for further reading.

Plato, *Theaetetus*; I recommend John McDowell's excellent translation (Clarendon Press, New York & Oxford, 1973).

Moritz Schlick, "Meaning and Verification" in *Philosophical Review* 45 (1936), pp. 146-170, reprinted in Herbert Feigl & Wilfred Sellars eds., *Readings in Philosophical Analysis* (Appleton-Century-Crofts, New York, 1948). Discussion of the main claims of logical positivism by one of its founders.

* Robert K. Shope, *The Analysis of Knowing: A Decade of Research* (Princeton University Press, Princeton, New Jersey, 1983). Wide-ranging survey of recent epistemology.

Bernard Williams, *Descartes* (Penguin, New York & Harmondsworth, Middlesex, 1978). Good discussion of Descartes' epistemology along with an interesting account, in Chapter 10, of the Cartesian view of the mind-body question.

Chapter 3: Language and Logic

Jens Allwood, Lars-Gunnar Anderson & Östen Dahl eds., *Logic in Linguistics* (Cambridge University Press, New York & Cambridge, 1977). Good introduction to the ideas of formal logic.

William Alston, *The Philosophy of Language* (Prentice-Hall, Englewood Cliffs, New Jersey, 1964). Fine introductory book in the Prentice-Hall *Foundations of Philosophy* series.

J.L. Austin, *How to Do Things with Words* (Harvard University Press, Cambridge, Massachusetts; Clarendon Press, Oxford, 1962). Modern classic, which introduced the theory of speech-acts.

* Simon Blackburn, *Spreading the Word* (Clarendon Press, New York & Oxford, 1984). Good recent introduction to the philosophy of language. Not an easy book; but it makes few assumptions.

* Susan Haack, *Philosophy of Logics* (Cambridge University Press, New York & Cambridge, 1978). Very good starting point for those who want to go further with some of the more advanced philosophical questions about logic.

Ian Hacking, *Why Does Language Matter To Philosophy?* (Cambridge University Press, Cambridge, 1975). A good place to start further reading on the philosophy of language. Highly recommended.

* David Lewis, *On the Plurality of Worlds* (Basil Blackwell, New York & Oxford, 1986). The most important recent defence of realism about possible worlds. The beginning of the introductory chapter is fairly accessible, but this is an advanced work.

* Richard Rorty, *The Linguistic Turn: Recent Essays in Philosophic Method* (University of Chicago Press, Chicago, 1967). Collection of many key works of the philosophy of language.

Chapter 4: Science

Nelson Goodman, *Fact, Fiction and Forecast* (Harvard University Press, Cambridge, Massachusetts, 1951). Contains the classic statement of the new riddle of induction. Very clearly and entertainingly written.

N. R. Hanson, *Patterns of Discovery* (Cambridge University Press, New York & Cambridge, 1965). Fairly accessible introduction to Hanson's views about theory-ladenness. A fascinating book.

Carl Hempel, *The Philosophy of Natural Science* (Prentice-Hall, Englewood Cliffs, New Jersey, 1966). Great introduction in the Prentice-Hall *Foundations of Philosophy* series.

Mary Hesse, *Models and Analogies in Science* (University of Notre Dame Press, Notre Dame, Indiana, 1966). Discusses the role of model-building in the development of scientific theory in a way that challenges the received view.

David Hume, *An Enquiry Concerning Human Understanding*, Eric Steinberg ed. (Hackett Publishing Co., Indianapolis, 1984). Great empiricist work, where you can learn about the problem of induction from the man who discovered it. Short and fun to read.

Thomas Kuhn, *The Copernican Revolution: Planetary Astronomy in the Development of Western Thought* (Harvard University Press, Cambridge, Massachusetts, 1957). Wonderful example of the way philosophical and historical study of science can be pursued in tandem. *The Structure of Scientific Revolutions* (University of Chicago Press, Chicago, Second Edition, 1970). The most widely influential criticism of the received view.

Bryan McGee, *Popper* (Viking, New York; Fontana, London, 1982). A good point of entry to Popper's work.

* F. Suppe, *The Structure of Scientific Theories* (University of Illinois Press, Chicago & London,

Second Edition, 1977). Contains a marvelous overview of recent philosophy of science in Frederick Suppe's Critical Introduction and Afterword; along with many good papers and discussions among leading philosophers of science.

Chapter 5: Morality

C. Dyke, *Philosophy of Economics* (Prentice-Hall, Englewood Cliffs, New Jersey, 1966). Very good introductory discussion of utility theory.

Jonathan Glover, *Causing Death and Saving Lives* (Penguin, New York & Harmondsworth, Middlesex, 1977). Philosophically sophisticated yet introductory discussion of moral theory as it is relevant to such issues as abortion, euthanasia, murder and killing in warfare. *What Sort of People should there Be?* (Penguin, New York & London, 1984). Discusses some of the ethical problems of genetic engineering and neuroscience. Both good starting points for further reading.

R.M. Hare *The Language of Morals* (Clarendon Press, New York & Oxford, 1952). Very influential work. *Moral Thinking: Its Levels, Methods, and Point* (Oxford University Press, Oxford, 1981). Introductory statement of Hare's views as they have developed since *The Language of Morals*. Hare is a clear, if not always an exciting, writer.

* Immanuel Kant, *The Groundwork of the Metaphysic of Morals*, translated and analyzed by H.J. Paton (Harper Torchbooks, New York, 1964) One of the two or three most influential works in philosophical ethics. Kant's style is not easy, in part because, unlike Hume, he self-consciously developed his own technical vocabulary. So it is important that Paton's edition is very helpfully annotated.

J.L. Mackie, *Ethics: Inventing Right and Wrong* (Penguin, New York & Harmondsworth, Middlesex, 1977). An extended argument against moral realism. A fascinating book.

Alasdair MacIntyre, *A Short History of Ethics* (Macmillan, New York, 1966; Routledge & Kegan Paul, London, 1967). Brilliant survey from classical Greece to the present time. *After Virtue* (Notre Dame University Press, Notre Dame, Indiana, 1984). Well worth reading.

Roger Scruton, *Kant* (Oxford University Press, New York & Oxford, 1982). In the *Past Masters* series. Good introduction to Kant.

Peter Singer, *Practical Ethics* (Cambridge University Press, New York & Cambridge, 1979). Deals with a number of important moral questions in an introductory way. Highly recommended.

* J.J. Smart & Bernard Williams, *Utilitarianism: For and Against* (Cambridge University Press, New York & Cambridge, 1973). Contains a pair of first rate essays on utilitarianism, with Smart *for* and Williams *against*.

Chapter 6: Politics

Morton Davis, *Game Theory: A Non-technical Introduction* (Basic Books, New York, Revised Edition, 1983). Very useful, clearly written book. Highly recommended.

John Dunn, *Locke* (Oxford University Press, New York & Oxford, 1984) In the *Past Masters* series. A very helpful introduction to Locke's work in its historical context.

* Brian Barry, *The Liberal Theory of Justice: A Critical Examination of the Principal Doctrines in A Theory of Justice by John Rawls* (Clarendon Press, Oxford, 1975). An important advanced discussion of Rawls.

Thomas Hobbes, *The Leviathan*, C.B. Macpherson ed. (Penguin, New York & Harmondsworth, Middlesex, 1985). Splendidly vigorous book and the beginning, in many respects, of modern political philosophy.

John Locke, *Second Treatise of Government*, C.B. Macpherson ed. (Hackett Publishing Co., Indianapolis, 1980). Very influential in determining the conception of rights that underlies the American Constitution.

Robert Nozick, *Anarchy, State and Utopia* (Basic Books, New York; Basil Blackwell, Oxford, 1974). Brilliant and fascinating book and a good point of entry to recent political philosophy.

Jeffrey Paul ed., *Reading Nozick* (Rowman & Littlefield, Totowa, New Jersey, 1981). Useful collection of papers on Nozick's work.

John Plamenatz, *Man and Society* (Longman, London, 1963). A useful two-volume survey of political philosophers from Machiavelli to Marx.

* John Rawls, *A Theory of Justice* (Belknap Press of Harvard University Press, Cambridge, Massachusetts; Clarendon Press, Oxford, 1971). A long and difficult book, which started a resurgence of interest in political philosophy.

Robert Paul Wolff, *Understanding Rawls* (Princeton University Press, Princeton, New Jersey, 1977). The best point of entry to Rawls's work; also a fine critical introduction to the use of game-theory in political philosophy.

Chapter 7: Law

John Arthur & William H. Shaw eds., *Readings in the Philosophy of Law* (Prentice-Hall, Englewood Cliffs, New Jersey, 1984) Very good collection of readings from authors including Aquinas, Austin, Hart and Nozick.

* P. Atiyah, *Promises, Morals and Law* (Oxford University Press, Oxford, 1981). Difficult but rewarding discussion of the relationship between the ethics of promising and the law of contract.

* D.J. O'Connor, *Aquinas and Natural Law* (St. Martin's Press, New York; Macmillan, London, 1968). Interesting discussion of this subject.

* R.A. Duff, *Trials and Punishments* (Cambridge University Press, New York & Cambridge, 1986). Very good recent defense of the Natural Law tradition as a basis of the criminal law.

* Herbert Hart, *The Concept of Law* (Clarendon Press, Oxford, 1961). Perhaps the most highly influential recent English-language work in the philosophy of law. A careful reader can gain a great deal from this book.

Ted Honderich, *Punishment: The Supposed Justifications* (Penguin, New York & London, Revised Edition, 1984). Excellent introduction to this important topic.

David Lyons, *Ethics and the Rule of Law* (Cambridge University Press, New York & Cambridge, 1984). Interesting, introductory work.

Chapter 8: Philosophy

Jack Goody, *The Domestication of the Savage Mind* (Cambridge University Press, New York & Cambridge, 1977). Marvelous study of the influence of the development of writing on intellectual style.

Edward Evans-Pritchard, *Witchcraft, Oracles and Magic Among the Azande*. Anthropological classic, which has received a good deal of philosophical attention. Best to read it in the abridged edition, Eva Gillies ed. (Oxford University Press, New York & Oxford, 1976), which has a very good introduction.

John Hick, *Philosophy of Religion* (Prentice-Hall, Englewood Cliffs, New Jersey, 1983). A good introduction in the *Foundations of Philosophy* series.

Michael Krausz & Jack W. Meiland eds., *Relativism: Cognitive and Moral* (Notre Dame University Press, Notre Dame, Indiana, 1982). Useful collection of recent writing on this topic, with very helpful commentary on each selection. You can also follow up the discussion of moral relativism in Chapter 5 of this book.

John Passmore, *Philosophical Reasoning* (Scribner, New York, 1962). Good attempt to introduce beginners to the style of philosophical argument. *A Hundred Years of Philosophy* (Basic Books, New York; Penguin, Harmondsworth, Middlesex, Revised Edition, 1968). A brilliant survey of the last century of philosophy.

* John Skorupski, *Symbol and Theory* (Cambridge University Press, Cambridge, 1976). Philosopher's careful discussion of the nature of traditional religions. Rewards close reading.

Index